A SHAMAN'S GUIDE TO
Deep Beauty

Blessings!

Rico

A SHAMAN'S GUIDE TO
Deep Beauty

Connecting with the Mojo of the Universe

FRANCIS RICO

A TRI S FOUNDATION BOOK

COUNCIL
OAK BOOKS

SAN FRANCISCO & TULSA

Council Oak Books, LLC
www.counciloakbooks
www.trisfoundation.com

COVER DESIGN/BOOK GRAPHICS AND DINGBATS:
   Ted and Peggy Raess, Raess Design

TEXT DESIGN: Carl Brune

Printed in USA

ISBN (paperback) 978-0-9823274-2-5
ISBN (ebook) 978-0-9823274-8-7

LIBRARY OF CONGRESS CATALOGING-IN-PUBLICATION DATA
   Rico, Francis.
   A shaman's guide to deep beauty : connecting with the mojo of the
universe / Francis Rico. — 1st ed.
      p. cm.
   ISBN 978-0-9823274-2-5 (pbk. : alk. paper)
   1. Spirituality. 2. Spiritual life. 3. Shamanism. 4. Civilization—21st
century. 5. Civilization—Forecasting. 6. Aesthetics. I. Title.

   BF1999.R5415 2011
   204'4—dc23

                    2011027488

Here, now,
with love, gratitude, and
this handful of wildflowers
I say **thank you**
to the Mother of us all.

Contents

Forward

As has long been predicted, we are entering a time when the world as we have known it is falling apart and a new world is emerging.

Ancient indigenous wisdom traditions as diverse as those of the Mayan, Hindu, Siberian, African, Native American and many others have predicted that this would happen. They were aware that time/space flows in long cycles, and they were able to calculate and project time and events with a degree of accuracy that is remarkable even in this age of atomic clocks.

The similarity of these predictions is astonishing. In almost every account, these traditions state that we're at the end times of the fifth "world" and at the beginning of the sixth — the previous "worlds" being advanced civilizations that we know very little about — civilizations that faced challenges that they were unable to meet.

What we do know is that we are *now* in a time when the elders of all world cultures are simultaneously hearing a call from within to speak up and to speak out.

As a shaman and elder, I can assure you that you are not alone in feeling anxiety, fear, and distress regarding the way the world is changing. But if you listen to any of us speak, what you will find is that we are encouraged by the *opportunity* that this transition presents, and our message to you is one of hope and light — there *is* a path to well-being and harmony that will bless our own lives and the lives of future generations.

My response to this time of transition is to offer you this guidebook. Most guidebooks provide you with maps, charts and photos of the territory being covered, along with descriptive highlights of what you can expect to see. Here, instead of telling you *what* you'll see, *A Shaman's Guide to Deep Beauty* offers shamanic practices that will help you remember *how* to see.

I encourage you to take heart and consider that we are at an extraordinary moment in the evolution of our species. We're moving *from* a world of ignorance, scarcity and limitation, controlled by greedy, frightening and frightened people, to an age of enlightenment.

We're becoming a world where thriving is replacing simply surviving, where love is overcoming fear, and where cooperation, collaboration and compassion will become key components of our global social, economic, educational, healthcare, political, and ecological structures.

Given the world's current state of endless war, famine, drought, floods, economic collapse and manmade ecological disasters, we can all agree, at the very least, that things are *looking* rough. However, it's not an impossible dream that places us at the beginning of a new golden age.

Humanity has more than a passing familiarity with this "new" world. It has been the territory of shamans, seers, saints, visionaries, and mystics since long before the dawn of conventional history. And yet, while we hold the highest regard for our visionaries, mystics and spiritual teachers, and we feel a great reverence for their messages of love and compassion, just take a look at the damage we have done to each other and to the living ecosystems of the earth in just the past hundred years.

It's obvious that we consider our spiritual teachers to be impractical dreamers. Their offerings of wisdom and guidance have been disregarded as being essentially irrelevant in the affairs of the real world. In a state of what can only be described as global hypnosis, our species continues to hold these messages of peace, love and brotherhood high, as lofty standards of what we will *someday* attain; meanwhile, the reality of our actions reveal that quite the opposite is true. War, fear, hatred and ruthless exploitation are the hallmarks of our modern world's dominant so-called civilization.

But, there *are* those who have searched and found a crack in the world's hypnotic trance. We could call them *practical dreamers*. Most often found in marginalized indigenous cultures, these travelers have slipped through the crack and have explored a magical realm of exquisite beauty and abundance.

These practical dreamers discovered a source of deeply relevant wisdom in a realm where rainbows light the path; where trees and animals speak with insight and clarity, becoming companions and guardians on the journey to the center of Creation; where vast fields of light sparkle and crackle with lightening bolts of inspiration. Within the radiant field of being at the center of this other world, situations presented for healing, guidance and resolution become illuminated. Then, with hearts true to their mission, these practical dreamers return back through the crack, into what we call "normal" reality with profoundly helpful gifts. They return with healing cures, solutions, and inspired opportunities that emerge from the light of awareness that underlies life in all dimensions — in every time and place.

The new world that is now becoming for us has always been present, but has remained hidden to those hypnotized by our civilization — and that's pretty much all of us. This mysterious field of awareness, hidden-in-plain-view, is called the *divine Presence* by shamans of widely separated cultures and times. It is called divine not in a religious sense, but rather in recognition by practical dreamers worldwide of the presence of the loving wild heart of Creation.

Around the world, these practical dreamers — also called shamans — continue to actively explore the mysteries of life, searching for healing and life-enhancing solutions, guided by the heart of Creation.

In indigenous cultures, becoming a shaman was not something that you could just decide to do. Creation selected her shamans, testing them for their capacity to care for the totality of life, and for their ability to *move energy* without cracking up. And, of course, having illuminated the DNA of these individuals from the inside, Creation has continuously evolved through established shamans and their lineages in the selection, initiation, and training of new generations of shamans.

Until now, shamanic wisdom, resources, tools and practices have always been held in reserve for the *initiated* — for those who, through training or natural giftedness, have learned to speak, hear, feel, see, understand and communicate in the ancient sacred language of Creation, Deep Beauty. Just as a practical matter, shamans have hardly been able to communicate their navigation of the indescribable dream-like wonders of other-worldly dimensions, even when they've wanted to, because most of the experience and knowledge gained in their travels simply does not translate.

Our modern languages are pale, weak, deconstructed imitations of the original sacred language, and are unable to communicate the information, energy and vibration of the original language. Visions of the world of magical divine Presence have always been highly valued by humanity, but their transformative power has been held safely contained in poetry, music and the arts, and is only marginally incorporated into the fabric of normal reality. Even trapped within these forms of containment, visions of divinity cannot be prevented from emerging and shining on special occasions like weddings and funerals

— moments when the sacred emerges with wings from within human life experiences and cannot be denied. But as far as our fluency in the language of Deep Beauty, it is rarely heard or understood in the modern mainstream media that dominates our daily consciousness with "if it bleeds, it leads."

There's an additional contributing factor that has until now prevented Deep Beauty from being included in everyone's education: shamanic allegiance to ecstatic wild beauty runs counter to the accepted moral, religious and cultural norms of "civilized" humanity — at least it has for the past five or six thousand years. Now, however, as the beginnings of a new world age overlap and gently rock the foundations of our troubled and distressed modern world, we are finding that the tools and resources that generations of shamans kept alive have become essential to our ability to navigate through this time of transition.

Yes, our world is in trouble. And along with shamans, mystics, visionaries, seers, saints, elders, and religious and spiritual leaders of every stripe, we are *all* being called to come present and be accountable for the care of all of life on earth.

Ultimately, we're a single family. We are all related — and the time has come for us to recognize that we're all in this together. The time has come for us to share everything, from resources to wisdom, and to include everyone.

Backward

Before we take another step forward, we have to take a step back to have a word about a word:

Shaman.

But first, allow me to share with you how one of the brightest lights that humanity has ever produced created magic.

Holy man Frank Fools Crow – a Lakota Sioux, and nephew of Black Elk – would *slow things down* so that there would be plenty of time to experience and become saturated with the importance and depth of what was being done.

For example, when offering a cup of healing herb-infused medicinal tea, he would extend it towards the person, and then would pull it back, then offer it again, and then pull it back again – so that by the fourth time the offering was made, all of the worlds – the physical, emotional, mental, and spiritual – had been included, and the moment of receiving the offering became charged, full of the magic and seriousness of the healing intent.

Frank Fools Crow was *the* grand old Medicine Man of the Sioux Nation. He was widely recognized as a holy man because of his total transparency. He was the elder that tribal elders turned to for guidance and blessings. He passed in 1989 and was perhaps the last of an ancient lineage. The divine Presence that he allowed to shine through his life was a supernova of light that continues to illuminate pathways in spiritual dimensions for all of us who travel the mysterious worlds spoken of in the ancient traditions.

In the spirit of Fool's Crow, here's an additional back and forth step *before* we move on to taking our original promised step back to discuss the meaning and place of shaman in our world today:

> Many elders, from around the world, have stated that Creation is calling from deep within our hearts — calling us to come forward within our traditions and our communities and to speak and act with wisdom and compassionate regard for the shared well-being of all of life on earth.

It would seem impossible that anyone would want to argue with that. However, there are always going to be those who protest, claiming that the old ways belong exclusively to them. Having guarded and held these traditions as a sacred trust, they are understandably reluctant to let go, and they continue to insist that this ancient heritage must be kept from those who would exploit it for their own benefit.

There is a genuine nobility to those who protest sharing their spiritual inheritance, but given the times we're in, it has become obvious that *we no longer have the luxury of thinking this way.* Both those that guard the old traditions and those that would exploit them, are too late. At this point, the survival of the world depends on our ability to share what we know and to work together, *now.*

Fools Crow's comment on sharing sacred knowledge and ways was: "The ones who complain and talk the most about not giving away medicine secrets, are always those who know the least."

OK, so are we ready to move ahead (and by that I mean backwards)?

"Shaman" is a word that was adopted by Western anthropologists from an ancient Siberian tribal language. It replaced witch doctors — a term used to politely describe those odd indigenous individuals that the academic world of the late 1800s and early 1900s clearly considered to be, at the very least, deranged and dangerous characters, even though they were held in high esteem as healers and resource people within their tribes. Witch doctors served as a good working description for those individuals who functioned as tribal healers, because their cures seemingly relied as much on primitive magic as on medicines.

In retrospect, we can see that the use of "witch doctor" also contained an underlying Western religious cultural bias against witches, which, combined with a scientific superiority and scorn for "superstitious primitive practices," exposed these academics for what they really were — narrow-minded products of the Victorian era.

But, the social scientists of the early 1900s were desperate to be taken seriously in the world of academia. Very soon after the intellectual discourse of the times suggested that the label "witch doctor" revealed decidedly unscientific ethnocentric biases and beliefs, they dropped it like a hot potato. They adopted "shaman" as a replacement, and hoped that the translation from the ancient Siberian Tungus language, of a shaman as "one who knows and is wise" would show enough respect for indigenous ways to settle the matter and get them off the hook.

There were a couple of problems with this solution.

The use of "shaman" in reference to all healers who walk the pathways of the Spirit Worlds assumed that all "primitive" religions were the same. This is an understandable mistake, because the core premises of the world's indigenous belief systems have striking similarities. However, just try calling a traditional Native American medicine man a "shaman" and you'll experience informed blowback and contempt for the Western academic world's myopia.

And, what is true within indigenous cultures in the Americas is also true in Asia, Africa, Europe, and Australia. The word "shaman" is meaningless to the Nigerian Drumming Healer, the Australian Aboriginal Koori, or the Peruvian Maestro. We might as well substitute "earthling" for "shaman."

But the real problem lies less in the glib assumptions made by these early social scientists than in the language of anthropological academia, English.

And of course, the language problem is so much larger than any one academic discipline; it includes the entire vast interlocking machinery of Western culture. English has become the dominant language on the planet because it was the language of imperialism, and it is the language of science, of industrialization, of commerce, of corporations, and, most unfortunately, of mass media. English is a language that parses and separates into subject and object all that it defines. As a language, English divides and conquers, killing what it describes.

I'm reminded of something that Eckhart Tolle said in discussing how to explain the unreality of the English language to a child. Using a tree as his example, Eckhart said, "We call *that* an *Oak tree. But that's not what it is!*" What we call an Oak tree, while thinking about how we like hardwood oak floors, or how we prefer using aged oak for firewood, is in reality a play of light and shadow, a breathtaking up-reach of limbs into the sky, and roots into the earth, a cool and inviting embrace, a haven for a glittering melodic feathered orchestra, a whistle of wind, and rustle of leaves, a touch of rough bark, a holy green cathedral of majestic living Presence.

What other choices of language do we have? Most of our beautiful old languages are dead, and more die out every day. It seems that the languages with roots in the sacred are now relics of bygone eras.

Given enough of an effort, English, along with our other contemporary Western world languages, can be pushed and shoved into the realm of the sacred. Occasionally the sacred can be found in poetry and in song lyrics, where the melody wings the words towards the divine. But in everyday spoken language, English is sadly one-dimensional and portrays a world of static objects.

Languages that actually succeed in fluent communication of the sacred, because they emerged from it and are still immersed in creative potential, are languages that are verb-based. And this is simply because verbs describe action, or flow, and flow is a more accurate representation of life than a collection of things could ever hope to be.

Native American Holy Man Joseph Rael once asked a small group of us to reframe our thinking into verbs, so that what we called a "chair" became "chairing," and what had been called a "cup" became "cupping." Soon, the table was tabling, the walls were walling, the teacher was a teaching, the sky was shining, the air was humming, shaman was shamaning, and we were verb-alizing.

We had begun, in a small way, to speak Tiwa, the original language of the first people. And, as the world we had once taken for granted began to flow in beautiful interconnected patterns of vibrating energy, we were well on our way to speaking the original language of Creation itself, the language from which sprang humanity's first language, the vibrational language of Deep Beauty.

This guide book can orient you towards the path to personal freedom, and it does so by helping you become a fluent speaker of the language of liberation, the language spoken by Creation from the very first word, fourteen billion years ago, at the time of the great origination that we call the Big Bang.

And the word was *YES!*

The ancient Siberian people's language was also verb-based. The word *shaman,* or *saman,* meant being excited, vibrating with energy, living and seeing in the realm of rippling, excited vibration.

The language emphasized the seeing, especially seeing the high vibrations, so that anyone vibrating highly enough to be seeing vibrations was shamaning.

By the way, the word "shaman" can apply to either a man or a woman, and it also can mean one individual or a group — and as the word came to us in the late 1600s via Russian, the "man" part of the word did not mean something attributed to "man" — this is not an English word like "human" or "woman." A shaman is an action, or state of being, not a title.

In an attempt to verbalize and reconstitute a definition that seemed static and fixed, Scottish Highland shaman Frank Henderson MacEowen describes people who enact traditional rituals, affirming the living, flowering, vibrating energy patterns of family, clan, community and culture as shamanists — those who shamanize.

I personally like this direction, and perhaps would have recommended shamanista or shamanerengos if it weren't for the suggestion of don Miguel Ruiz (who speaks beautifully accented Spanglish) that we make English a sacred language by being impeccable with our word. Don Miguel so eloquently expresses the truth that the power that shapes our world is contained in our thoughts and in our speech.

Instead, I recommend that we go along with an exquisite speaker of Deep Beauty, Martin Prechtel, and just call shamanism that old time religion, an ancient vine sprouting a sweet new blossom of ecstatic joy, releasing the otherworldly scent of profound gratitude just for the intoxicating pleasure of taking our next deep breath.

It is in this spirit that I offer you this guide to the spiraling path that leads us to the central presence of beauty speaking from the heart of Creation within us and echoed all around us.

We begin with a simple prayer:

> *Great Spirit,*
> *thank you for the gift of life*
> *opening in this moment*
> *within my heart,*
> *each beat an embrace*
> *of love,*
> *each breath a renewal*
> *of creation.*
> *Opening my eyes, my hands*
> *and my mind to Presence,*
> *let me become your love in action,*
> *and your beauty in this world.*
> *Aho.*

Introduction

Our attention follows our belief.

This insight into the way our minds work is the key to using this guidebook to seeing your world in a new way. This ancient shamanic adage is the result of deep inquiry into the nature of human consciousness. Essentially, what these early inner explorers discovered was that our minds continually gather evidence to support our conviction that we are right. And, we're convinced that what we believe is right, because we believe it, and because we keep finding overwhelming evidence that confirms that what we believe is actually true.

Yes, of course, this is circular logic. The problem is that in order to break away from going in circles, the mind would have to admit that it is fundamentally wrong, which it is entirely unwilling to do, because being wrong would invalidate it, threatening its very existence. Unfortunately, given this relentlessly tight focus on proving that what we believe is right, what we are able to see is severely limited. The result is that we're simply unable to see the infinite wonder, beauty and opportunities available to us in each moment. Sad, isn't it? The limitations we experience in our lives turn out to be self-imposed. We live our lives constrained within a prison of our own making.

But what if you could break out of jail? What if you could see the big picture? What if your attention was not restricted to searching for evidence to shore up your belief system while excluding everything else? What if your awareness greatly expanded and you were suddenly able to see a range of choices available to you in each moment that had simply not existed when you were only seeing what you believed was possible? And, what if the magic and miracles that seem to be impossible from within the limitations enforced by the trance state of your beliefs simply turned out to be available choices found within this greatly expanded field of awareness?

The most ancient shamanic wisdom passed down to us through the ages teaches that *we choose* the reality we live in. It also teaches that the magic, miracles, wellbeing, liberation, enlightenment, joy, unconditional love and divine Presence that we seek all exist within us. I'm not asking you to believe this, because you can see from the ancient teachings that believing is an expression and projection of the hypnotic trance that has overtaken us, blinding us to the world around us. So, this guidebook is not offering an alternative belief system. Rather, what is being offered here is a way of transcending belief itself — a way of moving simultaneously to the highest and deepest levels of awareness of what actually is, and a way of becoming adept at seeing, speaking and living in this new reality.

If it were up to me, I'd ask you to be skeptical of everything. But I would also ask that you commit yourself to actually doing the work suggested — and not just reading this book and then setting it down. The deceptively simple practices presented here are experiments for you to try.

Let's find out if there is magic within you. Let's discover the source of the call you are hearing. Let's face bravely into the unknown, and, acknowledging the deep longing we feel for a healthy, happy and fulfilled life, let's speak heart-to-heart in the ancient sacred language of Deep Beauty.

Where do we start? Let's take a look at the guiding principles that are fundamental to shamanic wisdom. Can you allow yourself the freedom to experiment and try shamanic perspectives on for size?

First, are you willing to consider that you are It? Can you consider the possibility that you are the precious gift of Creation to Herself, and that your entire experience of life is a dream that you are having? The rest of us are co-creating along with you, of course. But, the ultimate bottom line, end game, final conclusion is that *You're It!* And this guidebook was written just for you.

Second, consider that all of Creation is alive. We're not talking some sort of primitive animism here — our most sophisticated and advanced scientific research states that everything that exists vibrates with dynamic resonant living energy — an energy that originated fourteen billion years ago with an explosion of what can only be called *"Yes!"* Can you see that we're all connected? And everything is alive – the rocks, the trees, the waves, the water, the earth, you, humanity, microbes, worms, lobsters, whales, jaguars, eagles, gods, the sun, the moon, and the stars in the sky. . . . We are one living being.

Third, the only Absolute Truth is that truth is relative. When scientists experiment with light and determine to prove that it is a wave of energy, then it turns out that light is a wave of energy. But, when they posit that light is infinitesimally fine vibrating particles of energy in motion, then, what they find is that light behaves like particles. Even our most "objective" scientists now understand that the mind of the observer becomes an integral part of the experiment being observed. The study of Quantum Physics has revealed that there is no separation between us and what we observe, and like the ancient shaman from before history began, science has discovered that attention follows belief.

Put another way, imagine that you are bouncing a ball up and down in a moving train car, one of those tourist train cars with windows from the floor to the ceiling. To you, the truth is that the ball goes straight down and returns straight back up to your hand, with no sideways motion. But to an outside observer, standing on the ground a distance from the train, each hit of the ball on the car floor occurs hundreds of feet apart, and the ball sweeps through great arches of space, never landing in the same place twice. Truth is relative to our position on the spiral — or in this case, our position either in the train or on the ground. A spiral is an accurate metaphor for how a difference in our position and point of view revolving around anything can prove something to be true or not true.

Something can be true from one point of view, and not true from around the bend, and then, true again, and then, not true again. This *Shaman's Guide* does not assert a point of view to be Absolutely True, but asks that you be willing to release your tight grip on what you think you know to be the truth and to allow for some experimental flexibility. Nothing dangerous will be asked of you here! And we can all count on whatever is actually true staying true, no matter what we think about it, true?

Fourth, we're multi-dimensional beings with amnesia. We've forgotten our origins and we don't know our own history. Our amnesia

3

is so profound that most of us don't know anything about our great-great-grandparents, who lived a mere one hundred years ago! But worse than having forgotten our ancestors, we've forgotten our ancient deep connection to the earth. We've abandoned or been torn away from our indigenous roots, and we have moved into a disconnected world of isolation and separation. The result? We live our lives separated from the flow of energy emanating from Source. Humanity increasingly lives in a trance state of illusion and delusion, imagining the electronic hook-up of the television, computer screen, or hand held device to be an adequate connection with Life. We are held captive in this trance by a very large rotating gravitational field of assumptions and beliefs about ourselves and the world. It is an energetic system that traps and enslaves us and is almost impossible to fight.

The good news? We are multi-dimensional beings, and, while we may not be able to counter this trance on its terms, we're blessed with an inner potential to simply choose an alternate reality — choosing Love in the face of fear and hate, and responding to hostility and greedy self-interest with kindness and compassion.

Fifth, you know within yourself that there are ways to awaken from this trance! But they all seem to involve some sort of austerity, with long periods of meditation best done in cold mountain caves, or by adhering to strict spiritual practices that only a few are able to perform. Out beyond the temporary comfort of going to church on Sunday, there's a disheartening sense that real spiritual pursuits are impractical and pointless, and that seriously pursuing "liberation" would involve such a life-consuming struggle that we would no longer be able to enjoy anything.

And even worse than being cold and lonely in a mountain cave would be to be in a group devoted to a "master," "guru," "swami," or "awakened being," whose instructions that it's his way or the highway are enforced by a highly organized and political structure of disciples with greater access to the "enlightened one" jockeying for a position nearer to the center, keeping middle circle and outer circle devotees doing the same. These cults can't help but develop their own miniature gravitational fields, sucking people in, and occasionally, spitting them back out.

Would you be willing to consider that the path to awakening might involve something completely outside of the realm of what you know? Your intuition that there is a great mystery working within everything you see is correct. So, why not let yourself be surprised by the unexpected? Are you willing to allow yourself the spacious presence found in not knowing?

We're talking about a very practical matter. You are going to be asked to practice shifting your experience of doing things from *mastery* to *mystery*. And instead of working hard to get it right in order to advance through the ranks, you will be asked to switch your allegiance over to mystery — to allowing inspiration to guide you and to moving with the easy grace of a willing dance partner who dances with Creation. Here's a simple way of asking this: Are you willing to move from the rigid certainty of practicing the piano to the mysterious magical flow of playing it?

Finally, are you willing to dedicate five minutes a day, with an occasional half-hour here and there, to experimenting with shamanic practices? Will you dedicate a little time every day to cultivating your essential wildness? Are you ready to talk with Creation heart-to-heart and let your attention follow the deep beauty of pure awareness?

Yes?

OK, let's begin.

Enlightenment is Easy

THROUGHOUT HUMAN HISTORY, OUR SPIRITUAL GUIDES, teachers, and holy ones have all shared the same central message with us. They've done their best to share a blazingly obvious but mysteriously deep secret of life. They've come from different times and cultures, and they've spoken many languages.

Knowing the human potential for creating confusion and misinterpretation, they've resorted to the most basic of human languages — sign language — to communicate this secret. And the sign they have all presented is the open hand, held in front of their bodies, with the palm facing us.

Their secret message: "Enlightenment is easy."

Enlightenment is easy because it is a natural part of our human design. It is as much a part of our design as the rosebud's design is to open into a full blooming flower. We are designed to open and become present in life in exactly the same way — gloriously beautiful with our promise fulfilled. This flower, called enlightenment, has also been called awakening, opening, satori, or, becoming alive, aware, and awake in the dream. The early "flowers" of our human species, our spiritual teachers, knew and expressed this state of ease. They lived it. And they did their best to share it with the people of their time and place.

The old shamans, on the other hand, behaved more like a secret society of wilderness gardeners, cultivating the flowering of our species into the awakened state, starting with themselves, long before Adam and Eve and the Garden of Eden. Long before the civilized mythologies of the East and the West, long before the stories of the gods and the big flood, the old shamans had discovered the same foundational schematic of human design that modern neurological science now shows us — that we are organized as a three-part system. In fact, neurologists call our design the "triune brain" — the three-part brain — the three parts being the spinal cord/brain stem, the limbic brain, and the neo-cortex.

Around the world, from Australia to Siberia, and from the Americas to Africa, the most ancient indigenous wisdom describes this three-part organizational system as the *underworld,* the *middle world,* and the *upper world.*

The underworld is symbolized by the snake, because the snake is in belly-to-earth contact with the material world, with the jungle floor or with the hot desert sands. The snake symbolizes the undulating metabolic functions of heartbeat, breathing, digestion, temperature control, sexual reproduction, and our basic motor systems — all essential functions governed by the spinal cord and brainstem.

Then, there is the middle world, the limbic mammalian world, the world of the puma, jaguar, tiger, leopard, mountain lion. This is the world we live in, the world of mankind, comprised of relationships, of family and tribe — of being present, adaptive, and responsive to the shared needs of food, shelter, warmth, safety, companionship and belonging — these being the fabric of our "normal" reality.

And then, the upper world, the world of the eagle, the condor, flying high above and able to see connections, relationships, and patterns not obvious from the ground. With keen vision, the high flyer is able to spot opportunity from far above and to strike like lightening into the web of life — and then again to go soaring with inspiration and imagination, the two wings of perception in the upper world.

It is our blended projection of these three worlds, seen through the focal point of our own inner and outer life, that creates our perception of one continuous experience of life. The brain is, after all, just another organ like the liver, stomach, or kidneys, but what we call reality is created from these three overlapping interrelated physiological systems, as distinct as three alternative dimensions of being. The "reality" we create seems to be external, and we respond to the external creation with an inner world of feelings, desires, motivations, drives, attractions and memories. At the balance point between the inner and the outer worlds, our minds shimmer, a blend of emotions, history, and consciousness.

What can become illuminated, when a lightening bolt of awareness strikes us, is a vision of how we are doing, and of what our potential is. For a brief moment, in a flash, a bright mirror of light appears and affords us a look: What would our life be like if we took better care of ourselves? What if we all simply loved each other? What if we used our intelligence to improve the quality of life shared by all living beings?

Put like this, awakening sounds easy — after all, we're created to be healthy, happy, loving, kind, and generous. But that's not how we live. Looking around our planet, we all can see the damage that we humans have done, and are continuing to do. The idea that we are the solution seems far-fetched and daunting. Yet, when the flowers of our species — Buddha, Christ, Muhammad, Frank Fools Crow and others — prominently display their open hands, they are telling us that we have the same potential, that we share the same design, that we are their equal, and that we are equally capable of awakening.

Shamanic traditions include a practice we now call lucid dreaming in which our hand plays a key role in our awakening to the truth of who and what we are, and how we are made. Here's how the practice works: as you go to sleep, you direct yourself to look for your hand in your dreams. You set your intent to find and see your hand, and once you've found your hand, you locate your wrist, and then your forearm, your elbow, your shoulder, your body, your other hand, your face, your total being.

You know that you are sleeping, yet you have found your self. And with this discovery of your self, you come awake and present, with

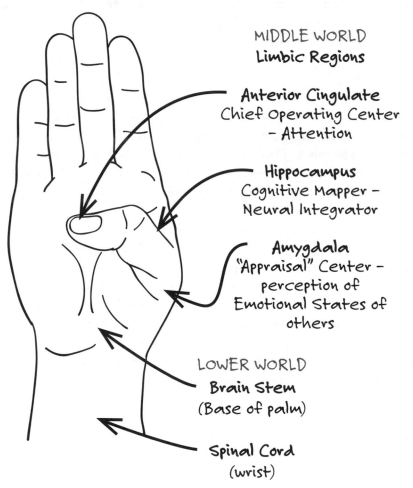

UPPER WORLD
Orbitofrontal Cortex

MIDDLE WORLD
Limbic Regions

Anterior Cingulate
Chief Operating Center
– Attention

Hippocampus
Cognitive Mapper –
Neural Integrator

Amygdala
"Appraisal" Center –
perception of
Emotional States of
others

LOWER WORLD
Brain Stem
(Base of palm)

Spinal Cord
(wrist)

consciousness, while you are dreaming — just like you are present and conscious during the day.

Shamanic practices, from journeying and shape-shifting to healing and magic, spring from the realization of the truth that we are dreaming at night, and that we're also dreaming during the day. Through deep inner exploration and experimentation, shamans discovered that our three part brains are designed to dream — designed to create, project, and believe our experience of the reality of the world around us, and within us, whether we think we're asleep or awake.

Now, we have an opportunity to work with this ancient practice of lucid dreaming in a slightly less otherworldly way — we can call this practical approach lucid living. This practice will support your awakening, in the dream of life that you're in now — and, yes, you are going to use your hand to help you do it.

On the diagram of the hand you see that the wrist and base of the palm of the hand represent the spinal cord and brainstem. The thumb is the limbic brain folded over inside — the center of the brain. And the fingers represent the neo-cortex or the new brain. This image is the very same image that neurologists and brain surgeons use when they describe brain functions and show you how your brain is constructed.

When something stresses us, we retreat from the stress, and our system compresses. In fact, that's what the word "stress" means. It means, "to shrink," "to pull back." Stress is a natural part of life, and a certain amount of stress causes growth and elicits creative responses that actually help expand our capacity to deal with whatever comes our way. But a shrunken and compressed position is very uncomfortable when held for any amount of time. And when we are constantly stressed — when we are chronically stressed — without letup, without relief, without a break — our capacity for creative responses shrinks and wears thin. We become exhausted, frustrated and less than gracious when we are under the influence of constant unrelenting stress.

And rather than fresh creative solutions to the situations of our life, we lose our resourcefulness and are driven back to adaptive strategies that worked to help us survive in the past — when we were infants. These early strategies come forward because they once worked, and the fact that we survived with their help is proof that they worked. Because these strategies are stored as implicit memories in the limbic brain, there is no sense of "time" attached to them — they are as immediate and available now as they were when we were two years old — plus, the self-fulfilling prophecy quality that comes into play reassures us that we have what we need. Even though the stressful situation currently faced might call for a completely different approach, what worked in the past emerges as we react to stress by closing down — and unconsciousness overtakes us.

Here's an example — and it is only one example — there are a great variety of possible scenarios:

> Faced with the stress of overwhelming responsibilities and multiple children, a mother numbs herself to the overwhelming

11

distress of being isolated and alone with a crying newborn, an attention-demanding two year old and a rebellious six year old who refuses to cooperate with her demands that he be quiet and behave himself. In addition, her husband, who is emotionally and physically absent most of the time, contributes nothing but his own complaints when he is home. She buries her feelings and just tries to get through another day. In an effort to be a good mother, she places the needs of her children ahead of her own needs, but then resents them for being so needy. And of course she resents and blames her husband for abandoning her to this overwhelming and desperate circumstance, even though in truth, it is she who has abandoned herself in order to keep her family going — in order to survive.

Her little two year old, distressed and frightened by increasingly infrequent, brusque, and mechanical care from her mother, observes her mother becoming numb and oblivious to circumstances, and absorbs and adopts this response — becoming numb emotionally — as a working strategy for escaping the discomfort of neglect and unmet needs — by abandoning the "self" that experiences distress — and by disassociating herself from her experience. A two year old does not have the capacity to think about her mother's situation or to come up with ways to help make things better. This is a period in brain development that is "preverbal" — the language skills and thinking processes required to be able to verbalize discomfort and distress in ways that appeal to reason for a solution have not yet been established.

However, two-year-olds are razor sharp limbically. The mammalian center of their brains are wide open and observant, noticing every nuance of their mothers' behavior and deeply imprinting the energetic moves of their mothers, fathers and families.

This process of bonding with the mother and absorbing and adopting an energetic constellation of emotions, attitudes, and responses — contained within unique familial styles of intimacy, safety, love and acceptance — is studied by a branch of modern psychology. It's called "Attachment Theory." This theory regards the mother-child bond as being foundational to the personality, future development, and wellbeing of the individual. This is the study of how an infant "attaches" to its mother — and the resulting world it creates for itself in response to the nature of that primary relationship.

When we are distressed as infants, we adopt the same strategies for dealing with distress as those used by our mother — the same strategies that she adopted from her mother, and she from her mother. This is how energetic patterns of sacrifice, self-betrayal, neglect and abuse get passed from generation to generation. We adopt and internalize these strategies limbically, as energetic patterns — like learning dance moves. When the music of our environment becomes threatening, discordant and harsh, we move to that music by doing the dance of survival and retreating out of our body, turning away from the distress.

If we were able, we would physically run away, or fight for our rights — the well explored "fight or flight" response — but as an infant, incapable of actual physical fight or flight, we escape the unbearable pain and distress of the present moment by leaving our body, or by protecting ourselves energetically by distracting ourselves. The moves we make in this state are contained and held as "implicit" memories — memories in this case referring to stored energetic patterns formed as a direct cellular transfer or imprint, without words defining the experience.

A couple of examples of this: We all know someone who at a dinner gathering insists that everyone serve themselves first, ahead of him — and we notice that this isn't a casual act of generosity, but rather that there is a compulsive quality to his insistence. The ghost of humiliation past, alive in the present moment as an "implicit" memory haunts this person — the humiliation of having been accused of being a selfish greedy little pig in front of young friends at a birthday party sank deep into the limbic brain, creating the compulsion to never be put in that situation ever again and to absolutely insist that others go first. Another example might be a neurosis stemming from an extremely traumatic haircut event, which generates such discomfort that the implicit stored memory directs that "no one will ever cut my hair again." And, when getting a haircut, the unfortunate person comes unglued.

These patterns emerge as "whole cloth," as completely formed strategies, as completely formed responses to stress. They are activated by stress, as if a button were pushed and an energetic command was issued — a command that our survival depends on. The moment the button is pushed by stress, there is no other option available — the command must be obeyed if we are to survive — and the proof of the command's validity is the fact that we did survive. The twisted logic of this self-fulfilling prophecy is invisible — the command demands that the person survive at any cost.

13

These energetic commands, held in the limbic brain, are not formed in words or pictures, like the stories we tell from our past — our "explicit" memories. They are held as energetic patterns, ready to be activated, but not accessible through language — so you can't uncover them through inquiry or analysis. But you can allow the system of energetic patterns to open and become available by allowing light and awareness to penetrate and illuminate it. And you can recognize patterns that no longer serve to ensure your survival — the self-protective purpose the pattern was adopted for in infancy.

Let's look at what happens in your life, and remember that there is an easy path to enlightenment — an easy path to lighting up the darkness of unconsciousness within. When you are stressed by some circumstance or event in your life, an energetic command quickly emerges. And if the command to survive is "go numb, and don't feel," then, when you are stressed you go numb and don't feel. Effectively, you have become unconscious and disassociated from yourself — and being numb is not a resourceful response to life, even a life that's dealing with extreme stress.

So what do we do? How do we deal with stress if we recognize that going numb and unconscious no longer helps us to survive in our present life circumstances?

When a stressful event occurs, we could notice the stress, rather than going unconscious. Yes, the gravitational field of our early adaptive strategies pulls us towards unconsciousness — but rather than allowing unconsciousness to overtake us at the first sign of distress, we can notice that we're uncomfortable. And then, we can use our hand to demonstrate to ourselves in sign language that there is an option available other than reenacting patterns from the past that no longer effectively deal with our stressful circumstances.

Place your thumb into your palm, and fold your fingers over it. This is a living representation of your own nervous system.

14

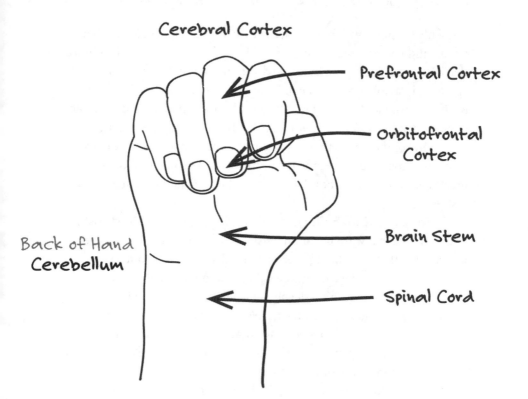

Cerebral Cortex

Prefrontal Cortex

Orbitofrontal Cortex

Back of Hand Cerebellum

Brain Stem

Spinal Cord

Now, squeeze your hand, making a tight fist, and feel the discomfort of this compressed and tension-filled state. Notice that blood is no longer flowing through your fingers — your hand is becoming white and stiff. The key is that you are demonstrating to yourself when you become uncomfortable that in fact you are uncomfortable. And now, allow yourself to gently open your hand. You have made a different choice — you have moved from the disempowerment and incapacity of an early adaptive strategy that no longer works in your life, to choosing something different.

As you open your hand, you have become spontaneously available and resourceful in the moment — to do whatever it is that you need to do. It is very difficult to serve yourself water, write something on your computer, or with a pen, or, to be intimate, affectionate and loving when you have a closed fist — especially a fist that is held so tight that it is shaking with stress. But with an open hand, you find that all of these things are very easy to do.

The resources that you need are nowhere to be found when you are disempowered, with a closed fist. These very same resources suddenly become available and are within your grasp when your hand opens, and you become capable of reaching for what you need. Solutions that you couldn't imagine in a closed-down state suddenly become apparent in an open state. The difference is simple and obvious between having closed hands, closed eyes, a closed mind, and a closed heart, and, having open hands, open eyes, an open mind, and an open heart.

One of the things that impacts us the most when stress drives us unconscious is that we stop breathing — we become shallow-chest-breathers, and as a result of that alone we become nervous, anxious and distressed.

The antidote to this increasingly toxic state induced by stress is to first notice that we're becoming distressed, and to send a message to ourselves that we're being overtaken by distress and about to go unconscious: we make a tightly clenched fist to represent the closed down state. Then, breathing deeply we open our hand, slowly and gently stretching and wiggling our fingers. We take a moment and notice in the waking dream of life that we have made a choice not to stay closed — our choice is to open — and we remember the message our spiritual teachers have shared with us — it's easy!

Here in an open state, we quickly reenergize and become empowered with a restored capacity to do whatever needs to be done, instead of spiraling downward and becoming increasingly incapacitated. And, we notice that around us are the solutions, tools and resources that a moment before weren't anywhere to be seen.

With every incident of stress that occurs in our lives, we have the opportunity to demonstrate to ourselves our newfound ability to restore our spontaneous capacity to be alive and present in the moment — alive to bring creative solutions to whatever faces us.

We get better and better at it, by practicing this new response — over and over and over. It's just like learning to play the piano or the guitar, or like learning new dance moves. With practice, you generate new neurological pathways that allow something new to play out — and you say to yourself, "When stress occurs, instead of contracting and becoming unconscious, my intent is to open my hand, to become more available and capable."

As used by shamans, the word *intent* means a state of awareness in which we are able "to reach, to stretch, to grow, to open, to expand." This meaning of intent originated as a description of the stretching of the open hand, the stretching of the tendons — a reaching and stretching that is necessary to accomplish any purpose. We share the intent to become awake, aware and present in our lives — and to not allow stress to drive us unconsciously into old strategies that no longer apply to our lives.

Because the process of being driven unconscious is so highly automated — it happens so fast that we don't even notice it — we have to counter it with a stronger, faster and more rewarding response — we practice and learn to mobilize in the moment and to come alive. And, this increased resourcefulness provides us with what we need to solve problems, deal with situations more effectively, become more spontaneous and free, and ultimately, to become more present, open-handed and intimate with every aspect of our lives.

So — how often do you practice noticing when you're distressed, and return to choice? At first, you must do it all the time. You do it in the supermarket, you do it when you're talking with somebody, you do it when you're driving, when you're at work, when you're dealing with kids, with your partner — every moment of our lives is an opportunity to practice becoming open and resourceful instead of closed and disempowered.

Remember, we're practicing lucid living. And in this dream of our waking lives, we first find our hand, and then we are able to connect with the larger reality of ourselves. This ongoing demonstration to ourselves — that we have the ability to move from being overcome by the trance of unconsciousness to being present and empowered in the awakened state — soon permeates every aspect of our habitual behavior, including our physiological responses to stress — from our breathing to our neurological and hormonal responses.

Yes, of course, this would be a worthwhile practice if the only benefits produced were improved health and an increased sense of well-being. But the real value of this practice is found in the increased awareness you gain of the creative potential of each moment — especially of those painful moments that we considered too stressful to bear. As you reclaim your awareness, you also reclaim the capacity to choose your response within the dream of life. In effect, each choice you make invites the next moment of the dream, and choosing to love, to care, and to act with loving-kindness creates the dream of heaven on earth.

And this is what the ascended masters and spiritual teachers have been showing us: enlightenment is easy because we are designed to open. As wonderful as it sounds, enlightenment is not the goal of our spiritual work. It is not the goal of the shamanic path to attain the awakened state. It is simply the first step, the place where we start.

When Children Have Children

"Marita! Get down Marita! It's the Police! Don't let them see you!" Laughter.

Marita's sisters, Juanina and Carmen, with friends, and her brother Joaquin driving, were all together in the car, on their way back from the movies, laughing — Juanina pushing Marita down in the back seat, claiming that the *Immigration Police* would arrest and send her back to the Philippines because she was so obviously *dark*.

Marita would flush, stung with embarrassment. Humiliated, her eyes would well up with tears, and she would begin to sob.

"Oh Marita! For God's Sake — it's just a joke! Please stop being such a baby!"

I inherited Marita's color — plus some. Even now, mid-winter, people will ask, "Oh, did you just get back from vacation? Where'd you go? Hawaii?" Because the tan I inherited from Marita is a year-round thing.

During the summer, my fair skinned younger brothers would turn red with sunburns, while *my* skin absorbed the sun like a sponge — dark skin, dark brown eyes, dark curly hair.

Color was a lifelong source of distress for Marita — because to be dark in Southern California when she was a teenager in the late 1940s meant to be second-class, to be a dreaded Mexican — a *pachuko*. Uncle Joaquin changed his last name from Fernandez to Ferrin in order to be hirable — even as a college graduate, one had to be white to get a job in the corporate world of the early 1950s.

The Fernandez family were Spaniards, not Mexicans. For the Fernandez girls, in the Philippines where they came from, being Spanish had meant being European — not Filipino natives but members of the ruling class, and *white*. When the American soldiers rescued the family from the Japanese prison camp at Los Banos, outside of Manilla, the girls considered them to be their saviors and heroes, and wanted more than anything in the world just to be with them. And the soldiers were more than happy to oblige. But now, back in the United States, the rules had been shifted under the Fernandez girls. They had come to the U.S. from the Philippines at the end of WWII to live in a little vacation cabin on Catalina Island. Here *Spanish* meant being Mexican, which was just as bad as being Filipino!

"Look at those cheekbones, Matilde! Look! Look at those eyes — now *they* are Fernandez! But those cheekbones, they certainly are *not* Jerry Hayhurst!" Juanina so enjoyed teasing her sister — it was fun, especially when it got such a big reaction. "Look at this baby, as dark as a little bear — don't you agree Matilde? And just look at those ears! We have a little alien baby here!"

There was a certain amount of jealousy as the sisters started having a baby boom of their own, helped along by the Catholic belief in the rhythm method. Matilde, the eldest sister, had already had Peter and Joanie, then I was born, then Carmen had Marita Lee, and Juanina had Buddy, and many more came after that.

With the parade of babies, each mother, certain that her baby was the most beautiful and intelligent, competed for the affection and attention of their parents, Mama Juana and Papa — *Papa* being *Pedro Angel Anselmo Simeon Fernandez Ormaechea*, the grand patriarch of the Fernandez clan.

Marita, the youngest of the Fernandez children, had emulated her older sisters and had gotten married in the flurry of post WWII marriages, and even though she was just 17. The excitement of everyone's lives sailing into a bright future, being *Americans*, and being married to American soldiers, overcame any commonsense objections.

The American military had rescued the family from the prison camp, and once again they were rescuing the family from the crisis of becoming Americans in a strange land. Three sisters were married within a one month period, the eldest, Matilde, having married several

19

years earlier to a navy doctor. Pedro, *Papa,* worked to speak English. He quickly became adequately fluent, but *Mama Juana — Juana Maria Puerto Fernandez Colomina del Piño* — stubbornly refused to learn and spoke only the most basic broken English. Spanish was her native tongue, and she was an artist, a singer and a Spaniard who didn't bow to passing fancies.

Matilde, who had escaped being interred in the prison camp by having left the Philippines before the Japanese occupation, had welcomed the entire clan into a little vacation shack home that she and her husband owned on Catalina Island. Joaquin was off to college, and the girls were placed in high school on the Island.

Along with a half dozen love-stricken soldiers and most of the males in the senior and junior classes at Avalon High School, 19-year-old Private First Class Jerry Hayhurst had avidly pursued Marita's older sister, Juanina.

Juanina was a firecracker — and Jerry was hot for the bright, sassy, flirty, fluent slang talking star of the *Three Sisters,* the Fernandez' McGuire-Sisters-style singing act that they had created to perform in the prison camp and later for the troops, and in the hospitals, as the war was ending.

Jerry had also corresponded with Marita, though she was too young — just a child of 15 when he met her in the military hospital at Muntinlupa. While she was a meek and self-conscious little thing, it *was* enjoyable to be so admired by a pretty young girl, and besides, it gave him an inside track on Juanina.

Unfortunately, Jerry arrived back in the States three weeks too late. Juanina had already accepted the proposal of Bud Oss. And no amount of sweet talk and cajoling could sway her; she was engaged. Half as a joke, and half not wanting to completely fail and see his well thought-out plans for the future dashed, Jerry hit on Marita. It was too easy; she had a tremendous crush on him. She adored him, and even though at this point she was just 16, she *was* a cute little hibiscus flower of a girl, trembling, but willing to do anything to please him.

Catalina Island was a dance hall and vacation paradise with the best of the big bands performing nightly and plentiful food and drink — and soldiers were treated like royalty. The sisters and their friends would go out to eat as a group, and Jerry would shamelessly flirt with Juanina, while holding Marita's hand. Juanina would scold him, and he would smirk and say, "there is a solution to this problem."

Finally, Bud had enough. Like a gentleman, privately, away from the sisters and their family and friends, he punched Jerry's lights out. Jerry concocted a story about how he had rescued a young woman being attacked by ruffians, but with his military skills he had saved her honor. This touched a soft spot with Marita, and when he proposed to her, black eye and all, she was giddy with joy. Her *American*. Marriage offered a way out of high school and out of the stifling old-world attitudes and control of Mama and Papa.

What? Her sisters, already hysterical with joy with plans for Juanina and Carmen's weddings were now over-the-top-beyond-hysterically overcome with the prospect of three weddings, all occurring within a month. Matilde was a little skeptical of this turn of events, but quickly became convinced that God was caring for her family, and that the solution to her prayers in the form of these snappy military men was fitting and right.

Marita's best friend in high school, Margie, was her bridesmaid. The wedding went off without a hitch — once Jerry showed up — an hour late. Immediately after their one-week honeymoon on Catalina, Marita came down with measles. Jerry returned to duty as an Army Recruiter in Long Beach, leaving Marita to recover at Marjie's house in Avalon, cared for by Margie's mother. After all of the excitement, Marita was alone and bored. Margie was in school all day, and her mother was extremely staid and reserved.

Her old high school friends invited her to parties on the island, of which there were plenty. She of course turned them down — she was a married woman. But when the brothers Ricardo and Jaime invited her to a party, when she was almost completely recovered, she was so desperate for something to do that she jumped at the chance to get out and have some fun.

They drank punch, listened to music, danced, laughed and had a great time into the night, although she must have fainted, because Ricardo had to carry her home to Margie's house, laughing and yelling. Margie's mother was none too happy, and coldly suggested that her home was not a place for that sort of inappropriate behavior, and that a *married* woman was not a suitable companion for her little Margie.

In late Spring of 1946, Marita came home from a doctors appointment to their little house in San Pedro with news for Jerry: "I'm pregnant." Jerry was *not* happy. Marita was terrified. Her world, her dream was collapsing in on her. "How could this be?" Jerry became more and more agitated and angry. "I have always used a condom! I have been absolutely careful! This is not possible! I left you alone for one week, and you were dancing and drinking with your old boyfriend!'

"But Jerry, he was only a friend. I was with all my friends, and we were only drinking punch, really! There has never ever been anyone but you, honest!"

And then, without warning, Jerry was gone. He went A.W.O.L. from his military post as a Recruiter, but was somehow certain that the Army would understand that he was right, that this was not his baby, that somehow he had been tricked into marriage, and that it could not possibly be valid. The brass would agree and would go easy on him, he was sure.

Marita moved back in with Mama Juana and Papa, now in a little house in Long Beach, an abandoned, pregnant 17-year-old little girl. Oblivious of the reality that Jerry had been merely playing house with her, Marita pursued Jerry back to his family home outside of Chicago, where she was certain he had gone. She had written Jerry's older sister, Mae, and her husband, Andy, begging for news about Jerry's whereabouts, certain that her love would find a way to have him stand by her again, and they had said that she was welcome in their home.

Jerry was the solution, and the *only* solution to the awful problem that her life had become. Disgraced, dishonored, shamed, embarrassed, she would succeed in convincing Jerry to take her as his again. So she went, in the dead of a mid-west winter, to their home north of Chicago on Lake Michigan. There, she had me, one week before her 18th birthday. She was devastated. Her search for Jerry had only revealed, by way of a letter accidentally sent to Mae and Andy's address, that he was seeing a girl, an old flame, who called him her *fiancé.*

The nurses handed the baby to Marita, and she broke down completely — here was a dark wrinkled little version of Papa — dark eyes, dark hair, dark skin. There was nothing even remotely Jerry-like about this baby. She broke down completely and cried, and cried, and couldn't move. Life was impossible. She couldn't relate to the baby. How could she? She was the baby. There were no maternal instincts to kick in, because *she* was a child herself. A week later, still crying, she returned to Long Beach, knowing nothing about how to care for an infant, or even how to feed an infant. The baby cried. And she cried.

Mama Juana took over the baby. This was her seventh child, and it gave her a renewed mission in life. She was once again needed. After having felt completely unwelcome, with no purpose, in a country she could not understand, *here* was something that she could understand.

And, as an infant, I knew who "Mama" was — it was Mama Juana. I had no concept that I was missing a father. There was no thought that Papa was my father, I was simply secure in the center of the love and care of a warm family, with Mama Juana providing the connected attentive engagement that she had been too overwhelmed to bring to her own children.

When she was a young woman in Spain, Juana had been a promising concert pianist and singer. She was very popular and respected as an artist in Valencia, and was beginning to tour Spain's other big cities and cultural centers when she met Pedro. Pedro was a dashing, handsome young man, and very worldly, as his family had business interests in the Philippines, and they often traveled back and forth from Spain to the Philippines.

Besides being a businessman, Pedro was a musician as well, a fine classical guitarist. He was also a vegetarian, a comedian, a mystic and free thinker, a lifelong member of the Theosophical Society. His interest in mysticism was a source of constant antagonism and dissension with Juana, who was a devout Catholic. Her girlhood dream was to become a nun — while his ambition was to solve the mystery of Creation.

In the Philippines, Juana would be continually aggravated by the steady stream of people requesting Pedro's services to cleanse their homes of unwelcome spirits, to do house clearings of negative influences and to perform blessings on everything from homes and cars to chicken coops. Pedro would say, "If you take care of the *place,* the place will take care of *you,*" and Juana would shake her head and say extra Hail-Marys for his soul.

Pedro had another specialty — the ability to put a positive energetic spin on circumstances and events for the benefit of his family, friends, and those who came to him. He called this spin, "Pookies-Smookies," and would deliver it by circling his hand in the air until a positive charge built up, which he then directed towards the desired outcome with a flourish, saying "Pookies!"

Marita returned to high school, then to a secretarial business school. She gladly handed the chores of raising a child over to her mother, and happily participated in the play and fun that an infant can be. But for anything requiring mothering, the baby reached for Mama Juana.

23

In church, or in the park, when people would comment to Mama Juana, "Oh what a pretty baby! So happy and laughing! How old is your baby?" Marita would have to interject, "I'm the mother!" Sixty years later, when Marita would leave a message on my phone answering machine, she'd say, "Hello, it's the mother!" Not "It's *your* mother." "The" mother.

She was still proclaiming, even after many years of intensive therapy and training, and even though she herself had become a brilliant psychotherapist, that the little girl standing next to Mama Juana was, in fact, the mother.

"Well, Marita," Juanina would continue with her examination of the baby, "at least Jerry will never be able to claim that this is *his* baby! You won't have to worry that he'll try to take *him*! Isn't that right Matilde? This baby looks like a little Indian!"

Which got the desired reaction from Marita — a burst of tears. This let the older sisters know that at least Marita knew her baby was *not* the perfect little angel Mama Juana said he was. Of the tribe of children that emerged right after WWII, I was naturally Mama Juana's favorite. I was *her* child as far as she was concerned. Her *Rico*; her treasure.

Rico, or Ricky, or both — I was a happy and well cared for little baby, the center of perhaps too much attention, meeting too many adult needs. I was also Pedro's favorite. He'd set me on his lap, and demand a response to his questions, and I would laugh and make up answers. Then he'd laugh. He'd say in a booming loud voice, "Where do you live little man?" and I'd say, "Here, Papa, here, here!"

He'd ask "*Look* little man, what do you see?" I would peer into the distance and proclaim, "Colors, Papa, I see moving colors!" He would laugh and say, "You see Juana, he sees spirits!"

That same booming voice made the other babies and toddlers, my cousins, cry and strain for their mothers. I was used to Papa, and they weren't. But the mothers felt impatient and distressed that their precious little ones were frightened by Papa.

Many years later, when Papa died, his ring — the ring that the head of the family wore, the ring that was kissed by obedient grandchildren as he held out his hand awaiting the respectful affection of his tribe — that ring, along with his fine classical guitar, was willed to me — given to me by Pedro as his spiritual heir. This made Matilde furious. Her eldest, Peter, was the first-born of the family's children, and by all rights, *he* should have inherited the ring.

Matilde examined my first kindergarden report card with a critical eye. It was all A's in every area — with the comment that "Ricky is extremely active and sometimes doesn't listen." Matilde exclaimed, "Ah-ha! Marita! You see? He doesn't *listen!* You have to deal with this Marita! He will never get anywhere in life if he doesn't listen. He really *must* listen, and I've noticed this very problem as well — it is much more of a problem than you are admitting. Marita, do you hear me?"

And Marita would panic. "He doesn't listen? He really must listen, I agree, Matilde," and she would go on and on in agreement — anything to take the attention off of her great fear that the fiercely critical, questioning mind of Matilde would delve into the past, and would ask uncomfortable questions about exactly what had happened with Jerry.

Marita's autobiography, *Marita — A Memoir,* written in the last few years of her life, carefully glosses over this period. She had learned to keep her dark secret to herself, from her father, who also had a dark secret that he kept hidden all of his life.

Although Pedro was a full-blooded Spaniard, he had been born in the Philippines. This was enough, if it ever had become public knowledge, to put his status as a European elite — a member of the ruling class — in doubt. And that would be catastrophic to his reputation, his business and to the family's status in society.

But Marita's edit of history began long before she wrote the story of how she had overcome the limitations of a Victorian era upbringing and dysfunctional marriage to an authoritarian alcoholic husband who resented the impositions and inconvenience that having a family made on his life. She had carefully erased the first four and a half years of my life from the family photo albums. There were baby pictures of me — then the photo albums show life in Ft. Campbell, Kentucky, with baby photos of my brother Larry.

Jerry had returned to Marita and had begged her to resume their marriage. He was partially motivated by a salty old Master Sergeant who gave him the choice of making things right with his family or spending several years in the brig. Marita desperately wanted a fairy tale ending with her hero — and he wanted to "do the right thing."

However, Jerry was shocked that the little boy spoke only Spanish, and had long curly hair and a dreamy whimsical attitude towards adults. A crew cut and some strict military discipline would straighten him out, so, as long as Marita kept the child completely out of sight and out of his way and made his needs a priority, he could tolerate having "it."

It would be a challenge for him, though, because even though Marita called the child "little Jerry" he certainly didn't look like a Hayhurst. *Hayhurst* was blue-eyed and fair-skinned, with fine straight hair, and this "little Jerry" looked like a little Mexican.

Marita's memoir was the culminating creative work of her life — containing her lineage, her story, and the wisdom she had gained over a lifetime. But towards the very end of her life she admitted that her memoir was only a fraction of what had happened, and that her focus was on telling the story of her *liberation* from a Victorian upbringing and an abusive relationship. It was not the story of *my* origins, and to her *that* explained *that*!

A little later, as I gently pressed her for more information on what had actually occurred, she angrily said, "Listen, I protected you from prejudice and gave you a life with every advantage of being an American!"

A point we agreed on was that she had been so single-mindedly focused on serving Jerry's every need and his every command, that she had been distracted and inconsistent in her mothering. At first, her inattentiveness was understandable, because she had been more my "older sister" than my mother. But then, after Larry was born, her focus became overcoming the inconvenience of having both an infant *and* a toddler in order to do a better job of attending to Jerry's needs. She accomplished this by enlisting my aid in caretaking and helping with the baby. Her priorities were Jerry's meals, his laundry, his peace and quiet, and keeping Larry and me out of sight and out of his way.

When I was eight and we lived in Fort Buchanan, Puerto Rico, I had a newspaper delivery route. I was a good worker, and because I was responsible, reliable, dedicated, and fast — and because I was saving up for a bicycle — I earned the rights to a *double* paper route. Every day I would load up my delivery bags with the *New York Times,* the *Miami Herald,* and San Juan's *El Mundo,* and, tossing in a handful of dog biscuits — part of my cost of doing business — I'd trek a three-mile route through the Army Base housing development delivering papers.

At eight years old, kids grow like weeds, and I outgrew my shoes. At one point, I ended up hobbling around my route with an infected ingrown toenail on the big toe of my right foot, the result of shoes that were outgrown, along with the tropical climate, and my inability to bring any attention to my developing problem. Finally, one day I couldn't walk. Marita took me to the military hospital — where a doctor clipped the nail in half, down to the quick, removed the ingrown side, stitched things up and sent us home. Once home, Marita had to immediately begin getting Larry taken care of, and dinner preparations for Jerry. She sent me out on my route with my papers in a little wagon. About half hour later, a horrified customer called Marita to inform her that I was leaving a trail of blood down the street, and that blood was bubbling up from my shoes.

The moment Jerry got home she took the car and drove out along my route to find me — leaving him fuming and furious, shouting "Where's my god-damn dinner?"

Eventually, with the birth of my second younger brother, Jimmy, Marita became a *mother*. She fell in love with Jimmy, and Jerry groused and complained that he was now a second-class citizen, and how the hell was *he* supposed to manage? My third and fourth brothers, John and Bob, had a whole other family dynamic to grow up in. Marita had begun counseling, and had started taking classes at the Junior College. She was growing out of her desperate need to maintain her relationship with Jerry at any and all costs.

Jerry, with a classic aggressive, impatient, and amped up type "A" personality, had a major heart attack, with one of the first quadruple bypass surgeries, and from then on was on medications that slowed him down considerably. For the first time in his life, he became interested in his kids. He still did not have an emotional or connected relationship with me, and he essentially ignored Larry, but he was proud of Jim's decision early on to go into the Air Force, and he began to connect emotionally, and in the nitty-gritty details of life, with John and Bob.

By the time John and Bob were growing up, however, I was out the door and living on my own. I went to college to avoid the draft, but my life revolved around surfing California's North Coast and being a full-time rock 'n roll musician.

I have a photo of myself at one year old, laying on top of Papa's guitar, strumming a string, my face transfixed. The sound, the vibration that was so fascinating to me *then* became my safe haven and escape as a child. Perhaps it was also my sense of security and connection with

Papa, because it was his "knock around" classical guitar that he sent along with me when Marita decided to reunite with Jerry.

That guitar was my refuge — I could strum it, and play different strings up and down the neck for hours. As what I "saw" — the moving colors of Spirit — became ugly, and even my "seeing" was disapproved of, I retreated into the safety of vibration, the sound of the guitar strings forming a universe of their own. My "dark secret" — kept even from myself — was that *who I really was* hid within the safety of music. And if growing up and becoming a *man* meant becoming like Jerry, I chose to become something different — a musician.

Marita and I began to reshape our relationship when I was 30 and she was a still youthful 47. With the youngest of my four brothers in school she was able to return to school full time. After having attended the Junior College, she transferred to San Francisco State and majored in psychology, searching for the same answers I was seeking. She was a straight "A" student, and her lecture notes could have been turned into textbooks. I was a rock 'n roll surfing shaman-seeker whose notes were loud and distorted, backed by a hard-driving rock 'n roll dance band.

Our conversations were extremely useful for me because I would come back from a remote place, having spent time with an indigenous elder, with some sort of unusual practical application of something that was mysterious and ancient — like sitting under a blanket in a tree reviewing every memory of every room of every house ever lived in, then blowing the memory away with a sweeping breath. Or, I would be immersed in the serious deprivation that led up to a vision quest.

We would discuss everything from inter-dimensional travel to shape-shifting, and oftentimes argue, because Marita was most comfortable with work that had strong empirical foundations, and what I was talking about seemed too far-out. She would direct me to the work that she was studying in child development and to new developments in neuroscience, and to the vast field of literature from the various schools of psychotherapy.

By this time in my life, I was no longer making a living as a musician. I had opened a musical instrument store, selling musical equipment back to my professional musician friends and to the local community. This gave me the income and opportunity to expand my travels, as well as giving me the opportunity to complete, by proxy, Marita's masters and PhD program: I studied whatever she was studying.

The development, or branch of psychology, that resonated most closely with what I was learning from the old-timers, the shamans, was called *attachment theory*. British Psychoanalyst John Bowlby — credited as the originator of this creative blend of psychotherapy and anthropology, created a model of human development that draws parallels between the bonding behavior of infant humans to their mothers, and animal bonding behavior. Of course, this was right up the alley of the indigenous elders who knew that we *are* animals — and that our lives are forever shaped by energetic inheritance we receive from our mothers, family and tribe.

While even our names reflect our family history, we suffer from amnesia and very few of us know anything about our ancestors and the nature of our energetic inheritance. What do you know about your grandfather or grandmother on your mother's side? What do you know about your grandmother's mother, and her mother? We're only looking back a hundred years — but for almost all of us, it is as if it were the dark ages.

In traditional indigenous cultures knowing your ancestry and your family tree is as fundamental as knowing your name. Everything about you — your hat, your shawl, your pants, your dress, your tattoos, your ornaments, your hair — *everything* displays your familial, regional, occupational, and spiritual lineage.

The shamans and healers of the old cultures especially revered and tracked the matrilineal lineage that I'm asking you to consider because a special energy — a special energetic essence of metabolic psychospiritual vibration — is passed down from mothers to their children. This essence, which modern science has identified as mitochondrial DNA, is the driving engine within ourselves. It is the animating spark of life within each of our cells, and it could be called the *song of life* that is sung by each generation, and passed to the next.

Like the universe we find ourselves in, we inherit this song, this music. It forms an inner soundtrack that we live our lives to. It is the soundtrack that we *dance* to.

We learn to move in the world, and dance this familial dance from our mothers. At a very young age between 14 and 24 months, we absorb and adopt the energetic moves of our mother as she responds to us, and as she responds to our father, to our siblings, and to the events and circumstances that occur during this time. The music of our genealogy plays in our DNA, and our mother dances the dance that *she* learned from her mother, and *she* from her mother, back through our ancestry to the mysterious times of origination.

Oftentimes a dance has some beautiful moves — moves that express life loving being alive. But more often, the dance reflects the limitations imposed on our potential totally free range of movement. These limitations, caused by abuse, betrayal, abandonment, self-betrayal, compromise, and being overwhelmed and overtaken by circumstances become the *rules* and key components of the family dance. The dance then pivots around avoidance and resistance, both futile gestures leading to depression, despair, immobilization, and even to the abandonment of the dance altogether — to disassociation.

Practices offered by shamanic tradition involve recapitulation of one's life, taking an inventory and methodically easing personal history, and becoming elusive. They all revolve around our discovering, *hearing* and learning the inherited music of our ancestry. By cataloging and reviewing the events of our life — of *our* dance — and seeing how they occurred in sync with the music, we can learn to *change* the music and to move from within ourselves — to dance our lives the way that the *gift of our life itself moves.* In other words, there is freedom to be found in being who we are, our true and authentic self.

You'll be rewarded in personal freedom beyond measure if you create a family history along with a personal history. For the family history, just make a chart and include your father's family tree — but focus on going back as far as you can on your mother's side. Include family birth order at each generation. For example, my mother was the youngest of six children with two brothers and three older sisters. Get their names, birth dates, age differences, and gather as many stories as you possibly can about their lives and situations.

You don't need to write a novel — just gather simple brief comments on your chart. Your intention is to gather the highlights and stories that make your family unique.

Consider yourself very fortunate if your grandparents, parents, and aunts and uncles are alive. They will help fill you in on these stories and the people in your family tree. But don't be surprised if you encounter reluctance to share information, or claims that there really isn't anything worth remembering and that nothing really occurred. This is of course a red flag that indicates, "dig here."

This chart of your ancestry will give you a clear sense of the music of your family, with a feel for how the dance itself moves. Is it a march? Are there snappy snare hits, a big bass drum with everyone marching to the beat? Is it a samba, with flashy trumpet bursts covering vicious elbow jabs and knee kicks? Or is it a waltz — sweet and genteel, but with only the most rigidly formalized contact permitted? Is it so loud that individual voices are drowned out? Or is it so soft that everyone is walking on eggs?

The second part of this treasure hunt that will reveal who you really are is a short outline of your personal history.

Take a couple of pages and outline the years from your birth to your present age. Leave a little extra room for the early years, from birth to three or four. List key events in your life: the birth of siblings, deaths of parents, separations, hospitalizations, housekeepers, caretakers, pets, first friends, significant teachers, first breakups, sexual awakening, injuries along the way, family moves, education, employment, later true friendships, partnerships, marriages, children — in short, anything traumatic, dramatic, or significant — the works.

Again, this is not an autobiographical work of literature. You could create that from this outline, but for now, the key is to focus on this document as an *outline.* Don't try to analyze or explain or justify anything about your outline — just look at it. Patterns will soon emerge — distinct repeating patterns that will reveal the scope and shape of the dance you learned from your mother.

31

Of course we would like to think that we were conscious, and that we made decisions based on the best information available at the time. Unfortunately, as we discovered doing the open hand exercise, the slightest stressor can drive us unconscious, and we return to the early adaptive strategies we absorbed and internalized from our mothers when we were infants — before the beginnings of language or thinking in our development.

These strategies are limited and simple, and based on the fact that we were too young to fight for ourselves, and too small to crawl away and live with our neighbors. Our only option was to observe our mothers, and to adopt her response to stress and events. Stressful events, along with stress in general in our lives, repeatedly drive us unconscious and back to these strategies, which once worked and allowed us to *survive* in our infancy.

The fact that we *did* survive seems to justify the instant implementation of these strategies — even though they are no longer appropriate responses to the circumstances facing us. Instead of fresh creative approaches and solutions, utilizing the wealth of tools and resources around us, stress triggers unconsciousness, and we restrict ourselves to the severely limited dance moves we learned from our mothers. What you see in your outline of your personal history is the patterns made by this dance.

Ultimately, the whole point of *this* work is the same as the work of noticing that you're under stress and that you're being driven unconscious, and responding by demonstrating that fact to yourself by making a fist — and then coming to choice and opening the fist, and having an open hand, as well as open eyes, an open mind, and an open heart. In demonstrating to yourself that you do have a choice as to how to respond, you become spontaneously available to see and utilize resources that had been hidden from you moments earlier.

The ultimate truth of who you are is this: *you* are a gift from Creation Herself, *to* Herself, and your primary responsibility here is to open that gift by coming present. Take off the ribbons! Open the package!

Become present as the gift of Creation to herself — *that* is the cosmic dance to the song of the universe! And this is possible because deep within us is the music of Creation, and there also, deep within, is the presence of the Mother of us all. And, her response to the challenges of life is to *care*, to *encourage*, to *nurture* and *love* us, and ultimately, to *enjoy* us — and to clap her hands in delight at our silly antics!

Forgiveness is the Key

You've got to be taught to hate and fear,
You've got to be taught from year to year,
It's got to be drummed in your dear little ear –
You've got to be carefully taught!

You've got to be taught to be afraid
Of people whose eyes are oddly made,
And people whose skin is a different shade –
You've got to be carefully taught.

You've got to be taught before it's too late,
Before you are six or seven or eight,
To hate all the people your relatives hate –
You've got to be carefully taught!
You've got to be carefully taught!

"You've got to be carefully taught"
— ROGERS & HAMMERSTEIN

Our second step along the spiral brings us into the dawning light of awareness. Here is an opportunity to see what you're made of, to see how you got to where you are now — along with how you have acquired the unnecessary baggage you've been holding on to. Here is an opportunity to set everything down, and to take a *look*.

Let's start by talking about domestication — what happens to us from infancy into early childhood and continues to determine how we live our lives from then on. We'll look at how you were brought up and how your parents, with the best of intentions, filled your head with their prejudices, beliefs, and assumptions — things that aren't necessarily true. In fact, their beliefs and assumptions about how life is to be lived are mostly *not* true — and at best would lead you to the same sort of life that they lived.

Yes, a serious case *can* be made for domestication of young humans. The little human has to be tamed and accustomed to living in a household with respect for cleanliness, table manners and established customs. Accomplished with love, domestication doesn't seem like such a bad thing — after all, we all have to learn how to live together.

But something more seriously damaging than simple *domestication* happens to us when we're young. We *internalize* the system of reward and punishment used to domesticate us, and this system directs the course of our life based on the arbitrary rules and regulations adopted by our parents. The bitter irony of this internalization is that while the *punishment*, or stick, side of the system effectively directs our behavior because of our innate desire to avoid pain, the *reward*, or carrot, offered to us is a mirage, and cannot satisfy us. So, on the reward side of the equation, we are motivated and directed by an illusion — the illusion that we are loved.

What we need as infants, as children, is the presence of *unconditional* love. The sense of acceptance, worth, value, welcome, "rightness" of the world that being loved unconditionally generates is absorbed directly into every cell of our being, and it nourishes that deep place within us that generates growth and well-being that can sustain us for a lifetime. Unconditional love recognizes the unique gift to life that we are, and celebrates it wholeheartedly.

On the other hand, *conditional* love — which is the love and acceptance that is doled out when we behave properly by satisfying the expectations of our parents or caregivers — is *not* satisfying or nourishing to us because it contains the indigestible condition that we

36

are not acceptable or loveable *as we are*, but worthy of love only to the extent that we are able to meet the conditions imposed by our mother, father and other caretakers.

What children need to thrive is unconditional love. What we need as human beings of any age is unconditional love — the presence of love without expectations or conditions. But that's not what we get. We get praise and conditional love to the extent that we are not a problem — to the extent that we behave. Then, as counterbalance on the other side of the domestication system, we are punished when we "misbehave."

This system of reward and punishment is how we've all been domesticated. But something much worse than being compelled to be inauthentic in order to be loved happens in the life of every human being. We're not just struck and punished — we're actually injured. We are *hurt* by other people — most often by the very people who are closest to us. It's not defensible or acceptable, but it *is* understandable – we misbehave, we're spanked, or shaken, and hit. We do something scary, and in a weird twist on concern for our safety, our parents totally freak out and begin screaming and hitting us as a result of it: "You should NEVER, NEVER do that again." *Whap!*

Oftentimes we are punished for acting out the family issues that the adults would prefer not to see or hear. We're "trouble" and have to be taught what is appropriate. Often times what is considered to be appropriate is something like "children are to be seen but not heard." Our misbehavior provokes anger and frustration on the part of our parents, who need us to obey and follow their directions and rules in order for them to keep control. *Our* behavior triggers *their* unconscious distress and out-of-control insecurities and angry hurt feelings of having their wishes ignored and violated. The result is that without thinking they strike back. Once again: *Whap! Whap!* Through infancy and childhood, injury after injury accumulates, even from our brothers and sisters, who sometimes know that they're injuring us, and sometimes really don't know that they're causing lasting harm.

And the abuse continues — physical abuse, emotional abuse, mental abuse — from our families, from extended family, teachers, coaches, friends, lovers, business associates — all of our relationships contain the potential for violence and injury. In such a world, in order for us to be wide open and fully functioning in a state of wellbeing and creativity, it is an absolute necessity that we learn how to forgive.

37

The shamanic perspective on forgiveness is that it has nothing to do with the morality of someone's behavior. Shamanic forgiveness does not consider ethical positions — forgiveness is simple and very, very practical. Forgiveness of all of those who have harmed you is also absolutely necessary if you are to recover from injury and move towards self-fulfillment, awareness, and joyful effective action in your life.

To understand why this is so, let's take a tour of what the word "forgiveness" means, and where it came from.

Forgiveness is a word that originates in the ancient Celtic languages, and it has come down to us in Old English. The same concept of forgiveness, meaning restoration of our wholeness and our full capacity, exists in other languages, but this particular example in English truly illuminates the shamanic practice of forgiveness — so we'll use it.

In English, the key action component of the word *forgiveness* was originally a nautical term. When the small boats were out fishing and maneuvering over a fertile fishing area, the boats would bob and weave and mill about around each other. The person stationed in the fore part, or front, of each boat would warn other boats of their course through the waters by yelling out "Fore!" — basically saying " Stand back! Push back! Push out of the way!" *Fore* migrated from the fishing grounds to common usage in many words — but it can be found in its original pure sense in the ancient Celtic game of golf — golf being a game where you hit a ball down the fairway and warn people on the course to watch out and stand out of the way, or chance getting hit. You can hear people call out this ancient nautical term on golf courses everywhere — "Fore!" They're actually saying, "Back away. Watch out. Push away."

Let's look at a couple of other common usages of "fore" so that you really understand how simple your task is going to be. Let's start with "forget."

"I can't find my keys! I forgot where I put them." I had my keys — they were in my pocket when I got home, and they're not there now, and they're not on the counter or table. In effect, somehow I have *pushed away* from my conscious mind the knowledge of where I left them. So, I forgot where I left them, and I'll have to reconstitute myself, pulling back the memory of where I left them — all because I forgot. And how do we actually find the misplaced keys? By searching through every possible place we could have put them — in effect pulling each possible hiding place *towards* us and looking — until finally we find them in the jacket pocket where we forgot we left them.

"Foreboding:" we live happily in our abode — we're at home and we're at peace, and then suddenly an unnerving chill overtakes us that pushes away our sense of well-being, replacing it with an eerie sense of foreboding. In the movies, shrill discordant music announces this moment — but in real life, it is our sense of the "rightness" of our world that gets pushed away and replaced by the anticipation of something dreadfully wrong. We're pushed right out of our home and into a dark and dangerous alley — our sense of safety and shelter have been pushed away, leaving us standing vulnerable and shaking.

Another word sharing Celtic seafaring origins would be "forsake." Let's say that our relationship is mutually beneficial — we're good for each other — and our individual lives are enhanced by our relationship. We're in love and we're together. Then — and this is a story as old as seafaring — you've heard the sad song — "Do not forsake me, oh, my darling." My darling pushes me away, and I am forsaken.

In the case of "forgiveness," what is pushed away is what was given to you. Unfortunately what was given was not a *gift*, but the blow of a harsh word, a cold silent stare of disapproval, a grimace of disgust, a slap on the face, the experience of being isolated and punished.

To forgive is a very simple act. Despite the many books written and massive confusion about forgiveness, there are no complex moral or ethical components to it. Forgiveness is a purely energetic transaction — a pushing back of what was given to you, a returning of what was given to whomever gave it to you.

And in the case of injury and abuse, what was given to you was toxic and harmful, something that you absolutely had to defend yourself against and hold off, because if you let the full force of the injury strike you to the core, it would poison you and eventually kill you. If you can imagine the Hindu goddess Kali, with all of her arms, each holding something — a weapon, a flute, a flower, a severed head, a bowl, and on and on, arm after arm — you've got a mental picture of what we're like energetically. We each have many thousands of energetic arms and hands. This is just a practical way of describing our energetic potential as beings of light — we're luminous beings made of an iridescent multi-stranded fabric of light.

39

When something shocking happens to us when we're very young, we're incapable of processing or even understanding it. We don't have the resources to counter the attack, and we can't metabolize something that is essentially toxic to us. So we come to terms with being injured by attempting to shield ourselves energetically, by holding off the trauma. In a way, we're able to encapsulate the injury and not allow it *in* by holding it at arms length away from ourselves. We escape total devastation by holding onto the injury so that it can't come loose and work its way into our hearts, but we also become progressively disempowered, because our thousand handed capacity to engage in the world becomes reduced by the mounting number of injuries we hold.

Forgiveness Ceremony

Gather some dried chili peppers — we'll use them in a special ceremony of forgiveness as a symbol of the many incidents of injury that have happened in your life.

My recommendation for this ceremony is that you start with forgiving your mother, and then you work with forgiving your father, your brothers and sisters, aunts and uncles — and then you will include your friends, your teachers, your lovers, and any others who appear. Eventually you may find it important to forgive grandparents, ancestors, and others that come forward.

The ceremony will initiate a process of re-energizing and re-empowering yourself with the recovery of the personal energy you have invested in holding injuries that you couldn't deal with in any other way. The sharp edged toxic barbs of energy that you weren't able to metabolize, that you had to hold away from yourself, can be returned to their originator, the person who injured you. And as you let them go, the energetic hand that you used to hold them away becomes free to be useful and helpful in your life.

Dried chili peppers work best for our ceremony, because, even though as adults we can enjoy hot sauces, as a child there was no way that you could ingest or metabolize large handfuls of these things. Can you see that the insults and injuries that you have endured are like chili peppers — things so toxic that you had to hold them away from yourself? Sadly, in some cases we continue to hold injuries for a lifetime that we don't even remember are there.

Let's do this together. To begin, find a private and quiet spot where you won't be disturbed for an hour. Light a candle, have some drinking water handy, bring in some flowers just for the sake of making your ceremony beautiful. Light some sage if you'd like, to create some holy smoke. Sit comfortably, with the chili peppers in front of you, in a bowl, or piled on a *mesa* — a brightly colored cloth.

Start with your mother. Pick up a large handful of chili peppers and, holding them in front of you, say, "Mother, I am returning to you all of your energy that I am holding — all of the things that you did or said that have injured and hurt me that I still haven't resolved, I now return that energy to you." And, turning your hands over, simply let the chilies that you have been holding drop, saying, "Mother, I forgive you."

Forgiveness means pushing away and pushing back what was given to you — simply returning *what* was given to the one who gave it to you. And when you simply turn your hands over, dropping the chili peppers while saying "Mother, I forgive you" the toxic energy you have been holding flows away from you, and returns immediately to her.

It is important for you to know that the very same energy that is toxic to you is an integral and *necessary* part of her energy system. It is a part of her that she misplaced, that she directed towards you when she was unaware that she was reacting to her projections, not to the real *you*.

Without this energy she is incomplete, a part of her missing. It is a great gift you give her to return her misplaced and missing energy — she can't continue or move on with her own evolution until she recovers this energy and mends herself — and this is true whether she is alive or in spirit. Your simple act of returning what is hers to her ultimately helps her move towards her own liberation. However, the most important thing that's happened is that *you* have recovered the use of your facilities.

As you let the chilies drop, your hands become free to attend to doing a better job of taking care of yourself. You recover your capacity to direct your energy in response to your own needs, instead of having it locked up in the past. This is an instantaneous healing. 41

With your father, repeat the ceremony, taking the time to call his image, his presence, before you. Take the chilies in your hands and say, "Father, I forgive you for the injuries that you've caused." This can include extremely serious injuries. For many of us, it is not just a case of being hit occasionally or having a parent that's out of control and mad, or of having a parent that goes unconscious and whacks you. The injuries that need releasing, that beg our forgiveness, include *all* forms of abuse, including sexual abuse.

Both big and small injuries impact our energy system. Energetically, we do not evaluate the degree of harm caused and calculate some formula based on that — the simple energetics of our design just have us do our best to hold each injury away from its target, and to keep holding it away in order to protect ourselves. Injuries can include misunderstandings, being accused of things that we didn't do, and incidents in which we were treated unfairly — we hold off *all* the things that deeply hurt us, because we can't metabolize their toxins. In each instance, we demonstrate to ourselves in ceremony that we are holding these things in our hands, and we turn our hands over and release the chili peppers, saying, "I forgive you."

Jesus said, "Father, forgive them for they know not what they do." In so many instances, things happen to us that are injurious, but the person that has hurt us is unconscious and unaware that they're even hurting us. We still have the protective effect of our multi-handed energetic design. In our many hands we hold these things because we're not able to absorb or process them. Not that we would want to, because doing so would be so toxic that it would kill us.

To these unconscious people we can say, "I return your energy. I forgive you."

This ceremony of forgiveness is a *practice*, and you use it to release the energy you have been holding, returning it to your brothers and your sisters, your aunts and uncles, your teachers, friends, employers, co-workers — you practice returning held energy to *everybody* who's ever been in the range of your personal history.

You forgive them, and you return their energy to them. If they've passed on and they're in Spirit now, it's even *more* important that you forgive them, because until they recover themselves, and recover the energy they left behind in the form of insults and injuries to others, they can't evolve further. They can't move on, and they remain in a state of anguish, begging for forgiveness. So, forgiving everyone who has ever injured you in your life is a real act of service.

This initial ceremony of forgiveness will lead directly to the recovery of your own life energy that was bound up in past injuries — and this is the energy that will allow you to take the next step in forgiveness towards becoming whole.

Now that you've performed the forgiveness ceremony for others, you are ready for the next level of the ceremony: you are now capable of asking for forgiveness from those that *you* have injured, purposely and accidentally, consciously and unconsciously. At this point you understand that you're asking to recover your own energy.

Put your hands together, and hold them out in front of you, palms open. Say out loud, "Please forgive me for having harmed you. I didn't know what I was doing, and I realize now that it was hurtful and that what I did and said injured you. I know that you've been holding on to it, and I am sorry. Please forgive me."

You're asking them to push back *your* energy that *they've* been holding onto — and it truly is a relief for them to be relieved of it. If you can meet these people in person and say, "Please forgive me for the harm that I've done to you," and ask for their forgiveness, they might remain angry with you, but they *will* forgive you, because nobody wants to continue to hold onto toxic distress and injury. Deep within all of our hearts, we *all* want to forgive and be forgiven, we *all* want to regain our full capacity, our very selves — we *all* want to be complete and whole.

Finally — on to the completion of the ceremony, and to our most difficult challenge: The time has come for you to forgive yourself.

We hold parts of ourselves aside within ourselves, because it is unacceptable to us that we've been so oblivious and unconscious that we've deeply hurt the ones that we love, as well as hurting ourselves in the process. And we can't or won't forgive ourselves for what we've done. This separation within ourselves renders us incapable of love and incapable of being truly present, because we're divided within. Energetically, we're holding ourselves at arms length. And to become whole, recovering our *own* energy that we've held away from ourselves in weird ways, we take handfuls of chilies and, after a moment of feeling our own remorse and pain, we let the chilies drop, saying, "I forgive my *self* for the harm that I've done to others and to myself."

In each of these cases the energetic action required to effectively shift the way that our energy is being used is simple — and the shamanic ceremony itself is also simple. It is very simply taking the energy that you've been holding in some of your thousands of hands and returning it. As you do this process of forgiveness, working with the chili peppers to drive home the reality of what is happening, you will recover more and more of your *hands,* and the full presence and use of your personal energy will return to you.

My recommendation is that the *first* thing you do with your

43

returning personal energy is to place your hands over your heart, and feel the inflow of unconditional love. This energy *is* unconditional love — because the conditions it met, loving you so much that it nearly died trying to protect you from injury, having been removed, allowed for the release of this energy back into circulation within you. So, allow yourself to hold yourself unconditionally — and allow the return of this vital life energy within yourself to overcome the trauma of domestication — recognizing that what your parents believed, and the pain that they inflicted on you because of their beliefs, was the result of something that they didn't even know they were doing. They were doing their best, and they didn't know any better.

Your forgiveness liberates you, and returns misplaced energy to those who injured you. However, we're not released from *responsibility* for our actions — and each of us must make whatever amends we can for our actions, conscious or unconscious. Being forgiven does not change this responsibility that each of us bears for our actions. No matter what things might look like, no one gets away with anything. But forgiveness restores our energetic capacity to mend the torn fabric of being — with others and within ourselves.

In light of this truth, the key to our evolution and liberation is the simple act of forgiveness. Use it.

There are hundreds of different schools of thought about what forgiveness is. At the bottom of it all, everyone agrees on how *important* forgiveness is — but there, hidden underneath the bottom, lurks the unanswered question: Why should *I* forgive those who have injured *me*?

Isn't it somehow the responsibility of those who injure us to make amends for their crimes? And to beg *us* for forgiveness? And to do the best that they can to undo the harm caused by the injuries that they've done?

Even the "spiritual point of view" takes a hard line here: *karma* — the intrinsic justice of the universe — will deal with these people by doing to them what they did to us. So, it's not *our* responsibility to deal with the people that have hurt us. They're going to get theirs in the big picture!

What all of the definitions have in common is the perspective that we must forgive someone else for what they have done to us. For most of us, this is just *not* a hot topic. Yes, we've had our share of bumps and scrapes, but nothing *that* major has happened to make us think that we really *have* to give the subject of forgiveness a deeper look.

Sadly, though, for some of us, abuse, injury, and serious damage *have* occurred. Some of us — victims of crimes for example — have been seriously overtaken by catastrophe.

But for most of us, the importance of forgiveness is slightly submerged below the waterline of normal reality, and it's not a part of our daily experience. On the other hand, a much more visible piece of the puzzle is the conviction that *someone* is to blame for the way things are! And, look around! It's pretty easy to see that *someone is to blame*!

Big corporations act like sociopaths with no sense of responsibility for any of the damage they cause to the environment or to people's lives. Add to that the fact that they are not held responsible or accountable for their actions, and they don't even pay their share of taxes. Instead of paying taxes, their lawyers and lobbyists have helped them buy the government, which essentially does whatever they're told to do by the corporations!

And the government! Our governments, along with being inept, ineffective, and corrupt, are equally abusive, and roll over people and their lives without any concern for the damages done.

The military industrial complex is to blame. The Illuminati are to blame. Reptiles from alien galaxies, disguised as human beings, have taken over our planet, and *they* are to blame. And let's not get started on war and who's to blame for creating war, and what sketchy reasons we are given for bringing the devastation of war to countries and civil populations far away from *our* homes. We still don't know who really is to blame for 9/11 — the collapse of the World Trade Center Towers — and how about Building 7? Who was behind the assassination of Gandhi, the Kennedys, Martin Luther King? *Someone* must be to blame for these history-altering tragedies.

45

Closer to home, as much as we hate to think bad thoughts about our own families, aren't our parents to blame for the way we turned out? After all, they were ignorant, alcoholic, co-dependent, abusive, absent, addictive, anxious, depressed, narcissistic, neurotic and uncaring — and essentially the ones to *blame* for what we have become!

Don Miguel Ruiz had a very different take on forgiveness, an insight that he shared with us on one of our early "power journeys" to Machu Picchu and the Sacred Valley in Peru.

Don Miguel, a Toltec *nagual* (shaman) in the ancient Eagle Knight Lineage of the Mexican highlands, had come from a family of healers, of *curanderos*. His mother, Sarita, was a well-known healer whose work was grounded in the ancient Toltec Nahuatl traditions of pre-conquest, pre-Aztec and pre-Mayan Mexico.

By the way — the "don" in don Miguel's name is an honorary title of respect, as in "don Corleone" from *The Godfather*. And the word "nagual," which we loosely interpret to mean "shaman," translated from old Nahuatl means "flesh puppet" or, one who is the living puppet of Spirit, one who is *empty*, containing only the presence of the space between the stars. Don Leonardo, Miguel's grandfather, had a profound influence on Miguel's education and training as a Nagual — a training that Miguel received in the realm of Spirit. Miguel followed his family's tradition of becoming a healer by joining several of his older brothers in becoming a medical doctor and surgeon specializing in neurology. This being the modern age, healers now based their work on science, not on mysticism or superstition, and Miguel was by nature curious and had a strong common sense approach to healing arts.

But Miguel found out that science itself was only a small part of reality when he had an automobile accident, and after helping his friends out of the vehicle and to safety beside the road, he noticed that *he* was still slumped over the steering wheel in the driver's seat. This experience reawakened in Miguel a deep sense of wonder about the nature of reality, because he had suddenly experienced himself as pure awareness, and he remembered that he was more than he appeared to be. He turned again to the wisdom of his family, and studied with his mother, adapting ancient Toltec tools to the needs of the students and apprentices that had begun to gather around him.

The first book that came out about don Miguel, *Beyond Fear*, was treasured and shared by those interested in indigenous ceremonies and the ways of shamanic wisdom practices. Whereas Carlos Castaneda, author of popular books on shamanism based on his relationship with the nagual don Juan, was elusive and unavailable, don Miguel was up front and actively presented information in seminars and workshops. *Beyond Fear* is *still* cherished as a container of real magic, of living shamanic energy, but the book that put don Miguel on the world cultural map — and became a *New York Times* bestseller for over seven years — was *The Four Agreements.*

The Four Agreements — *Be impeccable with your word; don't take anything personally; don't make assumptions;* and *always do your best* — is a magical book containing deceptively simple wisdom principles that are capable of transforming one's life.

Like his grandfather don Leonardo before him, Miguel had become a true nagual guide, assisting people around the world to find their personal freedom.

The turning point that began don Miguel's mission in the world was an experience he had on the top of the great Pyramid of the sun at Teotihuacan, in the High Plains above Mexico City. This mysterious complex of pyramids, temples, courtyards and broad avenues suddenly came into focus for don Miguel as he meditated on top of the great pyramid. He saw that Teotihuacan was a University of Spirit, and that the Toltec heritage was to live one's life as a work of art.

He saw that the purpose of this University was to guide individuals to the recognition of the presence of divinity within themselves.

And as he looked into the sky, into the light of the sun, he noticed a change in the light — a shift in color and intensity — and he was filled with love for all of creation, he was filled with joy, he was filled with deep gratitude, and the recognition that a new age had begun.

He called this the Sixth Sun.

With the radiance of love flooding from him, beaming from his eyes and radiating like sunlight from his very being, the ancient wisdom that he offered attracted an increasingly large following. His workshops, seminars, lectures, and journeys were sold out — filled with people who wanted to just *be* with this wonderful charismatic being.

Miguel took groups of people with him to the great pyramids at Teotihuacan, taking them through the same process that he had been through — the process of discovery of divinity within the center of oneself, and finding the freedom and joy that this discovery brings. As his organization grew, early apprentices became teachers and assisted him with taking groups through the pyramids. One of his teachers, who also organized and handled the detail load generated by all of this activity was Gini Gentry.

47

Gini was (and is) a brilliant flash of illumination — and like lightning, she was beautiful and dangerous. She had the capacity to shock the hell out of you, getting to the bottom line of whatever your issue was in an instant — like a knife cutting through a pear. She was also willing to go the distance with a student or apprentice, and would patiently and lovingly work through the gritty details of their egoic involvement in creating their delusional, or rather, *illusory* worldview.

Besides being a "brain," Gini had the capacity to contain and hold enormous fields of energy, and this natural capacity to allow Spirit to be present in a *huge* way made her a nagual. It made her the absolutely perfect ceremonial companion at times when energy *had* to be called present.

Leading a ceremony with Gini present ensured the creation of an energetic foundation of transformational potential that positively crackled and lifted participants into other dimensions.

And she was a cowgirl!

I was in Teotihuacan with don Miguel and a group the night that Miguel declared that Gini was a nagual woman — *the* Nagual Woman.

It was a choice that did not go over well with the inner circle of devoted apprentices. That became obvious in the evening's gathering, when don Miguel presented Gini to the group as a nagual, and had her begin to teach as his equal partner. In that gathering, Gini the lightning bolt came forward, speaking the truth, electrically, beautifully, and shockingly.

"My Darlings," she said, "the more you are certain that you know and understand what we are doing here, the more you reveal yourself to be under the spell of a great Pretender. And here in this circle are those of you who should know better, *pretending to know better!*

"There! Right now! In this moment! Do you see how the energy has just changed from *Love* to defensive posturing? My Darlings, if you are unable to stay in Love here in this room, what honestly makes you think that you know anything about Love in the world outside of this room?"

Taking offense, some of the inner circle of apprentices grimaced and shook their heads with disapproval. Their reaction was contagious, and soon the room grumbled with discontent.

Miguel decided to do a survey of people's responses to Gini's teaching.

He looked around the circle — almost 60 people — asking if they

48

were offended, if they were thinking that Gini had been rude, or mean, or simply offbase.

People were distressed, and expressed it. Perhaps don Miguel was having second thoughts on his selection of Gini as the Nagual Woman, and they did not hesitate to express their concern.

Yes, they said, Gini was *way off* the mark. They wanted to hear don Miguel talk about Love, magic, and freedom. They had come to Teotihuacan to hear *don Miguel's* teachings. They had *not* come to hear Gini Gentry talk about dishonesty, delusion and the ugly underbelly of personal transformation. The disapproval in the room was tangible. Everyone who spoke opposed Gini. It was like being at a Roman circus with hand after hand displaying their thumbs down. The consensus was: *off with her head.*

I raised my hand, and don Miguel invited me to speak.

I said, "I think that when a teacher speaks, they become a *target* for everyone's projections. That's what has just happened here with Gini. "We've made her a target. And underneath the disapproval that has been expressed, I see *fear.* I think that Gini's honesty is refreshing. Maybe it's a bit like ice cold water in your face, but it's still refreshing, and I think you would all do well to examine what you've said about Gini as an expression of *yourself*, and not about her."

I had no intention of being so direct and forceful. I was just going to express a contrary opinion and say, "Hey, take it easy here," but the torrent of words had gushed out. After speaking, I felt a rush of adrenaline that made me shake, and I felt flushed, suddenly hot and prickly. I had obviously crossed over a line with the apprentices and teachers. Suddenly, I was in big trouble. All eyes turned to don Miguel for his reaction.

Don Miguel was smiling like the Cheshire Cat, his black eyes glittering and throwing off sharp-edged faceted sparks as he looked around the room.

"Yes. Yes," he said, "*who* is the target? And *who* is missing the mark?"

Then Gini whispered to the now dead silent room, "Class Dismissed."

49

Those who were close to Miguel knew that he had an ongoing heart condition, and for all the mega wattage of love and joy that emanated from him, he was not in the best shape. Rather than the rugged, primitive, close to the earth accommodations that one might expect from journeys into the heart of indigenous cultures, we always stayed at the very best hotels and had the very best of everything. This actually turned out to be wonderful, because our journeys were so profoundly challenging and intense that having a hot shower, a really good meal, and a comfortable bed at the end of a hard day was heaven, and helped everyone recover for the next day's adventure.

On one of our first journeys through the Sacred Valley in Peru our group of about 40 people stayed at a five-star hotel at the base of Machu Picchu. The group was spread across a number of really lovely individual casitas, the restaurant overlooked the Urubamba river, the food was fabulous, and on the grounds were extensive gardens and Inca ruins, a small zoo, and a beautiful little restored chapel where we would meet.

One evening after having spent the day in Machu Picchu, don Miguel gathered us in the chapel. We settled in a circle with don Miguel sitting at the top of the circle where the altar had been.

He began to examine us with real curiosity, looking from face to face around the circle — his dark eyes sparkling. This look was always a sign that trouble was about to occur, that the Nagual was present, and that the yawning, gaping hole of the great mystery that underlies what we called *normal reality* was opening wide, and any perception we might have had that we were safe from anything was dust in the wind.

Silence. "Forgiveness" Miguel whispered. "Forgiveness."

None of us were sure that we had actually heard what he said correctly, because Miguel's Spanish accent would subtly shift and shape words in ways that left you uncertain of *what* he was saying until a moment later when the context of his train of thought became clear. This alone effectively short-circuited our minds, which was very useful for Miguel when he wanted to alter our sense of reality, because, as he often told us, *thinking is not perceiving.*

"Forgiveness." He whispered, and gestured that we tighten up the circle and come very close. He reached out to Luis Molinar, one of his apprentices, and placed him in the center of the circle. He whispered instructions into Luis's ear, and Luis began to speak to each of us in turn.

He said, "Please forgive me for using you to abuse myself."

"Please forgive me for using you to abuse myself."

"Please *forgive me* for *using you* to abuse *myself.*"

After the twentieth repetition, the message was beginning to sink in — the message that we create our own reality and mistakenly put other people in charge of meeting our needs.

"Please forgive me for using you to abuse myself."

By the thirtieth repetition Luis was sobbing, and we were all in tears. By the fortieth repetition we clearly felt and understood that we allow ourselves to be *victims* and then blame other people for our own abuse of ourselves.

This ceremony of don Miguel's took a more circuitous route to releasing the role of victim while simultaneously taking responsibility for creating one's reality than the direct experience of simply releasing held energy suggested earlier in this chapter. But such a ceremony *does* have the effect of taking us beyond blaming someone else for our experience, and it does alert us to the fact that, by continuing to be a victim, we have disempowered ourselves. It relieves the prickly needle-like cactus spines of the judgments, opinions, thoughts, and gossip that we continually abuse ourselves with, thinking that we are merely *commenting* on others.

From below the surface of normal reality, forgiveness comes on like a fire that consumes illusion, and, once the fire is lit and illusion is burning, definitions of forgiveness are no longer necessary.

As you know from the work that you've done with your familial inheritance and personal history, people act out of unconscious scripts, reenacting patterns adopted in infancy and replaying in the world the things that happened to them along with the strategies they adopted to cope.

From this point of view, you are merely collateral damage, and, while the injury you suffer is bad enough, a lifetime of disempowerment because you attribute to others the power to determine your experience and destiny is a tragedy.

51

The solution is to take responsibility for everything that you experience. Consider this just an experiment if you find it too overwhelming to accept that you are responsible for everything that you experience. Taking on this responsibility has the effect of turning the light *on* in your life – and as you begin, you'll notice two things:

First: You have been disempowering yourself by continuing to carry the toxic energy of injuries, along with holding *blame* for the perpetrator who caused the injury, in addition to feeding your energy to perpetuate the sense of injustice that *this* could have been done to you. Energy snarled and bound up like this obviously is not free to circulate in your system, in support of your life.

Second: By continuing to be a victim, and seeing yourself as a victim of circumstances and of others' actions, you effectively disempower yourself and put other people in charge of what you experience.

Don Miguel's ceremony *("Please forgive me for using you to abuse myself")* is a step towards taking responsibility for your own experience.

The next step is the *recovery* of the power that you misplaced with others, and you know from your ceremonies with the chili peppers that the recovery of your power is really the recovery of your capacity to be truly present and spontaneously engaged in your own creation — to *be* the artist and creator of your world.

We are so certain that we know who and what has injured us, that we think that we can make quick work of this business of forgiveness. If only it were that simple. The real work of forgiveness is to methodically take stock of not only what seem to be obvious injuries, but also of any instance where you blame anyone or anything for the way things are, along with any and every case where you see and feel that there is injustice.

And of course, we start with those closest to us.

For me, it was easy to forgive my mother. I had an adult relationship with her that involved looking honestly into areas where neither of us wanted to look.

She had been a child when she had me, and it was not hard to see that she had simply replayed what had happened to her. When she was only five her mother had placed her in a convent school run by unhappy French nuns, in the Philippines. Her mother thought that it was the best thing for her and her sisters, because it was what *she* had always wanted — to be safe and secure in a convent.

Because I had an ongoing relationship with her, I felt the genuine love and care and beauty that was her essence. It was much more difficult forgiving my father for not *being* my father.

Energetic *crossed wires* oftentimes look like this. How can you forgive someone for not being who they were supposed to be but weren't?

And yet, here was a real human being who lived a life full of resentment, anger and insecurity, who medicated himself into oblivion with alcohol and arrogance. How can you forgive *that*?

My own anger softened and transformed into understanding and compassion when my research revealed that Jerry's father had vanished when he was an infant. His father simply disappeared, leaving a large family and a floundering business, and he was never again seen or heard from. So Jerry grew up without a father, and had no idea of how to be something that he had never had. Forgiving him and returning to him his energy – his resentful, angry, bitter energy – allowed *him* to forgive *his* father for having abandoned *him*, for having left him alone and without guidance in the world.

His mother was so distraught when her husband disappeared that she became mentally unhinged; her world came apart and she never recovered from the blow. Jerry's older sister, Mae, had to take over the family and keep food on the table, the kids in school, and the laundry and everything else done. She had to drop *her* future to take over the role of mother in the Hayhurst family. It comes as no surprise that she deeply resented losing her freedom and resented being forced by circumstances to care for this abandoned family at the expense of her own hopes and dreams.

Along with the recovery of your *own* capacity to use the vibrant energy of life for your benefit and the benefit of those you love and care about, your repeated acts of forgiveness will not only heal yourself, but will also help heal others, and ultimately will heal the world.

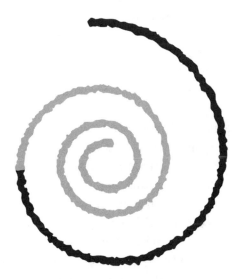

Suffering Is Optional

THE MOST RADICAL THING A HUMAN BEING has ever conceived is the notion that suffering could be optional.

The foundation of all of ancient wisdom — something said by the wise ones of all indigenous peoples, and something that was said by Jesus — is this: *the Kingdom of Heaven surrounds us.* And yet men and women don't see it. Is there a way for us to actually *see* that we are in heaven? And that, being *surrounded* by heaven, we can come to *live* there, no longer suffering? The answer is, of course, YES! There is a tried and true ancient path into heaven, well worn by the most practical of travelers, the shamans, medicine people, seers and Holy Ones of indigenous cultures worldwide.

All of us have had a taste of heaven in our lives — it is the "coming to live there, and no longer suffering" part that eludes us. So how do we start? What steps can we take to actually experience this in our lives?

The practice being shared here will sound easy, and you might think, "Oh, I can do that" while promptly forgetting that it is a *practice,* and that you have to actually *do it!* And the first step is the hardest because it means accepting something that we really do not want to accept. Taking this step amounts to being initiated into the possibility of a new life. Ready?

It's going to sound severe for me to say this to you, but this is the first step, and here is the truth: *you are responsible for everything you experience.* You're responsible for everything you do, and you're responsible for *all* of your actions and reactions in this world.

Yes, it's true that wild, random and accidental things just *happen* in our lives. Let's be clear that you do not choose these things, but you *are* responsible for how you react, and what you do from there. Having the ability to respond, and knowing that you have a choice of responses is central to the practice you will experiment with here. You know, you can *try on* being responsible for all of your actions and reactions. You don't have to *believe* it, you can just give it a try!

So — how can we possibly choose not to suffer, especially when we don't even know that we have a choice? Well, the truth is, there *is* pain in existence, and that pain is something that we inherit. It's almost the price that we pay for having a body. There's the pain of childbirth, there's pain in infancy and childhood, there's the pain of being an adolescent, there's the pain that we are as adults, and there's the pain of death. Pain is an ever-present part of our journey. We have knee pain, back pain, elbow pain, stomach aches — the list is long. We have pain attached to every part of our bodies. We even have pain attached to missing parts.

There is no avoiding it — pain does exist. We become ill, and serious things happen. When you are experiencing the reality of pain and having it dominate your life, the idea that suffering is *optional,* and that we can choose not to suffer, is very radical, and seems impossible. In fact, it is revolutionary. And the way that you continuously make the revolutionary choice not to suffer is a practiced and learned skill — something like learning to play the guitar or play the piano.

For this practice, we use a rock, a small rock.

I invite you to find a small rock. Don't get a round, smooth pebble kind of a thing, or a little round river rock. Get a pointy rock, around three quarters of an inch across, with some edges to it, so that when you step on this rock, you can actually feel the *presence* of the rock.

This small rock is a pretty accurate representation of the amount of pain that each of us inherits in our life. It's not a boulder, it is not overwhelming, and it's not monumental. We might not *think* so, and we may *feel* unfairly singled out, but the reality is that it is manageable. However, how we *handle* this pain is what causes suffering. The choices that we make about our pain determine our experience. Even simply *knowing* that we *have* a choice about it is close to being a liberating experience.

Using this rock, let's demonstrate the practice that I invite you to do every morning, as soon as you get up. It will take you two minutes, and you'll still have three minutes left over for other shamanic practices during the rest of the day.

When you get up in the morning, have your rock waiting and ready to be used, on a small altar on your nightstand perhaps, or on an altar somewhere in your bedroom (we'll talk about that in a moment). And for the sake of this practice, put on your socks, first thing, as you get up.

After you put on your socks, take the rock, and slip it into the sock at the bottom of one foot. Then, walk around in a circle in your bedroom. Make sure that the rock is in the most uncomfortable place underfoot that you can find. Right in the arch works best.

Real discomfort is not too hard to experience when you've got a rock in your sock. Walk around the circle at least three or four times. It is important for you to get to the point where physically doing this *hurts!* After walking around and around the room, there is going to be a moment where you say to yourself, "OK, this doesn't work, to be walking on this rock, and I'm going to have to do something about it."

Reach into your sock and pull the rock out, and hold it in your hand. Walk a couple of additional laps around your room – victory laps – and notice; you're no longer feeling pain.

When the rock is in your sock, every step of the "journey of 1,000 miles" is painful. You look around at people around you and you can see that everyone is moving through their lives in pain and suffering. You're suffering. You don't know why everything has to be so painful. It

57

is because the *pain of existence* is being held unconsciously. Experienced as part of every step we take, pain dominates our life, and we suffer. To bring this pain from unconsciousness, in your sock, to *consciousness* means to actually do something, to *notice* that you're in pain, and instead of being dominated by it, reaching down, removing the rock from your sock and holding this rock in your hand.

So, good enough, right?

Now, we're no longer suffering? Right? Well, not exactly. Because, here, now, you are holding this rock, and your hand has become incapable of doing much else. It has become greatly incapacitated for doing the things you need to do – preparing a meal, pouring water, stirring the coffee, writing, petting the cat, throwing a ball, brushing your hair. Yes, you can manage to do some of those things, but it's a pain. Literally, the normal activities essential to living your life are compromised by the pain held in consciousness, a pain which interferes with everything except holding it. Again, we are suffering, but in a different way.

Many people hold the rock — the pain of their existence — in their hand, in consciousness, and we hear them say things like, "See? I am the victim of abuse and that's why I am the way I am." "I had a really tough childhood and I didn't get an education, so that's why I'm not able to get a good job." They say things like, "I have to go to meetings because I'm the adult child of an alcoholic," or "I *am* an alcoholic." "The reason why I'm incapacitated, and the reason why I have these serious limitations is because this rock is in my hand, and I have no choice but to hold it. See?"

This place, of *empowered victimhood* — a place where we define ourselves by our injuries — is also only a step along the way to making suffering a choice, rather than something that is suffered through and experienced all the time, to the point where we define ourselves by it. Even though we have moved the rock from *unconsciousness*, where we step on it every day with every step full of suffering, to *consciousness*, with the rock gripped in our hand, we're *still* disempowered, because we're holding onto something that compromises every moment. Every act of our daily life — of working, of playing, of intimacy — has the pain of existence held in it. So we continue to suffer. Only, now we're suffering consciously instead of unconsciously.

Here, since we are conscious to some degree or another, we consciously try to adapt a number of strategies to deal with our suffering. We take the rock — the pain — and we try to throw it away, but it's just like a boomerang. It swoops out and around in Creation, and it comes back into our unconsciousness, and we find ourselves walking on it again. Every step of our life's journey is again full of pain.

For many people, dealing with suffering ends up being exclusively unconscious, with boomerang strategies like alcohol, drugs, sex, and work distracting us from the pain, or deadening the pain, which returns swooping back, amplified by the wear and tear of these ineffective ways of dealing with pain and suffering. Then, when things get bad enough, other people intervene, or, one "hits bottom" and finds an inner resolve to change. And with hard work, if one is lucky, one becomes conscious of the pain at the center of one's dysfunction with therapy and counseling. The less lucky become conscious in a rehab or prison setting. Trying to eliminate suffering out of their lives, given the best of circumstances, people take three steps forward, and then two and a half steps back, with the reactivation of the old patterns of suffering filling each step.

From your own experience you can see that there are many, many ineffective ways to deal with the pain of existence.

Back to using our rock. There *is* an ancient practice that you can utilize, and it is the next move we make with our rock. And it is a way that actually works.

All of the old traditions call this way *"Offering your suffering to the Divine."* Instead of holding the pain of existence in your unconsciousness, or in your consciousness, you place it on an altar to Divinity. You offer it to the Sacred.

You recognize that the price of admission to embodiment is pain, and you willingly accept it. You *respond* by offering the pain of your existence to Divinity, and you hold it on a sacred altar, created for this purpose.

Creating an altar for yourself is easy. It's simply a small place where you celebrate beauty and the gift of life — a place where you

59

put flowers, a crystal, and a bell, and anything that is beautiful and inspirational to you — a photo of a Holy One, or a teacher. A feather, a lock of hair. And, altars are flexible — they can be changed a little or a lot every day. It is a miniature temple to beauty, to life, to love — a small home for the Divine Presence.

Do you have to believe in a Divine Presence at the center of everything, including you, in order for this to work? No. What you *believe* has nothing to do with what actually works, and you don't have to believe anything for suffering to become increasingly optional in your life, but you do have to adopt this practice and become responsible for your experience!

This altar is where you will offer the pain of your existence, to be held in a new way, in awareness, awareness that you have a choice of how to handle pain. *This* is the practice, and you will do this over and over and over again. Morning after morning after morning, you will choose beauty, and you will celebrate the gift of life — as opposed to walking in circles of pain, or of pounding your fist in time to the ugly music of suffering as your life experience. The pain you experience is still your pain, you're not going to be able to get rid of it. But, by offering it to the Sacred and putting it in a Holy Place, a place dedicated to Beauty, to Life, to the Divine, you come to awareness and the recognition that you have the ability to live your life separate from suffering.

You don't need to suffer. Suffering is optional.

As you practice this, over and over and over again, morning after morning after morning, you embody the process of actually moving from *unconsciousness,* with the pain of existence in your sock, to *consciousness,* with the rock held in your hand, interfering with very aspect of your life, finally to *awareness* of the sacredness and divinity of life — awareness of the precious opportunity that life gives us. And offering our pain to the Sacred, we liberate ourselves from suffering because we have practiced doing exactly that.

Now, when something happens that triggers pain, you won't need to use the rock to demonstrate the movement to choice. You simply move through these three steps and continue to see Heaven surrounding you. You will still feel the pain of existence – there is no way around that. But you won't need to suffer.

A Talking Rock

I was just about to start this story, about how I met *Cho-oh*, a talking rock with a *lot* to say, with *"it's not every day you meet a talking rock."*

But I've learned that it *is* every day that you meet a talking rock.

How I learned this is a story in itself. And I know you'll want to get to the part where I tell you what Cho-oh had to say, so I'll be brief. I was introduced to Cho-oh on a mesa cliff site overlooking the Pacific Ocean by Joseph Rael — *Beautiful Painted Arrow* — a Native American visionary, mystic, shaman and Holy Person.

Joseph, whose real name in Tiwa is Tslew-teh-koyeh, had come to the San Francisco Bay Area to meet with his publisher, Paulette Millichap of Council Oak Books, for the purpose of searching along the Marin and Sonoma County coastline for the place where he had experienced a profound vision thirty years before — a vision that had informed his life's work.

Paulette and her partner at Council Oak, Sally Dennison, shared a vision of a publishing company that operated as a gathering place for wisdom, much like the oak that a Native American tradition gathered around to hold council.

They were driven by an inner commitment to find and present great writing in beautifully designed books, and they published really significant and important contributions to the field of shamanic wisdom, books like *Fools Crow, Wisdom and Power* about the great Sioux Holy Man, Frank Fools Crow, by Thomas Mails. They published don Miguel Ruiz's first book as spoken to Mary Caroll Nelson, *Beyond Fear,* and they published one of the richest, most beautiful, and deeply informed books to ever be produced, Joseph Rael's *Sound: Native Teachings and Visionary Art.*

Joseph and Paulette's plan that day was to drive along the coast and see if he could spot something familiar, and then to search out the cliffs and mesas for the location where a sweat lodge had been built at the edge of the ocean.

For Joseph, this search was equal parts an offering of gratitude for the vision he had received and of spiritual renewal and communion with the ocean. Some driving inner process was at work in him, a process that led to the creation of *Sound*, and for Joseph, real experiences of

61

connection and communion with the earth and the ocean were his guides.

I had met Paulette through a mutual friend, don Miguel Ruiz's teaching partner, the Nagual Woman, Gini Gentry. Gini had been visiting Paulette in San Francisco, and was alarmed by the weird energy and vibes in Paulette's apartment building. And when something like this bothers her, she cannot, and will not rest until it is dealt with.

I got the call from Gini: "Rico Darling . . . I'm in the City — and isn't it about time for a haircut, or a least let me give a little better shape to that wild-ass mop you call hair? Why don't you come over as soon as possible. Oh, and bring whatever you'll need to clean this place up. The energy here is yucky!"

I sifted through the options in my mind: candles, crystals, beautiful mantas, flowers, corn meal, tobacco, Florida water, copal, fresh mint, bells, special feathers, dried lavender, my medicine bag and a carved stone pipe — the works. If it's anything, shamanism is the cult of paraphernalia.

Oh that's right — I was going to be brief.

Anyway, no muss, no fuss, no trauma, and no drama, and very quickly the apartment building felt calm, peaceful, and solidly connected to the earth. If you can, imagine a sad, distressed apartment building as a cat with burrs and stickers tangled in its fur, and then imagine a happy well groomed untangled and sleek looking kitty — a little love and care — and that's all there was to it.

Paulette and I hit it off right away — and her grandson, Brian, who had watched the "clean-up" skeptically, finally said "OK, I don't believe it. This is much much better. This weird anxiety I always feel here is *gone!*"

Paulette was on my email list, and received my invitation to join with a small community of adventurers in a summer solstice ceremony at a sacred cliff site overlooking the ocean on the Sonoma North Coast, and the synchronicity of it convinced her to invite Joseph to attend the ceremony too. Afterwards, she figured, they could drive along the coast and continue their search for the place of Joseph's vision.

A small group of us gathered out on the cliff bluff, surrounded on three sides by crashing waves, looking out at the spectacular wide-open Pacific Ocean as far as you could see, to the curve of the earth at the horizon.

We rang Peruvian bells and inhaled fresh mint, blended with the sweet smells of sage smoke and copal. I led the group in a simple medicine wheel alignment ceremony — a realignment actually, casting off the "frame" of the dream of normal reality at each direction, until we faced the center, absolutely free and totally in the present moment.

Rogelio Herrera, a magical being, healer and musician, then blew the conch three times, deeply resonating and vibrating our bodies, and together we went into silence.

Joseph brought us out of silence a while later, with a very soft song, sung to equally soft drumming. It was the perfect accompaniment to the beauty of the day, and we concluded our ceremony with hugs, and enjoyment of Captain Mike's Holy Smoke smoked salmon on fresh French bread spread with guacamole and walnut pomegranate spread. Delicious!

Paulette hadn't done anything more than introduce us, so I asked Joseph what he was doing in California, what his plans were, and what was next for him. Joseph mentioned the quest for the place of his vision, and how he only had a few more days to try to find it. It's not every day that you get to hang out with a Holy Man, and I asked about his vision at the coast, and what he had seen, and how it had affected his life.

As he spoke, I got a clear image of exactly where he had been, and I told him "Joseph, I *know* the place where you had your vision, and I can take you there tomorrow morning."

A small group of us met the following morning at Muir Beach, on the South Marin headlands, and drove up Highway 1 to a place that is now called Slide Ranch, a place that back in my surfing days was a Sufi encampment, complete with a sweat lodge on the cliffs south of the community's shacks and sheds. Slide Ranch now provides day excursions and coastal exploration adventures to Marin school kids, and the place still has a sweet, innocent and fresh vibe that Joseph recognized right away.

As we walked along the trail to the cliff area where the sweat lodge had been, every one of us began to move into an altered state, saturated with beauty, breathing in fresh salt air, with every detail of the brambles, trees, bushes, and rocks brilliantly etched in the moment, walking along cliff edges that dropped down a hundred feet to crashing waves on a rocky shoreline below.

We arrived, and sat together in a small circle. This was not a time for formal ceremony or for anyone directing anyone's experience. Together we drifted into ocean dreams, and to visions of the ocean's deep beauty.

A little later, after we had shared a picnic lunch, Joseph began picking up small rocks — not just any rocks, but a very distinct type of reddish chert. When he had enough for everyone, he began handing them out, with enough ceremony to let each person know that this was a magical moment, and that the rock was more than just a rock.

When he got to me, last, he still had a small handful of rocks. He said, "These rocks are part of the solution. I don't know what you're supposed to do with them — maybe tie them to a small stick and suspend them in water overnight. Then drink the water. I don't know, maybe that's it. You'll have to ask them."

Then he placed one rock in my hand, and said, "This rock has asked to be placed in your medicine bag, and it wants you to know that you can talk with it at any time." Then handing me the other rocks, he said, "There are nine additional rocks here. They are for you to give to people who you feel will benefit from this blessing."

Then he put his hands over and under mine, and said a short blessing, quietly, under his breath, concluding with a soft "A-ho." I slipped "my" rock into my medicine bag, and the others into my jacket pocket. We gathered our people, and slowly, reluctantly, left this beautiful place, Joseph returning to the City and then heading back home to Colorado, his mission accomplished.

Back home later that day I placed the rock collection with a group of Peruvian bells, and opened my medicine bag, laying out the hummingbird cloth, the special crystals, the Nepalese temple cloth strand, and the small bundle that contained a piece of rock that glowed with black light from the four-leaf clover shaped cave deep under the center of the Pyramid of the Sun in Teotihuacan.

I set the rock that Joseph gave me next to the citrine crystal and turned to leave. Then I heard a squeaking chirping sound coming from the direction of the medicine bag. I stopped and looked . . . nothing . . . I turned to go, and again, squeaking. Did the cats drag in a mouse?

I had actually once heard a rather large crystal chirp with

happiness in the warm sunny courtyard at Tetitla in the Teotihuacan complex, and I flashed — this sound is familiar!

And it was not a mouse.

"Hey!" This time the squeak was absolutely clear. It had just said, "Hey!"

Now I can assure you that I've been in altered states before and have learned to navigate through dimensions and realities that can't be described or compared to anything we know about here. *This* was not that. In *this* reality, as plain as toast, with the tea kettle boiling, the cats coming in and out, the sun beginning to set, and thoughts of dinner just starting to rumble, a small reddish rock sitting on a mesa cloth with the contents of my medicine bag spread out had clearly said "Hey!"

"Hay is for horses!" I replied. I couldn't help it, the absurdity of the moment made me silly. But only for a moment, because something within me began tingling, then my fingers tingled and blood seemed to rush to my brain. Suddenly I was awake. I was *so* right here, right now, talking to a rock.

"I'm sorry," I said, "I didn't mean to be glib. Joseph told me that you would be talking to me, and I just didn't imagine that it would actually happen."

Silence.

"My name is Francis Rico. My given name is Francis and my family calls me Rico. I'm also called Frank. Listen, I am very pleased to meet you, and while *I* love rocks, my *mother* loves rocks, my *grandfather* loved rocks and my *whole family*, especially my cousin *Christina* loves rocks, I don't think any one of us has ever had a rock say "Hey!" to us.

Soft chirping sounds came from the rock. "Pardon me?" I said.

"OK, first things first," said the rock. "You can call me *Cho-oh* — but that's not who or what I am. We rocks don't think of ourselves as having separate names, because we are still one big rock."

"Oh!" I said.

"*Cho-oh* means, '*You might learn something*' in human language."

Now, I'm sure that you've had the experience of knowing that the Divine Presence was speaking to you through some sort of extraordinary circumstance or event, or you wouldn't be reading this book. This was not that.

Chirping sounds. "What was that?" I asked?

"I'm a poet, you know. That's the only reason we're able to communicate like this. Your language is impossibly awkward and stiff, and I really wish you spoke Tiwa, because then we might be able to communicate with each other."

"Cho-oh, I'm a musician, and I write songs. They're poetry too. I can't believe we're really talking! I'll learn to speak Tiwa if that's what it takes."

"Good. You'll learn to speak. For now, hold this thought when you hold me: *everything is alive.*"

Silence. I sat for fifteen minutes with this small red rock in my hand, not thinking, not amazed, not excited to tell the world — just sitting. Then I set the rock on the mesa and got up to make dinner. But over my shoulder as I left the room I said, "Thank you."

A number of days passed before I spent time with Cho-oh. I know, I know — here I've got a rock that talks and I go off to do other things? Isn't this a miracle breakthrough? Well, yes. But there didn't seem to be any hurry. After all, Cho-oh was a *rock*. Besides, I was going to need some time to brush up on my Tiwa.

"Cho-oh, how old *are* you?" I asked when I finally got back with my talking rock. "Do rocks talk with each other? Have you always been..."

Chirping noises.

"You have a 'body.' Doesn't that mean you have a personality?"

Swarms of questions were occurring to me simultaneously and I was trying to ask everything at once.

"Stop thinking!" Cho-oh commanded. "Thinking in language is *not* real. *Look* at me when I talk to you!"

We both laughed.

"I'm sorry. I was busy catching up, and I didn't mean to, um ..."

"Look Rico, it's not like I'm in a big hurry..." we laughed again.

"OK, Cho-oh, I'm looking at you, and what I perceive as most remarkable is not that you are talking with me, but that you are an opening into the Mystery even though you are an actual, real, tangible rock. I feel like I don't know anything."

"Good, Rico. We can begin."

Over the next couple of months I had regular conversations with Cho-oh, and collected a notebook of Cho-oh's teachings. If I had the notebook open, there would be no conversation — not a squeak. So, I had to remember and recall as best I could, and Cho-oh often sang long passages in Tiwa — very poetic and beautiful, but I'm just not enough of a native speaker to recount his songs for you. What I can offer you are the things that touched me — the illumination of areas that I had doubts and questions about. From my notes:

"You can have your personality, but that is not who you are."

"We are much more than this present perception of our state of being. We are pure, unrestricted divine potential. We are limitless, we are eternal."

"Our awareness is not a product of this moment. Awareness was in the beginning, it is everywhere, and it will always be."

"We are everywhere, right now in this moment."

Cho-oh certainly had a feel for the big picture, and there was a calm and peaceful certainty to what he said, a sense that these things were obvious to anyone who looked. I asked about his origins, and about evolution — if rocks evolved — and if he was an evolved rock or a regular rock.

"You're asking if there is some sort of forward motion towards improvement over time? Things are perfect, just as they are! Yes, of course there is motion, but it is not in a straight line, ever upward! Evolution is *energy spiraling* around the *center*, and the center is here, there, and everywhere.

"You and I were created as *gifts of spirit*. We're not here to improve the way we do things over so many generations. Energy in motion makes choices naturally. You see, Rico, the divine — the *YES* that began our cosmos — is *everywhere* across billions and billions of cosmoses. There have been billions of 'big bangs' and you and I are living all of it."

Cho-oh spoke in poetry, as if he was on stage at a cosmic poetry slam, and these notes do not do him justice. Maybe that's not important if you can feel that the core message that he repeatedly came back to is that *everything is alive.* It is only our language that defines things as animate and inanimate. In reality, those distinctions do not exist.

And in Tiwa, there are no *things* — everything is in motion. The mistake of calling a rock a *rock* exists in English and other noun/subject/object based languages, because what we call a rock is a *rocking!*

By this time, as I'm sure you can imagine, I was totally in love with this beautiful little red chert *rocking.* And the most endearing thing was that Cho-oh took great pains to stress that there was nothing unusual or special about him, again, that *everything* is alive.

It's hard to describe how cute this little rock was when he insisted that he was just another rock. His suggestion was that *anyone* could see this obvious truth, by simply stepping out of the self-imposed cultural trance that limits our minds, hearts, and relationships, especially our relationship with what we call *nature* and what we call the *divine*.

A lot of *our* relationship was very silly. Sometimes I'd pick Cho-oh up and begin tossing him up and catching him, and tossing him higher and higher, saying, "You better talk, Mister, or I'm going to toss you into outer space!" Tiny squeaks let me know that this was pretty amusing to him as well.

Cho-oh lived, temporarily, in my medicine bag, and because of this he went everywhere I went, and sat in on every conversation and event. He became intimately aware of every move that your typical Rico shaman makes in the course of living a human life.

The most serious conversation we ever had was about pain and suffering. I asked him, "Cho-oh, do rocks feel pain? Do you ever suffer, from not being able to get around and do what you want? Do you ever feel stuck?"

"Rico, I don't need to 'get around' because *I am around!*"

"Well, how about pain and suffering? You used to be a big rock and something happened. Were you smashed by other rocks? Did you roll down a hill and crash? Do you wish you were still a big rock? Did breaking apart hurt?"

"Rico! The problem is with your mind, and you are demonstrating it quite loudly! The problem is that you are thinking in English. Take some of the words you are using, "pain and suffering" — as if these were conditions or static states of being. The original word for what *you* are calling "pain" is *change*. Everything is always *changing*. That's the nature of all of this, of our cosmos, of the infinity of cosmos.

"When we move from spirit into manifestation, we move into the field of *change*, with everything *changing* at every moment, with everything changing as fast as light — faster even than light.

"And we are *all* subject to everything changing. This is the price we pay for admission into the manifest worlds — and you call experiencing being "in form" *pain*. Why? Is it because you want things to stay the way they are? You cried when you were born. Was it *pain*? Or was it *change*? Suddenly you were breathing air! Big change!

"Is it that you are comfortable and safe, and then *change* threatens your security? There is no safety! There is no security! Everything changes!"

"And 'suffering,' Cho-oh?" I asked.

"Resistance to change is suffering. When you *resist* the way things are, which is always changing, you *suffer*. And you get dragged along anyway. But you don't have to suffer. You can *accept* the way things are, the way that they are changing. And, the original word for 'accept' is *Love*."

"Sounds a little like fatalism and giving up to me...."

"This has nothing whatsoever to do with fate, or with giving up! When you accept change, and you Love, you begin to *cooperate*, you begin to *collaborate*, you begin to *communicate* with Divinity. When you accept Creation as it is, and no longer struggle to resist life, the opportunity opens for you to *co-create*, to participate in enjoying the deep beauty of the blossoming of Being."

That's a damn opinionated little rock, wouldn't you say?

Well, they say that when the student is ready the teacher appears. But they don't say what the teacher is going to look like. And after the student graduates, what happens then?

With Cho-oh, we continued to be great friends. We spent more time joking around and laughing than attending to the serious work of getting out of the prison created by misunderstanding and fear. I'm a pretty silly person, and it turned out that Cho-oh was a pretty silly rock.

About a year later, Joseph was back in Northern California, and we once again visited the site of his vision, on our way up Highway 1. We were going to be doing a ceremony for World Peace a little further north on the Sonoma Coast.

As I returned Cho-oh to his home mesa, I mentioned that within a couple of thousand years it was very likely that he would end up at the ocean's edge, being rolled back and forth by the waves.

He said, "That's what I'm looking forward to!"

That got a chuckle. Strangely, I didn't feel any sadness or sense of loss about returning Cho-oh to the wild. It was his home, and it was my home too, so, both of us were still right at home.

Our small group left the mesa, and we were walking up towards the parking lot to continue our journey. Typical of wild places, I'm always the first to get there and the last to leave.

As I turned to leave, over my shoulder I heard a soft, "Thank you!"

Wellness Flows Like Water

High in the Andes Mountains in Peru is a valley called the Sacred Valley. The Urubamba River flows through it, a serpentine torrent, fed by seasonal rain, high mountain snow, and sacred glacial ice melt.

The river makes a turn at the very top of the Amazon watershed, and, right at the turn, where it flows into the tributaries that become the Amazon river — flowing across the South American continent to the Atlantic ocean — is a sacred city called Machu Picchu, "The Crystal City."

Machu Picchu was never discovered by the Spanish, who 500 years ago conquered the Incan civilization. The Spanish made it their mission to destroy everything precious to the Inca civilization, hauling away as much gold as they could while wiping the slate clean for the introduction of Christianity — along with Spanish control of all other resources.

Machu Picchu was rediscovered (as far as the modern world is concerned) in the early 1900s by Hiram Bingham, an anthropologist and explorer with an interest in archeology.

Since that time, a massive effort has been made to clear the city of the jungle that had overtaken it and to restore the waterworks and ruins to some semblance of the glory they once were. Even today the restoration work continues — not that it is necessary, though, because the city glows with a vibrant energy not found anywhere else on earth.

At the very highest point of Machu Picchu, at the most sacred of places in the city, a large rock formation overlooks a spacious plaza and the beautiful grounds of the city. At the very top is a platform that can hold 30 or 40 people. A most unusual feature is the presence of several massive stone docking rings at the top of the stone steps up to the platform — as if dirigibles were tied off and anchored there — like boats docked at a pier.

At the center of one end of the top platform is a large *living* crystal, called the *Intihuatana*, with a very unusual multi-faceted shape that was carved in ancient times to be in alignment with all of Creation. It is not just in alignment with Earth's Solstices and Equinoxes, or with our local galactic system, but it is aligned with all of the galaxies of the cosmos — and in *tune* with everything.

Around the world, people recognize that this is one of the holiest places on earth, and that it is a sacred site, because of the special connection that is made here between the earth and all that is. Emanating from the crystal is a field of energy that flows outward in a spiral, and visitors can hold their open palms towards the crystal and feel a sensation of prickly heat. People can also feel the flow of energy moving from the cosmos, spiraling back, and connecting into the Intihuatana.

Intihuatana means, "The Hitching Post of the Sun." And the *sun* that is meant is the great central Sun of Being. The Intihuatana is not just a large crystal, it is made of the great light at the heart of creation — and the old Peruvian, pre-Incan wisdom states that those that touch it with their foreheads have their eyes opened into the Spirit world.

The energy flowing up from the earth, focused through the crystal, spirals up in a clockwise direction, and the energy flowing from the Sun — cosmic energy focused through our sun — flows down, spiraling in a counterclockwise manner, forming a double helix of light and sparkling, vibrant, flowing energy.

It is no wonder that this place where matter and light meet and intertwine is considered one of the most sacred places on earth. It was created to send a living message through all time that there is *one* unified field of being.

And what the Intihuatana represents is *you*!

The hitching post represents *your* connection with creation. It shows the flow of light *into* you, and the flow of life from your center *outward* into manifestation as the whole of creation. It is a working holographic model of the cosmic DNA from which all beings are created. It is beautiful, holy, and spectacular. It is a world sacred site visited by hundreds of thousands of people, and, it is simply a real block diagram representation of a single strand of the flowing energetic connectedness of which you are made.

Here on earth, we're made mostly of water, which we call *liquid light.*

Water *is* in fact liquid energy. And when water, this water of life, flows freely through us, we're in a state of health and wellbeing. Our life *flows.* But when this flow is obstructed, we become uncomfortable, and with continued obstruction, we become distressed. Eventually, our distress manifests as disease. In the East — India, Nepal, Tibet, and Siberia — the vibrant life force that flows through us is referred to as "Kundalini." It is represented by a coiled snake, usually a cobra. If you imagine a snake made of electricity, you get the idea of the potency of the energy available within us, and this lightening storm of energy is coiled at the base of our spine, its undulations creating the flow of life energy through our nervous system and throughout our entire body.

Practicing energetic work with snakes is a long-established shamanic tradition. While we don't have that many cobras here in our Western civilization to work with, we *do* have a lot of garden hoses. So, let's use a garden hose to demonstrate to ourselves the way that energy flows through us. A real garden hose is a pretty good representation of how life energy flows through the unique way that each of us are energetically *assembled* — the way that we are *organized.*

Shamanic wisdom calls the way that we are internally organized "the assembly." The focal point of our organizational structure, the point from which we organize our perceptions and look out at the world, is called "the assemblage point." Our Western civilization has overtaken much of the world with an external manifestation of our modern and commonly shared assemblage point, the television. The TV screen has recently morphed into the computer screen and is even now evolving and shrinking to the size of small handheld devices — screens which travel with us and demand constant attention.

We think of our "point of view" as being obvious. We think, and therefore, we are. For most of us, our point of view is held in our mind's eye, in our heads, behind our eyes. We look out at the world from a focal point that is the convergence of our domestication, the absorbed beliefs of our parents, our religion, our education, and our culture. In this example, how the world looks to us is a direct expression of who we think we are, and this view includes our notions of how the world works, of history, of evolution, and of what we consider to be normal.

This mental assemblage point is a recent development, and it is a view of life that is essentially passive. It is the point of view of the spectator and consumer, as opposed to that of the creative active participant in life. What once was the most common assemblage point is now held almost exclusively by the activists in our Western civilization — our athletes, artists, musicians and performance artists. This is the assemblage point in the center of the body, the solar plexus, the location of the dynamic core that active humans, like gymnasts, divers, bicyclists, basketball players, rock drummers and dancers experience as their center of gravity. Their life expression, their movements and relationship to the world flow from this center.

Along with the tellers of mankind's oldest stories and those imbued with folk wisdom, most healers and medicine people are assembled in the gut. And those with gut feelings, with knowing in their guts, express a high degree of intuition and practical common sense. Their worldview could be called grounded.

So far, we've been looking at the vertical alignment of our view of the world — mental, physical, or visceral. There is also a horizontal axis of patterns adopted in infancy and stored in the limbic brain as energetic commands that activate under stress. Included in the formation of this horizontal axis are the timeless relationships formed in infancy with our mothers and fathers, our siblings, and our other family members, like grandparents, aunts and uncles. These relationships are not stored in explicit memory. They're not stories that can be pulled out and told. They are stored as deep cellular imprints, patterns that we energetically repeat over and over in our lives in a constant recreation of the constellation present in our infancy and early childhood.

Your assemblage point is created at the point of intersection of these vertical and horizontal energetic flows — but it is important to remember that it is the way the entire energetic system is assembled and held that governs a person's experience of life. Usually, for most of us, the amount of life energy that flows through us is not enough. Stress and boredom take their toll, and we feel that our lives aren't as thrilling and fulfilling as they have the potential to be. We're depressed. We're anxious. And, there's a reason why our experience of life feels damped down, with occasional flares of intensity and beauty, but with a generally static and low level of vibrancy. If you could look at the way your assembly is working, you would not be surprised to find that the reason your energy flow is restricted and inadequate is because it is obstructed and its flow is twisted and restricted in a number of places within you.

But how is it possible to look this deeply within yourself? You could try some form of inquiry, but words fail at this deep level of our being. We could try to use meditation or a practice of self-reflection. The problem is that we are not our minds — even a quiet mind — and we can't use our minds, which are focused through our current assemblage point in order to see as deeply as is necessary. Our minds see continual recycled reflections of mind, and we end up contributing more distress to our already stressed-out systems by our minds' propensity to play memories of distressing incidents and injuries over and over again.

Bottom line: you won't be able to see the deep inner arrangement of your energetic system with your mind, and you won't be able to outrun, out-swim or exorcise limitations by exercising them. There *is* a way to illuminate this deep foundational organization of the flow of your life energy, and that is with a practice like yoga. There are a variety of forms of yoga that have developed to bring awareness into our bodies, and these include the arts of Tai Chi and Chi Gong.

The word yoga means to yoke, and what is being yoked is the physical with the divine inner presence. In this sense, yoga is a physical enactment of the Intihuatana. With yoga, you don't go in with your mind, and you don't try to understand the kinks and bound up places that you find. You explore within softly, with awareness of your breathing — and you gently find a way to move and stretch stiff, locked, and bound areas. And you bring awareness to allow the potential for opening the obstructed energy system that you find within. You begin to relax, open and flow.

With yoga, you *allow* what needs to be undone to find the source of flow within. And with practice, a whole lot more life energy flows through your assemblage. This is why yogis say that you are never too old, or sick, or too injured to benefit from the miracle of yoga. The practice of yoga will also allow for the inflow of energy and information from spirit — from Light. Creation herself rejoices as we become unobstructed and open to the flow of divine presence.

OK . . . you're sold. You'll start doing yoga immediately . . . well, almost immediately. Right? Do you still need evidence that there is a path to liberation within you? Let's go outside to where your garden hose is coiled at the side of the house.

You can see that the hose is roughly coiled and that there are bends and twists in it, the result of careless coiling and the fact that hoses just seem to have a natural propensity to get all tangled up. Let's turn on the faucet and see what happens. Well, how can you expect a free flow of water from the hose when it has kinks and twists in it? Exactly right! No matter how much you open the faucet, the kinks and twists in the hose will limit the flow of water, and there is not enough flow.

Obviously, you're going to need a better flow than this if you plan to wash the car, wash the windows, water the garden, sprinkle the kids, or live your life with overflowing joy. If we uncoil the hose, and stretch it out in the warm sun, allowing it to become soft and flexible in order to work the kinks and twists out of it, the full length of it, the miracle of adequate water pressure occurs. Then, with great care and attention to coiling the hose in open loops that avoid kinking, we are able to keep the flow going strong through the hose.

As you can see, the shamanic practice of shifting the assemblage point is practical and empirical. The world looks completely different from the shifted perspective of *caring,* and a new world of possibilities and opportunities opens before us. Keeping the increased flexibility and flow of vitality and life energy moving through our system requires care and maintenance of the unobstructed system, because the tendency of the hose that has been twisted and kinked is to return to the kinked and twisted position — a position stored in the cellular memory of the material of the hose — a position stored within *our* organizational structure as well.

Why was the hose coiled and kinked up so badly? You can see that each kink is the result of an injury, or repeated small injuries, but aside from the kinks there is the issue of the twists and poorly coiled coils. What happened?

It would be easy to say that it is the nature of the hose — it is our nature — and in a way, that would be right. As Frank Fool's Crow says, we are "the hollow tube — the evolution of the human is to being the transparent vehicle through which Divinity flows." And while we take care of our churches, temples, and mosques as homes of the divine presence, we don't take care of ourselves as if *we* were the home of divinity.

We've returned to *domestication* as the key to understanding what happened to create such poorly coiled hoses. We didn't learn to care for ourselves as the home of the divine presence because we were busy learning to fit in, in order to receive the love we needed to survive, love that was doled out by our caretakers on the condition that we behaved in appropriate ways. As a species, we've survived generation upon generation not giving our children the unconditional love that they really need in order to not only survive, but to evolve and grow into their full potential as the Divine Presence.

Can you see that evolution could be seen as the Divine Presence entering in to care for all of life? Those that experience the *transparency*, or flow, that Frank Fools Crow speaks of report a state of ecstasy combined with the deepest cherishing of the preciousness of all living beings. This level of caring is not something we've passed from generation to generation. Our legacy, our inheritance, has been one of rather badly coiled hoses. But you can learn to care for yourself at this deep level. It's not an acquired skill, but results from an inner exploration into the way we are energetically assembled. While there are plenty of teachers and guides available, it is impossible to teach this deep emanation of caring, because for each of us there is a unique universe springing and flowing into manifestation from the upwelling divinity within us. Finding this within yourself is an inside job!

You *can* care for yourself at this very deep level. It is also the province of shamanic healers, quantum healers, and energetic healers to support you in finding ways to un-kink your *flow*. Our real healers all report that *they* do nothing. It is the Divine Presence of life itself within each of us that accomplishes all healing.

Experiment for yourself — and do it right now. The step to take after choosing not to suffer is to go out into your yard, find your hose, and play with it. Turn on the faucet. See what happens when the hose is kinked, and see what happens when you open it and carefully recoil it, beautifully and elegantly, so that there are no kinks, twists, or obstructions to the flow. Life flows.

Go with the flow

If you're one of those people who really *don't like* being told what to do, you're going to dislike this section.

And even if you don't mind being told what to do, you may dislike what you're told here — because there is no avoiding the call to action. And what I'm about to share with you is absolutely essential to your health and wellbeing.

But first, let me tell you a story, about the most elegant and beautiful exploration of *flow* that I've ever seen: the work of Moshe Feldenkrais.

If you were to talk with a modern-day Feldenkrais practitioner and ask about the history of the method, you'd hear that it started when Moshe injured his knee so seriously that he was told that his only hope was surgery — surgery that had a 50% probability of putting him in a wheelchair for life.

To say that Moshe was brilliant is an understatement. He was a scientist and engineer, and he immediately applied himself to learning everything he could about anatomy, physiology, neurology, and kinesiology. He combined what he learned with his deep knowledge of electrical engineering, systems, physics, and mechanical engineering.

He was convinced that he had enough bone, muscle, ligaments, tendons, blood supply and nervous system to restore his knee without surgery. A sure sign of a genius is the capacity to be very simple, and Moshe decided that he would approach healing as if everything about it were completely up to him.

At this point though, the authorized history of the Feldenkrais Method props Moshe up in a suit and tie, noting that he healed himself, and that he then began to heal others, and he trained other people to do what he did. The authorized history presents Moshe stiffly presiding over his growing organization until his death in 1984.

You'll hear very little about how unpredictably wild, tricky, ribald and funny he was. Moshe was a shaman, a prankster and a coyote, i.e. a trouble maker. And while he hadn't come from a shamanic tradition that honors the trickster, he *had* explored the depths of human action, reaction, and interaction and had gained a deep respect for the genius of the human physiological system, as the first non-Japanese ever to earn a black belt in Judo.

Moshe realized through deep self-exploration that while his injury was indeed serious, the single biggest thing holding him back from being able to move freely was *his own nervous system*. In a flash of genius, Moshe had discovered that he was sparring with his own nervous system, that when we're injured, our nervous and vascular systems *protect* us from further injury by *splinting* the affected area, effectively immobilizing it, preventing further damage to occur, and giving the injury an opportunity to heal.

He had discovered for himself that healing from an injury was an inside job — and that *that* was part of the problem. Because, long after the crisis of the injury had passed, and long after the pain of the injury had subsided, our nervous systems still continued to protect us from potential further pain and injury by continuing to splint the area, keeping it as immobilized as possible. This is why people limp, shuffle, hobble, become deformed and stop physical activity. They are afraid, at a neurological level, that it will *hurt* to return to normal movement.

One woman that Moshe worked with had been a semi-professional tennis player. She was extremely talented, but hadn't spent

79

the necessary full time keeping totally conditioned, fit, and prepared. During a match, while performing at a peak level, she overreached a shot and threw her right arm out of its socket, tearing the ligaments and tendons that hold the bone at the top of the arm in place.

She immediately iced the injury and hoped that it would heal itself, like a sprained ankle. Over the next few months she became an aspirin junkie, and she became progressively stressed by lack of sleep. Every time she fell asleep, she would turn, and pain would shriek through her body, waking her up.

She learned to sleep on her side, with her injured arm up. Even after many months, her shoulder and arm were still tender and painful. She knew that surgery would end her career, and so she tried physical rehab. But in her case, every time she exercised even a little bit strenuously, she re-injured her shoulder, and she paid for it with weeks of disturbed sleep.

A year after this injury occurred, she heard about the Feldenkrais method from an old tennis partner, and, desperate to get off of the 12 to 20 aspirin a day she was taking, she went to see Moshe. Moshe laid her on her "good" side, and arranged her legs as if she were jumping a high hurdle. He had her curl her head down, into a fetal position, and had her cup the back of her neck with her right hand.

Moshe had been chatting with her about how he had tried playing tennis, but that tennis made him very tired. *Very* tired. *So* tired.

Then he let out a huge yawn.

Yawns are highly contagious, and as the woman yawned, Moshe gently guided her arm over her head, as if helping to stretch out the front legs of a stretching cat, and then, just as gently, with a big sigh, he guided her arm straight down, along the plane of her spine, and said, "There!"

He helped the woman to a standing position and had her raise and lower her right arm, then her left arm, then her right arm — both arms — straight up and down.

Surprised, delighted, with a big smile becoming impossibly wide, the woman burst out laughing. Moshe joined her, and soon they were both hooting and laughing so hard that they were in tears.

Moshe's second brilliant discovery had been the recognition that the human nervous system operated at the level of sheer genius when it came to energy management. You can perhaps attribute it to several hundred thousand years of experimentation with bioelectrical conservation and energy regulation, using energy in the most efficient way possible.

But the discovery that this inner *genius* could and would instantly recognize and register the absence of pain in an area where it had been holding an energetic splint, and that it would just as instantly *release* the splint, simultaneously returning the energy spent maintaining the splint to the biological system, was a *stunning* breakthrough.

Then, the work of regaining physical strength could begin, because the freedom of movement and mobility necessary were once again available.

Word of this breakthrough spread and dancers and athletes led the way to Moshe and his method. The most difficult thing for Moshe to teach was the necessity of surprising the defensively guarded and splinted energy structure of the client. This could only be accomplished by *tricking* the person, and *this* is what endears Moshe to shamanic practitioners. This is also what caused Moshe's system the most opposition from the orthodox medical establishment — their opinion being that *tricksters* are not reliable, stable or consistent in delivering measurable results.

I'm not giving anything away to let you know that *this* is why we elders maintain and cultivate personas of great calm, stability, and peaceful presence, reassuring our clients and respecting their needs for safety and maintenance of the status quo. When it comes to *tricks*, how else can we shake things up, encouraging the dynamic wild flow of passionate life to blow the doors off of the cage, drop-kicking the client into the free flow of life's vibrant energy?

81

Moshe was once invited to demonstrate his techniques in front of an extremely prestigious group of medical doctors and surgeons. This demonstration was to occur in a small medical theater used to present unusual medical cases for the edification of the attending doctors.

Moshe was given the challenge of demonstrating his techniques on a woman whose back was so compromised that she could not sit, bend, turn or lay down. The medical treatment being recommended for her was the insertion of metal rods to reinforce her spine in what was determined to be a degenerative condition. As Moshe's work revolved around injuries and arrested development cases, this presented more than a challenge — it was a setup that almost certainly assured his failure — a setup that would forever discredit his methods.

The appointed day came, and the demonstration was set up. The woman was wheeled into the theater in a hospital gown, with her purse clutched on her lap, and placed on the exam table at the center of the stage.

Moshe first helped to support her neck with several rolled towels, and then he began the gentle work of examination and exploration, finding where her body was holding the splints that rendered her unable to move. As he chatted with her he discovered that two years before, she had been hit from behind by a bicyclist while out walking, and that her lower middle back felt to her like her ribs were pinching the nerves in her spine, causing her shallow breathing and the feeling that even one deep breath would cause her to pass out.

He began working on gently moving her arms and her shoulder blades through the area that was being held rigid. He reached under her back and lifted her lower rib cage up and away from her diaphragm. He then pretended to massage her breasts, with circular motions of his hands, while taking deep labored breaths, and then panting. As a finishing touch, he leered up at the doctors with a lascivious grin on his face.

The doctors were of course *horrified*. They were shocked and indignant that Moshe could be taking sexual advantage of this poor immobile woman right in front of their eyes. They were so indignant that they barely noticed moments later that he had helped her sit up. And then, she stood up. He asked her to swing her arms from side to side, which she did without pain. She was giggling, and so was Moshe. She then bent over, picked up her purse, which Moshe had set on the floor in front of her, and walked off the stage. These were *all* things that she had been incapable of doing a short 15 minutes earlier.

What Moshe had discovered was that the free flow of life energy was in *itself* healing. He had learned to trust and work with the innate genius of the body. He understood that he would have to trick the patient into a neurological discovery that their protective splinting was no longer necessary. And, in direct opposition to the icily remote and removed attitudes of medical doctors, Moshe allowed himself to *feel* the joy flooding to the surface from deep within when obstructions are removed.

These same principles — of obstruction caused by splinting, and of energetic release based on an unexpected experience of ease from within the injured region — also apply to emotional injuries, as well as to mental and psychic injuries. This is not complicated stuff: fluidity and the free flow of life energy, blood, lymph, chi, sexual energy, and breath, equals *wellbeing*.

And the *obstruction* of flow creates discomfort, distress, and eventually, disease.

Another point worth noting is that the free flow of life energy within us is the true *fountain of youth*. And the opposite of the fountain of youth, the source of aging?

Again, it's simple: *stress*.

Five Point Plan

Here is a simple five-point plan for increasing flow and vitality while lowering stress — and I insist that you begin with this plan immediately, if not sooner:

1. Deep Cleaning. Beauty begins from within, and a regular program of detoxing and cleansing will work wonders for keeping your flow going.

If you smoke, stop now. No kidding. If you drink alcohol, go easy. Skip three or four nights a week. If you drink less, you'll need less.

Don't do drugs. The exception would be for sacramental purposes under the guidance of an experienced guide. And, consider that the "highest" beings on the planet use *water* as their ceremonial sacred drug.

Add additional *fiber* to your diet. Most of our diets are woefully inadequate in fiber, and fiber is essential to carrying out the toxic waste products from your cleanse.

2. Deep Nurturing. Eat fresh organic foods. Drink fresh, non-chlorinated water. Basically, with food selection, avoid anything packaged, and anything with a list of ingredients. Get rid of the microwave.

As important as what you eat is how you eat. *How* you eat determines how your body feels about what you are taking in. Express gratitude! Bless your food.

Appreciate every bite, and let your body know by saying, "Ummmmm!" at least two or three times a meal.

Sugar causes your blood to cry. Do you really want to cause your blood to cry?

Salt lowers your intuition, insight and sensitivity. Do you really want to become dull?

84

3. Deep healing. Healing is an inside job, and the best support you can give yourself is plenty of restful sleep. Do not deprive yourself of sleep in order to keep a *busy life* going — the busy life is really just *stress* in disguise.

Create rest breaks for yourself during the day — create opportunities to enjoy a moment of sunlight, a moment of fresh air, a moment of beauty.

Exercise, but don't beat yourself up. As mentioned earlier, *yoga* is the oldest and best practice you can do to truly inhabit your body, encouraging spirit to flow freely within yourself.

4. Deep Peace. You could call it meditating, or prayer, or napping. Whatever you call it, take several opportunities during your day to slip below the weather patterns on the surface of your life and go into the deep waters connecting us with all of life.

This resource — your connection with source — is available 24/7. It is a priceless *gift* to us from Creation herself, and it allows us to counteract the wear and tear of the grinding details of life by bringing the ease and flow of the Divine Presence welling up into our lives.

5. Deep Awareness. When we're in awareness we recognize that there is an auspicious time for all things. There is a time to take action, and there is a time to wait patiently.

When we operate from our minds, and are full of our goals and our agendas, we oftentimes grind away trying to accomplish something that has no energy behind it.

When we're in awareness, we can easily see the waves of energy that move, not only through us, but through our environment.

You'll feel much less stress if you stop burning yourself out with needless and pointless effort.

Dedicate your energy instead to cultivating awareness, and you'll easily catch the waves of energy that allow you to apply a fraction of the effort to accomplish many times the desired outcome.

The Great Mystery

For most of us, when we consider the Great Mystery, we become overwhelmed by the sheer size of it, as if the very words "Great Mystery" refer to something too large to be comprehended and too mysterious to understand. Great Spirit is another example of our tendency to keep anything that big at a safe distance.

But there is an optional definition of the word "great" that more accurately describes the original intent and meaning of the phrase, and that is great in the sense of really excellent, as in: we ate dinner at a great restaurant. In this sense, the Great Mystery becomes so much more accessible, without losing any of the majestic power that ultimately governs the reality of our lives. Yes, there is the uncertainty of a mystery at the bottom of everything — but it's a great mystery!

How it could possibly be that *you*, the individual, precious *you* reading these words right now, are the sun, the moon and the stars. You are the far-flung galaxies in space, and you are the waves on the ocean, and the wind in the trees. *You* are the trees, the open sky, the sparkling ice of the high glaciers, the hot breath of the jaguar – and, simultaneously, the jungle that the jaguar slinks through.

It's a mystery. You are every heart that beats, you are every eye that opens, you are every mother loving her child, and you are every child — with fins, scales, fur, skin, feathers — you are *her* child. And you are the Father of creation, the great *light* that illuminates everything that is.

At this point, you've got to admit that this is starting to sound like a *really* great mystery. And, it is your next step in the spiral, a step that will bring you to a direct experience of the reality of your place in the center of the Great Mystery. Shamanic practitioners have been taking this step, and have supported others in the discovery of the Great Mystery at the foundation of being for hundreds of thousands of years.

It has been easy for shamans to respect the *mystery* of the Great Mystery, keeping this path hidden and protected. Once a person experiences deep alignment with the Great Mystery, the ordinary hierarchal political, corporate, religious, and academic structures and organizations that govern our lives lose their compelling, attractive power. To add further mystery to the Great Mystery, people who are focused on working within these structures simply cannot *see* the mystery. They are also not able to see the nature of the societal structures that they have bought into. These organizations and structures look like so many ladders, placed up against high walls — ladders leading nowhere, covered with people attempting to do whatever it takes to climb to the next rung, with the lure of eventually, with enough dedication and single-mindedness of purpose, being able to make it to the top. And this phenomenon is as true today as it has been for every human organization for thousands of years, from the ancient Egyptian courts to the United States Senate, from the governments of Babylonia and the Incan Empire to the Mayan, Ottoman, and British Empires, along with NATO, the United Nations, Dow Chemical, Wal-Mart, IBM, and other multi-national corporations, along with the "Seven Sisters" — the global oil companies that have controlled the energy destiny of our planet.

How could it be otherwise? Those who are intently focused on the next rung on the ladder don't see the great rejuvenating and healing secret that is contained within the Great Mystery. Even though it is hidden in plain view, it is invisible to those who would protect their position on the ladder by viciously kicking at those below. It's true that occasionally — rarely — a ladder is leaned into the upper branches of a tree, and something productive happens — fruit gets harvested. But most human ladders are placed in ultimately useless and wasteful ways — as if fighting wars, initiating corporate takeovers, advancing through the ranks, becoming the king, or being promoted to upper management really contributed anything to the wellbeing of life.

You can see that the Great Mystery remains a hidden secret, because those who take the step that you are being offered here no longer allow their lives to be directed by the circumstances they find themselves in. Instead of following orders, they follow their bliss, their destiny.

In preparation for what we are going to *do*, let's take a look at what we will have to un-do. First, there is a common thread that runs through the major belief systems that humanity has been indoctrinated into: Do you remember the earlier description of how we were domesticated in our families? That our psyche and inner worldview was shaped by a system of reward and punishment, with *conditional love* as our reward, and with disapproval and the removal of love and acceptance as punishment for bad behavior? You can think of the belief systems that we'll investigate here as having the capacity to domesticate entire populations. Let's look at a few examples:

We've been taught by science that we are just a tiny speck in a vast universe. In fact, we've learned that we are microscopic little specks living on a minuscule speck, circling a minor star in a single small spiral arm on the outside of a medium size galaxy in a vast infinity of galaxies, most of which are billions of times the size of our home galaxy.

89

And that's just the *visible* cosmos, a tiny part of infinite space, a space that is also inhabited by monstrous black holes that bend space and time, eating entire galactic systems in huge bites. The idea that we might end up being dessert for a black hole doesn't sound that great, and we hope that science will come up with the technology to prevent the tragedy of us becoming a small snack in a large hungry universe.

But it gets worse. In an effort to take the terror out of the Great

Mystery and to replace it with the safety of knowing our place in the grand scheme of things, humanity has only recently turned to science. Before that we turned to religion, theology and philosophy — systems of thought and belief that were originally based on mythology. Mythology, however, proved to be too disturbingly complex, ambiguous, and full of double meanings and unexpectedly bad outcomes. The world's creation stories and mythologies contained stories that too often referred to the Great Mystery, even as they outlined the hierarchies and agendas of the Gods.

Religion and philosophy are the children of mythology, and while we live in an age of TV sitcoms and rarely are touched by the ancient fires of mythology, these children have shaped our world, both the emotional climate we live in and the very nature of our thoughts. We live in a modern world that is based on pale simplifications of the allegorical stories of mythology, stories that were unacceptably full of unclear motives, strange twists, and dangerous pursuits.

The world's major religions have only been around for a few thousand years. The oldest, Hinduism, has been around for perhaps 5,000 years. Religions are relatively recent innovations within what we call "civilization." An honest appraisal of the function of organized religions would be that the offering of faith that there will be an eventual reward for those who follow the program and behave has the functional effect of maintaining the stability of the status quo by keeping the focus of people on attaining the reward, climbing the ladder ascending into heaven.

On the organizational side, religions offer the safety of coherency and meaning, with a year-round calendar of rituals, celebrations and events, designed to tightly focus one's attention on compliance with the rules and regulations handed down from God himself, closing and locking the door against the insidious presence of *mystery*. Everything from church cupcake fund raising drives to building the pyramids has been accomplished by driving the *flock* to whatever purpose is desired. Religion enforces the acceptance of one's lot in life as a minor cog in the big wheel of Creation.

Western religions teach that the divine presence, God, is a remote, all-knowing and all-powerful figure, and that we are at best miserable little sinners. Once again, we are specks, but in this pre-science version of the big picture, we are specks with the opportunity to kindle our tiny little flames into adoration of the remote figure called God. This opportunity is called being *saved*, because the assumption made within the belief system is that *of course* God will take care of those that serve and adore him, but space is limited to those that believe in him.

Philosophically, we've learned that there is no God, that at best, *he* is a projection of our "better" instincts. At worst, He is infantile, indifferent and uncaring — letting bad things happen to good people, and not raising a finger to help the starving, the diseased, or the suffering. The idea that the Christian version of God was a viable source of morality was tossed out in the early 20th century — but the reality of a Divine Presence eluded philosophers, because they were safely snarled up in their own self-referencing *thoughts*. Theologians continue to argue the case that there *is* a God with atheists who argue that there is *not* a God — the common denominator being that both sides love to argue.

We've come this far. Let's go all the way, so that you truly are prepared to step away from the tangled web of delusion and into the clear light of the truth about yourself. OK?

From the East comes an entirely different notion: the idea that you are an individual is an illusion. In the great dream of the divine One, universes flow out into manifestation and back into the dream, the in and out breath of Vishnu, the dreamer. Individuals, or rather, individual manifestations, are dream vapor, formless, empty foamy bubbles, and the path through the illusion of individuality leads to escape from the endless wheel of birth and death. This system also stresses that the caste, or socio-economic strata, that you are born into is your destiny. This caste system keeps everyone effectively busy at their respective tasks, on the rungs of their designated ladders, from the untouchable street sweepers to the unreachable members of the ruling class.

And let's not leave out "ancient conspiracy" theorists who speculate that what we call the Gods were simply a more advanced species who modified earth stock creatures into what we call humanity in order to have slaves to do their dirty work. According to this belief system, we were designed to serve and worship this Master Race, we were designed to be humble servants, which we've remained down through the ages.

A certain amount of traction for this version of our origins is in fact told in the mythological stories. The Epic of Gilgamesh, for example, tells the story of a half-human, half-god who went looking for the way back to heaven, the home of the gods, in search of immortal life, and along the way encountered technologies that we have only recently employed — space ports with launching pads, airplanes, and laser fences guarded by robotic machines. He also incurred the extreme displeasure of the gods, because he was a "created being," a human, attempting to claim the rights and inheritance of the gods.

Mythological tales of highly evolved ancient civilizations, Atlantis and Lemuria being two notable examples, blend the presence of the gods on earth with men, sometimes referring to the advanced civilizations as being of another world, and sometimes to them being from another world but also being here on earth. The common theme of these tales regards the eventual destruction of the civilization by the inappropriate use of technology, fueled by arrogance, greed and a lack of concern for consequences. There are many structures, pyramids, temples, and vast earthworks and undersea complexes that are unexplainable by modern historians, and thus have essentially been ignored or relegated to the realm of — get this — mythology.

Whatever happened, and whatever you think about it, the thread of civilized, organized beings mastering their environment, including using their own people as a resource for the benefit of the few at the top, can be found across all times and places. Even among what we would call primitive indigenous peoples living in remote corners of the world, belief systems based on rewards and fear of punishment have the effect of maintaining the tribal system and societal balance of power. Those who pursue power for their personal advantage are called sorcerers, or witch doctors. They believe that their self-serving agendas are justified in light of an on-going battle raging between ancient demonic beings from deep space that are hiding within the DNA structure of all living beings here on earth, and those who would fight them and reclaim their sovereignty, i.e. the sorcerers. This creation story of life on earth as being "seeded" long ago by an advanced species that came to earth to hide out is a very different vision of the origins of life, but it is found in many parts of the world.

One additional thought regarding secret societies and so-called

Mystery Schools down through the ages: In the late 1960s the CIA and
FBI infiltrated anti-Vietnam war protests and civil rights organizations
in the United States, often times keeping the groups funded, and
organizing their meetings and providing access to resources — just to
be able to collect information and keep an eye on the protestors, and to
be able to anticipate any *real* threat to the nation's war machinery that
was creating huge profits for the elite power wielders of that era. This is
exactly the same tactic employed by the church and state "powers that
be" in the creation of mystery schools that attracted and taught non-
conformists of their day carefully constructed versions of everything
from alchemy and the Tarot to the esoteric mysticism and rites of the
White Brotherhood and the Free Masons.

This co-option of the tools and methods of transformation was
spotted and dodged by shamans in the same way that wolves and foxes
wouldn't be caught dead moving into the barnyard to live with the
pigs, goats and chickens. And the revealing, telltale sign of co-option of
those who would explore the Great Mystery was the systematic use of
hierarchy and mastery as models for attainment — shifting a would-be
explorer's focus from mystery to mastery, from discovering the truth of
the self to climbing the ladder of spiritual achievement.

Shamanic practices predated all of these modern belief systems,
with one foot planted firmly in creation and the other in destruction,
and balanced between two worlds, light and dark, day and night, birth
and death, shamanism emerged from the crack between the worlds,
from the very sophisticated realization that the lines of destiny of life
itself could be influenced by the act of seeing.

This potential is being explored by modern science; we now call
it quantum physics. Besides the newly re-discovered reality of multiple
overlapping universes, alternative realities, and the fluid and permeable
nature of what once was thought of as solid and fixed, the most dramatic
leap forward into what shamans have always known in their bones
regards the way scientists look at light. The scientific argument revolves
around the nature of light energy: Is light made up of particles of energy,
or is light a wave?

93

It was accepted and agreed that where it was previously thought
that light had to be one or the other, only a paradoxical state of duality
could account for the behavior of quantum scale constructs. The
disturbing result of experiment after experiment was that light acted like
particles of energy when the experiment was devised to find particles

of energy, and light behaved like a wave when the experiment was designed to find wave-like functioning.

The hard science behind the experiments could not create an experiment that would prove that light could be both a particle and a wave simultaneously. But the accepted compromise is that particles could have wave-like functioning and waves could exhibit particle-like characteristics.

This is important to us because hidden behind this irresolvable paradox is the Great Mystery — that you could be your self, still reading in the here-and-now, while you are simultaneously the center of Divine Presence, the almost fourteen-billion-year-old explosion of primal energy we can only describe as *YES!* that is upwelling and blossoming into manifestation as All-That-Is.

Shamanic practitioners applied their understanding of the power of envisioning to see flow within form, in order to care for members of their families and communities. The oldest form of medicine involved holding a vision of a healed and thriving individual. Shamanic healing is the calling forth of a stricken individual's inner resources to conform to the fully recovered healed image held by the shaman. This tradition of healing as the love and encouragement of the divine flame within, and of an individual as essentially being made of light, differs completely from the view held by religious systems — that the human role in creation is to fit into a pre-existing stratified structure and to work to better or advance oneself within that system.

94

"How is it possible that you are all of it?" We've looked at a few of the ways that this question has been approached. As far as organized human belief systems and organizations are concerned, the answer has been, "You're *not* 'it.' You're just a small little cog in a very large mechanism."

From a shamanic point of view, almost all of these ways that we have attempted in order to find our place in the universe share a fatal flaw that totally skews the resulting answer: they are all based on a foundation of progressive mastery of the world. A little mastery, in the sense of proficiency and skillfulness is a good thing. We want our brain surgeons to be skillful, we want our guitar players to pick it, and we want to be able to improve and speak Español like a native. But mastery in the sense of controlling and dominating our environment, of exerting superiority over others, and of reveling in our mastery over nature, are examples of how our species has gone mad.

Yet this model so dominates our world that we think of it as being normal. The mastery model has come to dominate every aspect of our lives, from competitive sports to our educational system, from our relationships with other people to our relationships with other nations. The imposition of degrees of mastery, of your position on the rungs of the ladder, has completely infiltrated our sense of anything having value *as it is* and has replaced it with everything having value only as it pertains to assisting our achievement of mastery.

In the world of spiritual endeavors, the mastery paradigm is particularly insidious — especially wherever an organization forms. Charismatic leaders making bold spiritual claims form the tippy-top of an organization, with their generals, officers, and troops in a pyramid below them. And in a weird twist, the ultimate claim made by these spiritual leaders is that they are It. Actually, this is true, except that they then add the condition that for you to get to *It* you will have to go through *them*, as the only way to It. You are required to work your way up through the levels of mastery of their organization.

There is one further caution about the claims made by spiritual leaders, teachers and gurus: one of the great realizations made in the early jolting and erratic stages of awakening is the realization that there are no rules, that there is no ultimate judge of our good or bad behavior other than ourselves. When this realization is carried back by the ego into "normal" life, it becomes a justification for arrogant self-serving manipulation of others. When the same journey beyond duality returns in the heart, it becomes an inner imperative to care for the earth and for all living things. You can easily tell the difference between arrogance and integrity.

95

The journey beyond duality, into the realm of the Great Mystery, is not as far away from your own practical experience as you might think. When we were kids we had a homemade paper loop that we played with, that looked like it had two sides, an inside and an outside, but seemingly impossible, much to our surprise, it really did have only one side! I invite you to make one now.

Cut a long rectangle of paper, a couple of inches wide and 14 inches long. When simply taped end to end, it forms a loop that has an inside and an outside. But then, the same paper rectangle placed end-to-end and taped with a simple half twist forms one continuous surface that has only one side and one edge. This is called a *Mobius strip*, named after August Ferdinand Möbius, a nineteenth century mathematician and astronomer.

Now, take a pen and hold it to the paper on the "inside" of the Mobius strip, then pull the paper along under the pen. You'll find that you can traverse the entire paper loop with one continuous line, without lifting the pen from the paper. What looks like inside and outside are the same side. This practical experiment demonstrates the truth of the self that is contained within the Great Mystery. It defies belief and it makes no rational sense, but there is not an inside and outside to *you* either, there is only one radiant being of light comprising the totality of the cosmos, and the Mobius strip is a magical clue left in plain sight for us to play with.

Shamans didn't use Mobius strips to prove this point – they used their own experience traveling within the *One* — and the travel agent that sent them on this journey was the drum. They beat a pulse on the drum and got *inside* the beat while simultaneously being *outside* the beat. They transported themselves into the Great Mystery, transforming themselves from being a limited small person, to being the One within everything, connected with everything, the heartbeat of Creation.

Try it. Use a hand drum, a frame drum, or any small drum. You can use a mallet or stick to play it, rather than your hands, because being able to maintain a steady beat for a half hour or more is essential, and we don't want to cause you any discomfort. Work in a private space, either a darkened room, or an isolated spot out in nature. Start a *pulse* beat, or heartbeat, at a moderate rate, approximately 80 beats a minute, two beats followed by a rest of equal length — just like a beating heart: tap-tap . . ., tap-tap . . ., tap-tap . . .

> *This beating heart is my beating heart. I am that I am.*
> *This beating heart is my beating heart. I am that I am that*
> *I am that I am that I am that I am that I am that I am.*

The beat transforms us, transporting us to a place where we are on the inside and the outside at the same time. We're the stars in space, we're the wind in the trees, we're us, and we're the beating heart at the center of all Creation.

You are the Great Mystery.

Two Scoops of Great Mystery

OK, I get it. You want to know if it's really true that *you* are It.

Because, if it *is* true, there are some things that are going to change around here!

Here's the difficulty: the part of you that wants to *know* is the same part that will do anything it can to block you from knowing, from having a *direct* experience of divine source within yourself.

Because *it* — the mind that wants to know — is in *charge* and in *control,* and it certainly doesn't want its hard-earned grip on reality to be loosened, even a little bit!

Of course, it *will* let you drink and take drugs, read books, and go out to experience whatever fantastic entertainment — spiritual and otherwise — that is around. Because it knows that once your little "vacation" is over, it will be back in charge, with a tighter grip than ever!

You noticed that I mentioned that your mind reads the same books that you read?

97

It is *very* interested in what you read, because its survival is based on staying one step ahead of you. It co-opts everything and anything you take in, and presents it back as something you already know about. Our minds are very sophisticated in their arrogance, and they know that the most effective tactic to maintaining their tight grip on our life energy, experience, and perceptions is to "divide and conquer" *us*.

The mind allows (and even encourages) a steady diet of self-help and spiritual books and videos on everything from NLP, tapping, and meditation to shamanism and the I Ching, because it knows that our desire to live, love and enjoy life will without a doubt be pulled up short by the "reality" that we live in a cold, harsh, competitive and scary world where there is not enough to go around, and where everyone must aggressively fight for their share.

Yes, the game is rigged!

But we are *not* our minds! You can prove this to yourself right now by simply observing your thoughts. *They* are not *you*. And, as you know all too well from your own experience with harsh inner negative commentary and criticism, our minds are not even our friends.

In Toltec mythology, what the Western world calls the *mind* is considered to be a *parasite*, an entity that is *not* us, but feeds on us, and sucks at our vitality, eating our distressed energy, stealing our joy and happiness in order to continue its dominance over us.

Just to be very clear, the *mind* is *not* our natural intelligence, our capacity to perceive and experience with awareness.

How is the game rigged? (See how curious the mind is as to how we might be *on* to it?) The conscious mind's delusion that it is the *self* prevents us from experiencing the true self, and every technique found in the self-improvement field aims at turning "you" into a *super-self*, an evolved super-being.

But the reality is that those seeking self-improvement and self-empowerment in spiritual areas are repeatedly disappointed with their string of failures to find the real thing, and become addicted to trying *one more thing*. And the game of pretense that one actually *is* evolved, enlightened or liberated and that self-improvement actually works is *exactly* the goal of the mind. No wonder it lets us read these books! The path to Mastery is paved with the stumbling blocks of this core delusion — that one can become One by being *better at it* than everyone else!

Is there a way around being dominated by the mind?

Well, yes. And, the "mind" can be such a useful and wonderful ally to have working for our best interests.

So, right now, you and I can experiment: let's invite the mind to curl up at our feet, like a good mind, and let's all relax and listen to a story or two, about how two very different people became their own best friends.

The first time I met Eugene Albright was at a Toltec gathering in Berkeley, at a presentation lecture by Heather Ash.

Heather had mentioned to me that Eugene Albright and his partner Brooke Kaye were going to be attending, and that Eugene was a spiritual teacher who had taught for many years in the Southwest. They had expressed some interest in joining with us on an upcoming journey to Peru and were there to check us out and get to know us.

I had arrived at the gathering late, and was sitting at the back of the room. Seated next to me was an older gentleman, in his 70s at least, in a threadbare jacket, sporting a scruffy beard. He had a slightly stooped posture and was holding on to a pair of squirming Chihuahuas with some difficulty.

I whispered to him "would you like a hand holding your dogs? I can take one for you." I was a little concerned that a pair of Chihuahuas running loose during Heather Ash's talk would at the very least be distracting to her, and perhaps to the important guests visiting.

"No thanks — they'll just get more amped up and start yipping, yapping and nipping — it's better if I just hold 'em."

His accent was pure Oklahoma, and even though I knew better than to make assumptions, I jumped to the conclusion that somehow this scruffy old Okie had somehow wandered in looking for a place to sit down for a spell. Oh well, that's Berkeley for you!

After the presentation had concluded, Heather Ash rushed to the back of the room and proceeded to make introductions. "Gene" she said, "this is Francis Rico, my teaching partner, and he has been to Peru many, many times. He'll be with us, with Gini, when we go to Peru! If you have *any* questions, you'll definitely want to talk with Francis."

"Francis" she continued, somehow ignoring the wiggling, squirming, licking, panting bright-eyed little dogs, "this is Gene Albright, the Spiritual Master I told you about."

At that moment, Brooke had worked her way through the post-presentation gatherings of people talking and snacking. Interrupting Heather Ash, and pushing her way between us, she said to Gene, "I'm sorry but after I went to the bathroom I couldn't, I just didn't feel right about walking in front of all of these people interrupting Heather's talk."

She took the Chihuahuas from Gene, and said, "I'll just take these guys out to the van."

Gene said to Heather Ash, "Please don't call me a 'Master.'" He paused, took a wheezy breath, and said, "One time I actually met beings of such beauty and golden light that I recognized them to *be* Spiritual Masters.

"I was so overtaken by their Presence that I fell down on my knees before them, and bowed my head. I noticed a moment later that they too were on their knees with bowed heads.

"They too were looking at the ground. The one right next to me said, *"Did you drop it right here?"* I said, *"What?"* And the being said to me, *"Your contact lens . . . did you lose it right here?"*

Gene had had a death experience when he was 34 years old. Not a *near-death* experience, but rather, an actual experience of dying, where he was dead for over eight minutes. The experience was frightening at first, but quickly propelled him into a realm of pure love, oneness and connection with everything.

Time had ceased to be important or binding. He could see yesterday and tomorrow as parts of the same time. He reviewed his past, he looked into the future and saw the rest of his life on earth. He knew what he would do and how he would fulfill his task of showing people what life can be when ignorance and fear have been removed.

No words could describe the experiences he then began to have. He saw vast forms of energy and pure light, and he began to understand what Christ meant by "I and my Father are One." Gene could see energies forming interlocking fields of the most beautiful colors and sounds — greater than the finest music played by masters — and, he learned more in those eight minutes than he had in his previous 34 years.

He learned what love is and how it worked. He found that life itself is One energy, which is life to us and is Love in the cosmos. He found the teachings of Christ, that they were an expression of Love, and *this* is how Christ could touch the heart of anyone and everyone who turned to him. This was the great secret of Christ consciousness: Christ was the energy of Love made manifest.

Gene also recognized that *this* was the only way that he was going to be able to repair his body and come to life again.

It wasn't until the following morning that his doctor examined him. He said, "Very honestly this is a hopeless case. There is too much damage to too many vital organs. He has a collapsed right lung, his liver is badly damaged, there is too much damage here to operate. Too much is wrong. And, there are gross infections in every part of his body, plus, his blood pressure is less than 40."

The doctor turned to Gene and said, "I've never tried to treat a dead man before. I can't understand how you are alive at all.

"Here's what will happen if we operate. We'll open your chest, try to re-inflate your lungs, and then will try to repair as much of the damage as we can. But at this point, you probably won't survive the shock of the surgery."

Gene decided on the spot that if he was going to die again, it would be less traumatic to skip the surgery, and stay at home.

For months he was in constant pain. And then, he gradually began to heal. He used the knowledge that he had gained during his experience with death, and step-by-step, he recreated his body from within. He learned how every organ, duct, nerve and muscle was constructed, and how everything works together. And with his *mind* he learned how his mind worked — how it continued to produce his fears, his suffering, and even his illness itself.

He began to remember the glowing fields of light revealed in his experience with death, along with the information the light carried and revealed, and he gave a name to this body of organized knowledge. He called it "Uni-Chotometrics."

This is what Gene called "the method of oneness" dealing with the principles of *unichotomy,* as opposed to the *dichotomy,* which means split and opposing, contradictory and opposite — essentially, *dualistic* thinking — the foundation for *separation* of the mind.

Gene began to teach Uni-Chotometrics as a scientific method for acquiring the knowledge of oneness. His teaching of the psychology of becoming whole and undivided included a scientific method for integration of the senses. His method, founded on the knowledge and

101

understanding of physics, metaphysics, theology, and ontology, is most succinctly expressed in his absolutely brilliant and rare book *Uni-Chotometrics, A New Way of Life*. This book, a hundred years from now, will be considered a bright light in a dark age.

Oh great — another book to read! Right?

The absolute essence of Gene's message is simple, and can be understood right here, right now:

"To be one, to love, and *to do."*

To be one is to recognize the fact of our oneness with all of life and *act* like it.

To love is the very nature of our life energy and when expressed it creates health, sanity and wellbeing.

And *to do* is the action of putting into practice the teaching of the great living divine presence, Christ.

And *this* is the person I had assumed to be a misplaced Okie Chihuahua walker! By the way, regarding the accent, Gene was from *Texas!*

From your experience earlier in this chapter, making your own Mobius strip, you recognize that it is possible to hold a representational model in your hands of the truth that proves that there is no *inside* and *outside, there is only one side.*

We have a built-in, almost compulsive belief that everything has two sides, that everything has a beginning and an end, and that there is some sort of balance between light and dark, good and evil, and all the other pairs of opposites. This dualistic thinking underlies thousands of our concepts, which form the foundations of the systems of knowledge that make up what we *know* — or rather, what we *think we know.*

Even to the most advanced minds in science, the simple concept that *the Universe is One Whole* seems impossible to accept. Yet the simple Mobius band provides proof of the factual and measurable existence of an object in our three-dimensional world of matter that demonstrates this truth.

If you didn't stop and make one earlier, do it now.

Because this object breaks every commonly accepted law we can name: It does not lie on one plane, it has no center, it does not divide in two when cut, it has a mathematical system related only to itself and similar structures, it moves in all directions at one time when spun, it faces in all directions when it is still, there's always an uneven number of twists in it, and it proves that what was believed to be impossible *is* possible.

And, in switching your allegiance from "Mastery" to *Mystery*, it is good training for you to directly participate in breaking all of these rules!

The Mobius strip demonstrates that all energy expressions are unique, circular in structure. This means that energy expresses in all directions equally. Light, sound, and other energies do not move in a straight line, from one point to the next. Energy makes a twisting motion before it arrives. You can observe this for yourself in the next electrical storm: lightning forms a jagged stroke, a turning, twisting spiral of electrical energy.

The idea that love is the energy that drives the universe may be difficult to accept if you still think of love as an emotion. But keeping this rule-breaking concept of Uni-polarity in mind, love and life can be seen to be the same vibrating energy that moves *through* us, the energy that *is* our lives.

And, it moves in a spiral, which is the point of the book you now hold in your hands — that you *align* yourself *with* this spiraling energy.

Another scoop? OK, maybe a small one.

Onye Onyemaechi dresses in traditional Nigerian Agbada style, bright, festive Dashikis, with small brightly colored round hats, and he is a dramatic presence.

When he hits the drums, explosive bursts of energy radiate in all directions, shocking flocks of birds into flight, driving the alligators back into the river, and bringing people from miles around to dance to the joyful, grooving village rhythms.

He can also be very gentle, just *touching* the drum, eliciting a soft cooing sound that speaks sweetly to the birds nesting in the trees and to the sleeping babies held in their mothers' arms.

Onye is a healer, a man of God, a maestro, a world musician and performer, whose lightning strikes spark deep within our DNA.

He told me, at the Peace Ceremony that we held with Joseph Rael on the California North Coast cliffs above the Pacific Ocean, "It is a misperception that drumming puts you *into* a trance, or that the purpose of drumming is to *induce* a trance. The truth is quite a different story. Drumming is a heartbeat of flowing energy, and when your heart is beating and your energy is flowing, you are *healthy* and capable of taking action in support of your family, your friends, and your own life."

"Drumming," Onye said, with a sharp *POP* of the drum, "awakens one *from* the trance."

The sound of drums, of the rippling flow of rhythms and repeated patterns, awakens our cellular, visceral knowledge of Oneness, of connection and dancing synchronicity with all of Creation. We hear and feel the beat *within* us, *surrounding* us, and we experience the truth that the *outside* and the *inside* are the same.

"This is why, when the deep groove is played, the stars and galaxies can be seen in people's eyes, the trees dance, and the light of God's love reaches to wherever healing is called for."

In the village communities of Nigeria, the certain knowledge of belonging within the community, of belonging to the land and to the sky, the inner sense of belonging to the cosmos, provides a foundation in Source that our hyper-mobile modern Western so-called civilization simply does not offer. It is part of our core misunderstanding about indigenous cultures that we think that they are *quaint* and *colorful.* And we assume that their dances, music, art, and ceremonies expressing vibrant communion with the Divine all evolved because they weren't able to get TV reception out at the edge of the world. We're the ones who need better reception!

104

Onye describes his personal evolution, "Even as a child, as a *very* young child, I was drawn to the drum and took part in all of the *welcoming ceremonies* — nonstop drumming for the village newborns, drumming that would go on for days and days outside of the pregnant mother's house in the village.

"New life was welcomed into the center of the village, into our hearts, into the center of the community, and held in the embrace of the drumming. The new mother would be brought into the circle, to be celebrated, and the baby would be passed from person to person, each saying 'Welcome! You are wanted here. We are so happy you have come!"

Contrast this with the Western medical model, of children being born to anesthetized women under the supervision of gowned and masked men, with the baby immediately placed in sanitary isolation.

In Nigeria, the common greeting between people is not a cursory "Hey, how're ya doing?" but rather, "My friend, are you dancing in your life? Are you full of music? Are you flowing? How is your health? And your family?" There is no rush to move on and get to the next thing, because life is not a series of serialized disconnected events, life is *flowing.*

Onye still teaches drumming — drumming for healing, for transformation, for transcendence — his method is to teach drumming as *love in action.* He is a highly educated man, but because his *intelligence* was shaped by *drumming* rather than by *words,* he is not run, or overrun, by his mind. When he needs to think, he thinks. Otherwise, his mind is set aside, like a special drum that is played only when he wants to hear a lot of opinions or figure out an airline flight schedule.

With the divine presence invited to join in every beat of the drum, obstructions are loosened and energy begins to move. As any dancer can tell you, when we *move* we're healthy.

Ancient tribal cultures understood that many problems are unsolvable. Things become broken, and are unfixable, but whatever the situation is, no matter how badly things have turned out, the problem can be accepted and transcended, and the experience can be included and shared in the life of the village.

"Yes!" Onye says, "Each beat of the drum says *yes* — each heartbeat says *yes,* each breath says *yes,* Creation opens and says *yes,* and so do you, when you say *yes."*

Please notice that Onye does not say that you must be accurate, precise, on target, on time, without fault, perfect, competent, or that you must *work* to become a Master. He only suggests that you say *"yes!"*

I trust that it's encouraging to hear that no amount of hard work and Mastery will lead you to a direct experience of your connection with Divine Source. Can you feel it? At this point, even *your own mind* is rooting for you to make a Mobius strip, and to take up drumming — after all, it's curious too. So, you can relax about the degree of difficulty involved in discovering the truth about yourself as the Great Mystery, because the very thing that makes it *so* great is right here, right now, even as you prepare to turn this page.

Alignment with Creation

THE QUESTION YOU MUST ANSWER BEFORE TAKING THE NEXT step in the spiral is this: "What are you aligned with in your life?" How aligned or out of alignment are you with the things that are most important in your life?

When I speak with people who grew up in our Western civilization, this question of alignment gets "heard" and understood to be something like, "What are you doing with your life?" and the even more basic, "What do you do?" — as if I'm asking you to justify your existence.

Why would we think this? Because in our shared Western cultural experience, what we do — our personal productivity, contribution, and accumulated resources — defines who we are. What you do is who you are, as in "I'm a doctor, I run a business, I'm a lawyer, a banker, a sales associate." A keen sense of limitation plays a role as well, as in "I work for a big insurance company to pay the bills, but I'm really a musician . . . an actor, . . . a poet, . . . an artist, . . . a dancer."

In the ancient view of things, however, who you are informs *how* you do whatever you do. This is a complete turnaround from having *what* you do determine your value and your identity. In this older view of the human condition, the very gift of your being is the essence of whatever contribution you make. Yet we become very insistent that our compromise with the ways of the world is based on practical necessity. We claim that the necessity to earn a living and pay the bills has pushed us into being reluctantly satisfied with getting by. We regard being true to ourselves as a luxury that we can't afford right now, and we tell ourselves that we will get it to when we have the time and resources. Then, to ease the pain we feel of being in this prison of our own devising, we medicate ourselves with alcohol, drugs, work, or sex, and we distract ourselves with TV, movies, computer games, internet surfing, and constant attention to Facebook.

In shamanic terms, this cluster of addictive behaviors is called the *trance.*

We've learned, while exploring the Great Mystery with drumming, that shamanic practices may look from the outside like we are going *into* a trance. But the truth is the opposite. These practices take us *out* of the trance of compromise and reduction of our capabilities. We awaken from the trance of conformity to the expectations of our parents, families, partners, friends, employers, colleagues and peers.

And what do we find upon awakening from the trance? We find that we have fallen under a spell and have aligned ourselves with an insane system of domination, force, exploitation, and abuse that is characterized by a hierarchal structure that commands us to obey orders and carry out actions as if we were expendable — to be used and disposed of like any other throwaway resource. This male-dominated, authoritarian, patriarchal insanity is the source of the destruction, exploitation and toxic waste that we see devastating the world around us. The current political, economic and societal structures of our world all evidence this insanity, and when challenged, those who are invested in maintaining these structures protest that everything is normal, that it is just business as usual.

But the world has not always been organized around domination of people and natural resources by this three- or four-thousand-year-old system of masters and slaves, of exploiters laying waste to the living systems that they raid and plunder for their own benefit. There was a time, before this insanity infected humanity, when men and women were considered true equals, when issues were considered and decisions were made by a *circle* of people, with each person's contribution considered a gift to the community. This circular organizational structure ensured that all points of view were considered and all voices heard. Everyone was included. Elders ensured that decisions were considered in the light of their impact on future generations, while young people contributed their ideas along with the energy and willingness to do whatever was needed by the community.

This system was not an idyllic fantasy, rather, it was, and still is, a viable alternative system of human organization. However, it had one structural characteristic that made it vulnerable to being overtaken by the domination system. Reaching a consensus from all participants, and selecting a wise course of action, took *time* to accomplish. What we call "shamanism" today was simply one aspect of this circular council that included all voices and all points of view. Shamans represented the interests of the unseen and invisible, and they were responsible for caring for the healing of the earth, for healing the occasionally torn fabric of families and of the society, and for attending to those individuals stricken by distress or illness. They did this by consulting with magical creatures and alternative realities that brought them ultimately to the great burning fire at the heart of Creation.

We could call shamans the "medicine people" of the society; however, it was understood that they represented, and were allied with, the deep, *wild* energies of Creation herself; and that they were *selected* by Creation for this purpose. From the beginnings of time, shamans have been severely tested by Creation to ensure that they had the capacity to direct energy, which to this day is the key to a shaman's effectiveness. The methods utilized by the circular council system were collaborative, cooperative, and reciprocating, with the highest value placed on caring for the interests of *all* species and natural resources involved. This care and concern applied to human activities like hunting, growing crops, using land, water and other natural resources, and minimizing the impact of human activity by recycling wastes and by conservation.

Some of the principles of this earlier human form of organization, an ancient comprehensive wisdom that we call ageless wisdom, are incorporated into our contemporary green movement, our modern ecological and energy efficiency movements. Essentially, those who care for the earth today are asking the same question that the old ones asked: "What impact and consequences will the actions we take today have on the lives and resources we all share? Now, and for seven generations?"

This *caring* for everyone and everything involved can be extended to an alternative view of our use of the resources our world offers us. We have the capacity to end hunger, provide clean and safe water, provide education and health care for all, offer globally beneficial employment, while sharing wellbeing and abundance, and live together in peace on earth. But if we look around at the world we live in today, our species doesn't seem to be aligned with these seemingly commonsense principles; in fact, we seem very badly misaligned to any kind of sense. As a species we have created an ongoing state of war, with people whose hearts are full of hostility and hate, convinced that there is not enough to go around. As a species, we live in a perpetual state of lack, causing needless destruction of resources and habitats everywhere we go. This ongoing destruction creates benefits for the very few at the top of the economic ladder, while causing intense poverty and suffering for the many on the rungs below.

We've allowed ourselves to become aligned with poverty, with lack of resources. We are impoverished and starving. And if we look deeply into our world, we can see a horrific pattern of slavery and domination that is as present and active today as it was in the dark days when it emerged. What makes this pattern of abuse and devastation so insane is that ultimately it leads to the destruction of all of us, along with a great many of the world's species, and even the world itself. The questions that have long been asked of those who would become initiated into shamanic wisdom have become immediate and urgent for us all:

Are you willing to move out of alignment with this insanity, and with your present imprisonment within the world of hierarchy? Are you willing to do whatever it takes to move into alignment with Divinity, to move into awareness, aligning yourself with the abundance being offered to us by Creation?

The old timers had a tool for alignment called the medicine wheel. Its use has continued, carried forward by shamans and medicine people, to the present where it is still being used by indigenous cultures today. The medicine wheel is laid out on the ground as a circle, with the directions marked: the north, the east, the south, and the west. Contained within these lines of intent, connecting the medicine wheel to the whole planet, are the principles of spirit, mind, body, and emotions. The medicine wheel contains the potential to support healing. It works as *medicine*, because everything is represented, included, and available to be reconnected with. All of the directions come to a center point, and all of the attributes of being human are present. The medicine wheel is a pharmacy made of energy, made of Light.

But if you could really talk with an old shaman, what you would hear is: *there are no directions*. There is only One. There is one interconnected web of life, one life.

Please understand that this view from the center of the circle is the place from which whole universes emerge, the place from which Creation celebrates existence by *being*. As a practical matter, for us the medicine wheel is a useful tool, but it is not a static thing like a hammer or an electric drill. When created, a medicine wheel springs to life, and we find that it is spinning; it is a living spiral of energy.

Within this field of Light, we're able to see ourselves, sometimes with the help of a shaman as a guide who prepares us, but it is Life itself that illuminates us. The first thing we see is that we are obstructed, locked down, immobilized, and stuck — as if in a prison surrounded by rigid steel bars. We cannot help but see the truth about how we have allowed our lives to become aligned, because Life sees and knows the reality of our condition at all times. The fact that we don't see the truth is called ignorance — a state of self-deception — because we are ignoring the truth that is always right in front of us.

And then, at that ruthless moment of clarity and self-revelation, the secret grace, or healing potential within the wheel reveals itself, and by moving clockwise around the spiral, we can release ourselves from

113

the tight grip of our attachments. We can move out of alignment with our misunderstandings, and into alignment with the Presence at the heart of Creation, coming alive, awake and present within ourselves.

As we turn, portals open where previously iron bars stood firm — and the opening to the east floods us with light, the light of the rising sun of awareness. The portal to the south opens with an embrace, moving us to gratitude for our own body, and for the gift of life we have received from our parents, grandparents and ancestors. Next, the portal of the west opens wide, offering us a spacious opportunity to surrender what no longer serves us. We can let go, and lay our burden down, returning it to Creation, unburdening ourselves of the heavy load of our own misunderstanding. Then, turning to the north, the clear cold wind of the Great Mystery blows through us, revealing the presence of pure infinite Spirit within us, moving through us, surrounding us, and without effort we experience the Great Spirit as our true nature.

Where there used to be locked cell doors, lightning bolts flash, illuminating open portals where inspiration calls us to break free and move in unexpected new ways. Where we once were trapped, we see freedom opening a path for us to take, a path out of prison and into life.

But you can't escape the prison of your present alignment — of your *mis*alignment — by reading about it. The next step for you to take is to create a medicine wheel, and to experience it by stepping in and doing it.

You can do this ceremony anywhere, because all places are sacred, but you will energetically be greatly aided by Creation if you choose a quiet place in nature where you can work undisturbed, away from people, cars, cell phones and the trappings of modern life. Mark a circle on the earth. Use your creative instincts. You can make it small and walk around it, or you can make it large enough to stand within. Locate and mark the four cardinal directions, north, south, east, and west. You can just make simple cross marks on the circle or you can place small rocks, shells or beads to mark the spots.

Burn a little sage or copal before you start. The smoke is an offering to the Great Mystery. Stand quietly for a moment, and, out loud or in your mind, invite Creation to come to your circle. Invite Light to illuminate and bless your circle. Invite unconditional love to well up from the center of your circle.

First, face into the east. The east is a place of sunrise. We usually approach life with a little flashlight beam of attention that is very small. Our minds keep finding evidence that proves that what we believe is true, because that is all we allow ourselves to see, and so we find the evidence that what we believe is true is a self-fulfilling prophecy. This is the time and the place to put the little flashlight of attention down, and to welcome the glorious dawning of Awareness. Stand in the rising sun, in the rising light of Awareness.

Next, face into the south. The south is the place of embodiment. The south is the place of our ancestors, of our great-grandparents and grandparents and parents, and of our teachers and our mentors and all of the people that have helped us in this embodiment, in this life that we've led, as we've grown up and become the people that we are now. It's time to say goodbye, to let go of *all* of these people and of all of the wisdom and all of the beliefs that they helped us with. It's time for us to move into a *new* experience of life, and with love and respect, letting all of them go, move out of alignment with our personal history as easily as a snake sheds its skin, and move into alignment with the truth of who we are.

Next, we face into the west, we face into the setting sun. This is the end of the day, the place of surrender, of letting go of what no longer serves us so that something new can enter into our lives. We look out into the ocean as the sun sets and we notice that every wave is an individual wave, but every wave is a part of the ocean. Every wave is water. And we see that we too are each an individual wave, and we too are water. We are the ocean, we are the source of wave after wave that moves across the ocean, surrendering at last at the shore, becoming refreshed again and again, what we always have been, and always will be, the water of life.

Now, we turn and face into the north: turning to the Great Mystery, to the place of Spirit. And we let the wind of Spirit blow through us. We let the wind whistle through us, sweeping away all of the teachings, beliefs, and certainties that we have adopted during our life. Allow the wind to blow clear through you. Let your spirit rise, upwelling from the center of your being, and let go of everything you have ever believed. There is nothing you have to do. There is nothing you have to prove. There is nothing but you and the Mystery.

Again, we face into the east. In the light of awareness, everything is simply what it is. Now we turn to the south. Step into presence. Step into the body as the portal, as the opening, as the open gate. Turn to the west, and face into the great unknown, the setting sun, and simply let go. Again, turn to the north, to the Great Mystery. This little self that is us is the open gateway through which all of Creation manifests.

And again, to the east, to the rising sun, to *ignition*, to allowing light to flow through us, to no longer seeking and searching for the light. And turning to the south to enjoy our bodies, to be present, *embodied*, the presence of Divinity here on earth. Turning to the west, surrendering to the present moment. And turning to the north, into the Great Mystery, into alignment with the great beauty of Divinity.

. . . Turning to the light. Turning to the joy of Being. Turning to the Water of Life. Turning in tune with the universe . . .

Jump the fence, and run for it!

As a species, we humans really do prefer to be comfortable.

And, typically, we resist getting up at 3:30 AM to go outside, and stand in the cold dark night.

So you are not alone in thinking that I'm out of my mind to suggest that you do exactly *that* — tonight!

The rational mind, Joseph Rael tells us, says, "Oh, that's not really important, it's ridiculous." Or, "I don't need ceremony because I understand what is *behind* ceremony."

And our minds, overlooking the truth that our souls are dying of thirst, continue to keep the status quo maintained — keeping the guards of the gates of perception well fed, with their electric cattle prods fully charged.

Our imagined security, and preference for the known and routine to the unknown and unexpected, is called "the safety of the barnyard." Barnyard creatures — chickens, ducks, geese, turkeys, pigs, sheep, cows — are most concerned about when their next meal is coming, because, they know *where* it's coming from. It's coming from the "Master," who brings it to the feed trough. Even under the best of circumstances, in which the "Master" cares for his animals and is not abusive, the bottom line is that domesticated animals provide food, fiber, and raw materials — they are an economic resource to be exploited for the benefit of their "owner," the Master of the barnyard.

The Master provides security with a containment system of fencing designed to keep predatory wild animals out, and designed to keep the domesticated creatures *in*. What the barnyard animals are incapable of imagining, until it is too late, is that they exist and are cared for in order to be slaughtered and eaten.

If *you* — the beautiful, loving, wild, funny, precious, unique and irreplaceable *you* — were to suddenly hear, whispered in your ear from somewhere outside the boundaries of this seemingly normal reality, *"Jump the fence and run for it!"* would you look longingly towards the feed trough and say, "But where will my next meal come from?"

Or, catching the scent of freedom, would you hop over the fence and *run for your life? That's* what we're talking about!

OK, let's deal with the fear factor. How can you trust that you'll be better off living in the wild with the other wild creatures? After all, isn't the tradeoff of your freedom for *safety* worth something? At least you're safe, right?

As if!

117

We've been hypnotized by those at the top of our modern financial, societal, cultural, and structural hierarchy — by those that *we* could call the "Masters." They are masters of war, and they are the masters of our world's resources. *They* create scarcity, and then they dole out just enough resources to keep us focused on their "system" as the source of what we need to survive. They manipulate media with what is called "entertainment" — imagery, cautionary stories and subliminal suggestions, designed to enforce the induced trance state necessary to maintain compliant and obedient slaves, ensuring that the needs of the "system" are met. They make the "news," and they report the news that they determine to be newsworthy. And we eat it up.

These global corporate and financial organizations have made a huge investment in centralizing and controlling both oil, our primary source of *energy,* and water, our planet's *lifeblood,* along with every and any other resource of value. They intend to continue to gather and control world resources and to continue profiting from the trance that keeps us imprisoned in the barnyard. So singleminded is their focus on their own needs that they do not see the increasing damage they are causing to the fabric of life itself, with an ever-escalating disappearance of species and habitats.

To them, *we* are really not much more than chickens and pigs. *They* create the stress of constant unrelenting fear for our lives, and then, *they* offer us security and safety from the very forces that they have unleashed to frighten us! The "trance" that keeps us docile and unresisting also keeps us distracted and powerless to stop their control of world resources and their greedy consumption of everything worth preserving.

They are successful *because* — and this is the heart and soul of the message being whispered into your ear — *they* are successful *because* the *enforcement* of the trance has become internalized. The guards that keep us in line are *within* us, and we live imprisoned within a virtual fenced-in barnyard of our own making.

Joseph Rael describes this situation: "There are *gatekeepers* in the four directions, keeping information *out.* They keep information out so that everything can stay the same. There are mental, emotional, spiritual, and physical gatekeepers. Joseph, *Beautiful Painted Arrow,* is himself a messenger of the unexpected. People naturally call him Grandfather, because he exudes the quiet dignity and no nonsense aura of a gentle man who has held his own in the world with love and affection for his children and grandchildren.

Would you be surprised to learn that this gentleman *is* your Grandfather?

When all hell is breaking loose and frightened prophets from every tradition are predicting doom and gloom, with catastrophe and devastation of most of life on our planet coming soon to a neighborhood near you, *Joseph's* vision is of a solar-system-size spiral of bounty and abundance, entering our local galaxy and coming into synchronization with our reality. In Joseph's vision of the near future, the Divine Being has seen what a fix we humans are in and has decided to provide us with *more* than plenty of everything we need, just for the asking. His vision of the coming world shift is that the people of earth will discover that there is more than enough to go around, and that with divine assistance, we will be shifting from a model of life based on scarcity and limitation to one based on shared abundance and love for each other.

Joseph's life has been dedicated to peace, and he, more than any single living Holy One, represents what is waiting for *you* out in the wilderness and beauty of Creation. He is our Grandfather.

"Energy is coming in and going out, but the gatekeepers won't let anything *new* in unless we can slip things past them, and, *ceremony* is one way to slip things past the gatekeepers."

You might say, "So, you want me to stand out in the cold and dark tonight to 'trick' my gatekeepers, who are only trying to keep me safe?"

Joseph explains: "What comes in is the unexpected — something new! That is what brings about evolution — the necessary unexpected. I live my life *praying* for the unexpected, because the unexpected always brings wonderful gifts that I never thought were possible or could happen. The unexpected re-charges my energy as it gives me a whole new idea about the way things really are."

By jumping the fence and making your way out into the wild beauty of creation, into the dark cold night, you are inviting a moment of direct contact with the unexpected, with the deep mystery that is just beyond the fence.

Can you hear this, whispered in your ear?

You can be free from the tyranny of hierarchy; you can be free from the prison of unrelenting fear.

You are the wild child of Creation herself, and it is your right to be free, to be in the world as it really is — magical, beautiful, precious, delicious. You are free to be happy for no reason.

The world outside of the confines of the barnyard is not to be feared. Here we share the gifts of life, and we are free to be loving, kind, caring, helpful, considerate, compassionate — living in peace.

And a little louder: *Wherever you are, set your alarm, leave the comfort of your warm snuggly bed and stand outside in the incoming light of the unexpected!*

119

There is a magical wilderness available for you to do this ceremony, wherever you live. It's as close as your own backyard.

I love to go to a place of great wild beauty on the Pacific North Coast for ceremony, because I've found that the wilder the place I go, the higher the voltage of the connection I feel with the heart of Creation. And being in a place of wild beauty, the greater my *appreciation* is for the living presence of *All of Creation*.

I have heard this presence all of my life — calling to me to come out of the trance, and into unexpected *gratitude* for the gift of life.

Listen!

earth

south

Freedom

WHETHER WE KNOW IT OR NOT, WE'RE ALL ON THE *path of return* in this journey of life. We came from the Great Mystery, from Spirit, into manifestation — and we're on our way towards a destination. Ultimately, we return to Spirit, to our home in the Great Mystery.

Step by step on our journey, the choices we've made have created the *momentum* that has brought us to where we are today. Another popular name for this condition we find ourselves in, that is the result of the choices we have made, is *karma*.

According to Hindu and Indian religious theology, your karma results from the choices you've made for good or evil, and your life circumstances are the consequence of those choices. *This* definition of karma and the resulting way the concept of karma is used within the Hindu system is a classic case of an energetic reality — called *momentum* within the shamanic community — being co-opted for its own purposes by a hierarchal system. Within the Hindu religious belief system, the concept of karma has been turned away *from* its potential to

123

awaken us to the power contained within every choice we make *to* the purpose of keeping the societal status quo maintained.

Karma keeps the power elite in control — their position at the top of the ladder is justified and reinforced by *karma*, with the merchant, agricultural, serving and "untouchable" classes kept in place by the very same twist — that a life of servitude is their *karma*, and that their rung on the ladder was preordained.

We Westerners may think "how self-serving" that the original intent of the concept of karma could be so perverted — but the fact is that what happened in India is no different than the stratification found between the "classes" in European and British society — with the added horror that adherents of the Western caste system believed in their god-given right to capture, sell, and keep slaves. And, the only people in American society that don't believe that there is a caste system that includes slavery still in place in our modern economic and social structures are those so privileged that they have been blinded by their own wealth.

If you detect a certain loathing of the master-slave, master-indentured servant, or even benign-despot-and-grateful-subjects scheme of things, you'd be right. Shamans have always placed their allegiance with nature, with the wild and free, rather than with the "safety" and well fed organization of the barnyard. No matter how well cared for, barnyard creatures are still dinner for the master of the farm. And shamans always advise the creatures of the barnyard to *jump the fence and run for it!* This would include the vast majority of us who dwell in the barnyard of our current social, political and economic system.

What is important is the next step that *you* take.

You can always slip back into the barnyard to alert your loved ones that they can escape the confinement of the "safety" that is offered by those whose actual intention is to use and abuse them for their own benefit. You can let your loved ones know that they too can live life free of fear, domination, and servitude — but you'll have to find *your* personal freedom first!

So, getting down to the particulars of your situation: while it is true that the sum total of the choices you have made have determined the momentum of your life, it is always possible, even in this moment, to completely change the direction of your life, simply by making different choices.

124

You may have just experienced this shift when you created a medicine wheel, and, step-by-step, you repeatedly chose to untangle yourself from the insanity of the trance induced by the domination and control systems that govern our world. And then, spiraling deeper and deeper, at a moment when you began dancing the dream of the universe, you *ignited* — and experienced the intense ecstasy of life illuminated by Divine Presence.

This moment of ignition is the moment you broke the spell of the trance — it is a moment of recognition and remembrance that we are energy beings, made of Light, that have become manifest in the gift of our bodies, our lives. Many shamans call this iridescent upwelling dazzling Light-being the rainbow body — and all shamans recognize that our essence is Light.

Around the world, we use a small bell to represent the human condition. A *bell* is a metaphor for what we are, for how human beings are designed, for how we are made. We have a shape, we have a form. We are unique and recognizable, and we have a pattern. Like the bell, we have some mysterious parts within us that we don't quite understand the purpose of, but there they are.

The cultural trance we live within keeps the mysterious potential of our design safely in check and hidden, supposedly for our own good. Distracted, immobilized and trapped within one religious, political, or economic system or another, we hardly even wonder what it would be like to be liberated and free of oppression. Yet, in each of us, our heart longs to be free. We long to let freedom ring — and we long to reach for and achieve wonderful things in our lives.

However, the practical facts of who and what we really are don't make any sense, until we get into motion. Our potential is not revealed until we begin to move — just like the design of the bell seems static until we swing it back and forth, moving the clapper inside, which strikes the inner surface of the bell and causes something wonderful to happen — something that happens in an entirely different dimension from the material world of gold, brass, copper or steel that the bell is made of. Getting in motion and swinging the bell gifts us with the beautiful and sweet sound of the bell ringing.

We're just like the bell — and there is no way to discover or move towards freedom until we start moving towards our freedom. We begin to move by choosing to move — at first by deciding to move away from participating in any further destruction, abuse or compromise of our selves. Then we move away from abuse or destruction of all beings we share life with. Once we have begun to move towards caring for all of life, we quickly discover that we must be willing to assume complete and absolute responsibility for every choice we make, and for everything that we do.

This willingness *is* the clapper within the bell. Without it, the bell will not ring.

What prevents us from being willing to assume total responsibility for our choices is the cultural trance we live under the spell of. This trance has infiltrated us and has taken control of our minds, telling us that we could not possibly be responsible for the creation of the reality we experience. The siren song of the trance hypnotically suggests that we are victims of circumstances beyond our control — and as victims of events and forces totally out of our control, the best we can expect to do in life is to hunker down in a place of safety in order to avoid suffering "the slings and arrows of outrageous fortune."

Choice by choice we can escape this prison that is the creation of the trance that has dominated our lives. With the increasing realization that we are responsible for what we do and for what we create, we are able to walk away from fear, from hell, and we walk in love to heaven, step by step by step.

When we are motion, the gift of another dimension of Presence is given to us. This gift is something that is completely unique to you. The sound of the bell ringing is the sound of your freedom.

There is a saying that is a central tenant of ageless wisdom: "As above, so below."

Shamanic wisdom adds, "As below, so above."

This piece of practical wisdom translates into your next step in the spiral. Get a small bell, and while reading this chapter again, ring it. Then, take a walk — and take your bell along. Each time you catch yourself noticing something beautiful, a flower, a tree, a rainbow, a soaring hawk, ring the bell.

Yes, we must create a world free from hunger, lack, and oppression, but to accomplish this, we must liberate ourselves first, becoming free to be in the world as it really is — awesome, magnificent, profoundly mysterious, beautiful, and occasionally frightening.

Your journey will take you to additional dimensions. Power animals will join you. Power objects will find you. Creation will provide synchronicities of the highest order — you will meet people who have freed themselves from the trance, people who stand free in the light.

You're *in* motion. You'll be able to move towards healing, towards collaboration and true communion with plants and animals. Your connection is with all of Being.

Step into the Sacred.

In the Garden

My earliest journeys through the Sacred Valley in Peru with don Miguel Ruiz would culminate in a visit to one of the most sacred sites on earth, Machu Picchu, the Crystal City, the Lost City of the Incas.

In those days, we could still gather a group around the Intihuatana, the Hitching Post of the Sun, the *heart* and most sacred of places within Machu Picchu, and do ceremonies of love and gratitude. We would also do ceremonies in the plazas and would work in a few of the more remote caves and ledges around the far edges of the grounds — if you could call learning to spring from normal reality through the crack between the worlds and into alternative dimensions "work."

As if *any* aspect of being at Machu Picchu could be considered to be normal! We were in an altered state to begin with, just being there. And the Crystal City itself generated high levels of vibrational energy that shimmered, crackled and sparked, focused by the exquisite blending of perfectly cut and fit stones blending into the natural rock of walls and buildings.

These days, the guards discourage and break up any ceremonial activity that they see developing. They've been instructed to not allow ceremonies because they block visitor access to walkways and points of interest and sometimes scare the tourists, especially if there is loud howling, chanting or strange dancing involved.

This makes sense. Machu Picchu is a world treasure, a world sacred site, visited by people from every country on earth. It deserves to be treated with the utmost respect. And while these "new-age" ceremonies may be heartfelt, they are hardly indigenous.

But ten, fifteen, twenty years ago, in those "good old days," it was wonderful to be able to go into Machu Picchu after dark, to just *be* there in the quiet of night, under the moon and the stars, or to go in before dawn and greet the sunrise from the Intihuatana. At times like these, the whole City becomes a quiet, magical blessing.

Imagine spending the night at the top of Huayna Picchu, the mountain peak that rises 1,000 feet above Machu Picchu, providing a spectacular view of the City from above; and at dawn, to be standing at the top, in bright sunlight, as thick swirling fog shimmers with rainbows as sun rays warm the City, creating a rainbow cathedral of brilliant rainbows within rainbows over Machu Picchu. Remembering that beauty brings tears to my eyes even now.

These days, only 400 hikers a day are allowed to climb Huayna Picchu. You have to sign a log-in book at the gate to the trail up the mountain in order to gain entrance, and the guards track you, making sure that you leave the top with plenty of time to depart for Aguas Caliente, the little town at the base of Machu Picchu, before closing.

Now, 700,000 visitors a year tour Machu Picchu — an average of almost 2000 people a day. That's a lot of people, and, given that there has been talk of closing Machu Picchu altogether to foot traffic and allowing people to view the grounds from platforms around the perimeters, it turns out that *these* are the good old days.

I still go to Machu Picchu frequently, and I recommend that you go too. The ethereal beauty and vibrating crystalline Presence of Machu Picchu continues to far outshine any rules and regulations superimposed by humans. This has always *been* true and will always *be* true. Machu Picchu is a treasure.

Here is proof of this, from down through the ages: when experienced travelers from those "good old days" would refer to the "ruins" at Machu Picchu, we knew that they were referring to the *hotel* at the base of Machu Picchu that used to be operated as a dilapidated youth hostel. (They certainly weren't referring to Machu Picchu!) Now, there is a luxury hotel at the entrance. It's expensive, it's booked far in advance, and it's as close as you can get these days to spending the night saturated with the mystery of the Crystal City.

The good old days ended abruptly when *J. Walter Thompson*, a publicity and advertisement production firm from the United States, accidentally dropped a thousand pound camera boom onto the Intihuatana, clipping off a silver dollar size chunk of the ancient rock while they were shooting a Cusquena beer commercial at night. Cusquena, by the way, is the beer of Cusco, and about the color and taste equivalent of Miller beer, so even the stoutest defender of beer was unable to come to the defense of the ad agency. Even though they had acquired a permit (everything's for sale), the permit specifically prohibited the use of a crane — only the lightest of portable gear was authorized for use.

The world was outraged, both by the damage done to this precious heart of the heart of Peru's archeological heritage, and by the fact that something so precious could be for sale for a *beer* commercial. Imagine an equivalent act of damage: a Morreti beer commercial being shot in the Basilica of St. Peters Cathedral in the Vatican and a thousand-pound camera boom accidentally taking a chunk out of Michelangelo's Pieta! So how did this thousand-pound boom get brought into Machu Picchu? Perhaps a *propina* or two was involved. After the accident, the Peruvian government, seriously embarrassed by the worldwide wave of indignation and disbelief, fired most of the guards, demoted site management, reassigning them to remote train stations, and created a new security organization to protect the sacred site.

The Peruvian government cleaned house in every area of Machu Picchu's operations, conservation and restoration, including kicking out the hotel mismanagement company and putting the hotel location up for international bid. Now it is the very nice *Sanctuary Lodge Luxury Hotel*.

One small positive outcome of the damage done to the Intihuatana is that it revealed that the ancient brownish grey stone, carved before history in alignment with the Hatun Inti — the Divine Central Sun of Creation — *was in fact made of radiant sparkling white crystal!*

Those early journeys with don Miguel Ruiz were such a rare treasure, because under his guidance, a journey through the Sacred Valley also became an inner journey that was just as remarkable — the harmony of the ancient Incan and pre-Incan vision, of humans and nature cooperating, complementing and completing each other. With impeccably built temples, fountains, stairways, open doorways to the infinite, and buildings that emerged from *within* a natural alignment with the cosmos, this harmony became an inner discovery and inner vision as well.

129

Don Miguel inspired us to look within, to find the beauty there, to heal and become complete, to come into harmony, into balance, and even to help heal the wounds of others. But this was just one of don Miguel's gifts. He could also become so vibrationally attuned to the environment that he could relate the intent, history, and use of a place in astonishingly accurate terms.

Don Miguel's *Nagual Woman*, Gini Gentry, who co-led and co-taught these journeys, was a vibrant and ruthless force for inner change. Her vision of the magnificence of people did not allow her to compromise with their "less-than" images of themselves and their potential. She lovingly pushed the hot buttons of illusion and delusion, and helped jumpstart many souls towards finding their inner truth.

Over many years, I visited Machu Picchu so many times that the local guides and I began to call out greetings to each other as we escorted our various groups along the Incan trails. We'd meet for beers in Aguas Caliente, the little town at the base of Machu Picchu, after a hard day's hike. I got to know every rock, every set of stone stairs, every beautiful little fountain, by heart. I fell in love, and felt like I had come home, adopted by the Incan legacy — a child of Light, who remembered past lives in the pre-Incan times.

I began leading journeys, with Gini and with Heather Ash, a Toltec pixie-goddess and firewalker of the highest degree. Together, we made quite a team, a Nagual, a Pixie and a Mystic, and led many journeys to both the Sacred Valley and to Teotihuacan, the ancient Toltec University in the high planes above Mexico City. Kirsten Hardenbrook and I also led a number of journeys in Peru as well. Kirsten was a wild woman — perceptive, sweet, and tough as nails. She regularly took groups of women on ten-day horseback wilderness journeys, so the hardships of high altitude, iffy food, questionable and possibly dangerous water, and long hours of travel didn't faze her a bit.

All of our journeys magically flowed seamlessly through the inevitable strikes, catastrophic weather occurrences, hotel misunderstandings, and the full range of typical travel mishaps and problems, thanks to one person: Our journeys were blessed by the presence of *Jorge Luis Delgado*. Jorge is one of those rare individuals who have *both* sides of their brain working simultaneously. He's a mystic *and* a successful businessperson, a seer *and* practical problem-solver. A Peruvian, Jorge created, owns and operates Kontiki Tours and has guided a great many groups thorough the Sacred Valley, the Altiplano, the Royal Andes, Lake Titicaca and other parts of Peru. He also has several hotels that he built and operates as a way of ensuring the best of care for his groups. What makes him unique is the fact that, as an indigenous Peruvian Indian — a pure descendent of the Incans, with an Aymara mother and a Quechua father — he started life with the disadvantage of having no resources other than his ability to help tourists with their luggage. Jorge had no opportunities available to him other than those he found in his own imagination. Everything he has created has been the result of his spirit illuminating the path ahead of him.

On journey after journey, Jorge would relate to us what he was learning from the Kallaways of Lake Titicaca, who were the Wise Ones of the Royal Andes, and the Q'ero elders of the Cusco region, the mesa carriers of the old traditions, the descendants of the original people. Jorge never called himself a *shaman* — the word created by Western anthropologists to describe ecstatic medicine people found in indigenous cultures. His experience was that self-described shamans considered themselves to be special, with special powers and abilities. Part of this feeling was the result of the development of spiritual tourism exploiters, individuals that we came to call "showboat shamans." These individuals would try to work their way into spiritual groups touring Peru's Sacred Valley, advertising their gifts and powers and putting on extravagant and dramatic displays, with feathers, smoke, drumming and chanting done to impress the tourist clients, proving that they were delivering the goods, for a healthy fee.

On the complete opposite extreme, Jorge has always been extremely humble about his contributions. He feels that *all* people have special gifts and are capable of magic. The term for what Jorge discovered to be true within himself is *Chacaruna* — or "bridge person." This Quecha word describes one who connects one side to the other and is able to be a bridge between the heart and the mind, between worlds, between dimensions, between people, between the human and the sacred.

Jorge is a bridge between the contemporary world of groups like ours, seeking spiritual connection and the ancient world where Spirit lives in every rock and is present in every moment. More than a guide, Jorge has lightened many a difficult moment with his simple eloquence. Our nickname for him became Maximo Sabor — Maximum Flavor.

It didn't take many journeys before Jorge had me convinced that *every* part of Peru *was* sacred and worth visiting. As much as I loved the Sacred Valley and Machu Picchu, the wonders of Peru were vast and deep and well worth investigating.

We added extensions onto our journeys, and we would often include extra days in Cusco, the heart of the Incan Empire, in order to explore and meet with the Q'ero, the vibrantly wise indigenous elders of the Peruvian Andes who lived in small villages at the base of the glaciers. Or, we'd go to Puno, on the edge of Lake Titicaca on the Altiplano, the high plains of Peru in the region where Jorge was born and grew up.

From Jorge's beautiful Hotel Taypicala, just outside of Puno, we would take journeys out on the lake to visit the Uros, the people who live on floating Totora reed islands, and fish, hunt and travel in small reed craft made of bundles of the same reeds. These people of the lake are of a different lineage than the local populations. They're pre-Incan, and are neither Amayra nor Quechua. They have maintained their waterborne lifestyle for a thousand years. Then we'd head out across the lake to visit the temples of the divine feminine, *Pachamama* and of the Father, *Inti* on Taquile Island. We would spend a few days and nights exploring the temples and pre-Incan ruins while enjoying the hospitality of the local community. The Taquileños run their society based on community collectivism, and on the Inca moral code *ama sua, ama llulla, ama qhilla*, Quechua for "do not steal, do not lie, do not be lazy."

This code, Jorge related to us, was actually the *Spanish* version of the true Inca Laws, as they were simplified and shaped by the Spanish to help keep the native population subservient and obedient to Spanish authority. The *true* Inca Laws were natural laws of the universe, and were transmitted from deep within the heart of Creation — starting with *Munay*, which Jorge described as being the flowing natural love of Creation for all things.

"*Munay* is Love; it is the divine presence, God, within *your* being, expressing itself in *your* life. It's difficult, because not everybody lives in a loving way, but even so, you can respect others and treat them as if they were your brother or sister, because everyone and everything *is* an expression of Divine Love," Jorge explained.

Jorge also pointed out that the Spanish version of the Inca Laws were *negative* — "do not — do not — do not" and that the true Inca Laws come from *Munay* — the Divine Love of the Cosmos. "The energy of the loving vibration is *positive* and is capable of raising the vibration of everyone and everything around you. This is the foundation for the next two laws.

"*Llancay,*" Jorge said, "is service. Every *Child of the Sun* has a gift that they can use to help their fellow man, to help their community, to help the world. This service, or *work*, is a blessing, not a burden, and it is a way for each of us to assist Mother Earth, to bring prosperity and abundance to everybody."

The third law, *Yachay,* is wisdom, the wisdom expressed from connecting with the inner spiritual, authentic self. Jorge's view of wisdom is refreshing: "Every morning, greet the dawn, the rising of Inti, the sun, with open arms, with thanksgiving and gratitude for the opportunity of another day. Drink in the love and light. Place your right hand over your heart, and say '*with Love*' — and place your left hand over your solar plexus and say '*without fear.*' It is little things like this that can have the most life-changing impact. The Divine will begin to offer many gifts and insights to you in response to your gratitude and intentions."

With Jorge, deep conversations about these wisdom traditions were a natural part of our journey, and he would flow effortlessly from describing a vision of the Cosmos as loving to negotiating the purchase of tamales from street vendors for the group as we headed into Bolivia. On our way to Copacabana on the shore of Lake Titicaca to visit the Island of the Sun and the Island of the Moon, Jorge made sure that there were enough tamales to ply the border guards with, as well as the extra cash it would take to facilitate our group through the border crossing.

"Francisco," Jorge whispered as our group returned from our visit to the pre-Incan temple on the Island of the Sun, "how would you and Heather Ash like to spend the night at the Doorway?" Jorge was referring to the portal carved into the solid rock face that was one side of a large outcropping in the hilly mountainous area inland above Lake Titicaca. Inspired by recurring dreams of this mysterious doorway, Jorge had for years searched the high plains between Peru and Bolivia until he found what is now called Aramu Muru's Doorway.

133

The local people never talked about it; it had been abandoned for many hundreds of years. The Spanish had successfully deterred people from even visiting it by labeling it the Devil's Doorway, and its presence had been forgotten by everyone except for the few farmers whose remote fields were nearby. The ancient traditional name for this doorway was still remembered in legends. It was called Wilka

Uta, the House of Divinity, or, the House of the Sun. The name Aramu Muru's Doorway derived from an interview Jorge gave with a European journalist. Jorge had described a vision he experienced at the doorway, of seeing Aramu Muru, a Lemurian Master of great magical wisdom, walk through the doorway, disappear into the wall, and walk off into the distance within what appeared to be solid rock. The legend had it that when Aramu Muru decided to leave this world's reality, he came to Lake Titicaca and walked through a doorway into an unknown mystical dimension. The name stuck, and it is now internationally known as a mysterious and magical portal. The vision of Aramu Muru wasn't the *only* vision Jorge experienced. His discovery and visionary experiences at the Doorway have deeply informed and supported his life and his work.

Now, he was offering an unheard-of gift to us. He would provide the sleeping bags, some firewood and other supplies that we needed, and Heather Ash and I could spend the night at the sacred doorway, under the light of a full moon.

What happened was *cold*. It was *freezing* cold, once the sun went down. The slight breeze off of the lake contained just enough moisture to drive the cold deep into our sleeping bags, and we huddled, miserable and alone. Jorge would send a driver to pick us up by mid-morning, but that was more than twelve frozen hours away. Our small fire was out by 10 PM. We had run out of wood, and decided not to scramble around the countryside looking for scraps to burn — we interpreted the spent fire as our signal to get to sleep.

To add to our misery, as the full moon rose from behind the massive outcropping that the doorway was cut into, we felt that we were being illuminated with the same bright white light that turns on when the refrigerator door is opened.

Yes, it was spectacularly beautiful, but we had retreated to our mummy sleeping bags. I pulled the face opening of the bag closed, and tried breathing into the interior of the bag, attempting to spread some warm breath in there. But each breath became a shivering battle to get to the next breath. It was so cold that breathing through my open mouth hurt my teeth, and breathing through my nose created a sharp wincing sinus headache.

Finally, I could take it no more. It was only midnight, and, forced by the increasingly insistent pressure of having to pee, I came to the conclusion that I would have to get up and get moving to generate some body heat. I didn't know what I would do. Jumping jacks? Run out into the fields and back? What would it take? I just knew I had to do *something*, and anything would be better than to be frozen solid in a stupid sleeping bag. I checked Heather. She was still, sealed inside her sleeping bag like a caterpillar in a cocoon. I could detect breathing, but I wasn't going to disturb her if she had managed to get to sleep.

Out of the bag. Pulling on frozen shoes. I should have worn them into the sleeping bag, I thought. Now I'm so cold I'm thinking crazy thoughts. Is my hair going to break off? Pulling on an extra windbreaker jacket. Having to take gloves off of stiff fingers to blow my nose, then struggling with getting them back on.

I paced back and forth in front of the rock wall . . . back and forth . . . trying to generate some body heat, trying to feel my feet. At one end of the rock wall, a little run-off stream from the edge of the rock face had frozen solid across my path, and where I turned to walk back, I could spin on the ice. My high school swim coach, Coach Gus, would have been proud of my flip turns.

On perhaps my twentieth trip back and forth, I noticed a diffuse warm glow coming from the Doorway. A trick of the moonlight? I climbed the step up to the ridge directly in front of Doorway, looked in, and noticed that the glow wasn't *warm* after all. It was just the reflection of the moonlight on a snowy path that led across a ridge. In the near distance was a small snow-covered adobe house. Its windows were blocked with adobe bricks — windows were sealed in the winter — but I could see a white plume of smoke coming from a clay chimney at the top.

It would at least be warm, I thought, as I headed through Aramu Muru's doorway and across the ridge. It was further than I had guessed, about ten minutes of strenuous hiking uphill in foot-deep snow, before I arrived at the wooden front door if the little house. I knocked and called in Spanish, "Hola! Hola! Por favor," I knew that it was unlikely that the Amarya or Quechua inhabitants spoke Spanish, but I was cold, and they would at least hear that a person was at their door.

135

The door pried open a crack, and a short, elderly native woman with a shawl wrapped around her face, exposing just her nose and her dark shining eyes, looked out at me. She quickly pulled the door back and said, "Come in, come in my child. I have been so worried! You're late! Where have you been? You must be freezing! Here, sit next to the fire and warm yourself. I'll get you some tea."

Grateful, I did exactly as she said, and huddled next to the fire, feeling my face for the first time in hours.

The moment I thawed enough to feel my fingers again I realized that I *still* had to pee, now more intensely than ever. I began to formulate how to ask the old lady if there was a bathroom connected to the house from the inside or if I'd have to bundle up and go back outside, when she said "Yes, yes, of course child, go. There is a porcelain bowl in the corner," and pointed towards a small side room with a cloth drape covering its doorway.

As I went in, *so* urgently compelled by the urge to pee, and pee *now*, I still was able to wonder for a second, "how is it that she is speaking and I understand everything she says?"

Then, in the very next moment, as my cold fingers fumbled with my clothing, I was struck forward by a bolt of lightening of such intensity that I fell to my knees, seeing sparks and swirling stars, and peed in the bowl. As I had reached for my frozen but familiar penis to aim into the bowl, I had found instead that I was a girl! Not just a *female*, but a ten- or eleven-year-old girl. I jerked back, still peeing, and looked at my hands — they were small, and the backs were brown. I gingerly reached under my clothing again, and *felt*. *No doubt about it, I am a girl.* Everything went dark. I fainted dead away.

"Sweetheart! Sweetheart! Drink this. Come my child, drink."

I awoke next to the fire, with the old lady hovering above me, pressing a cup of hot coca leaf tea to my lips. The pungent smell, which I had never really liked, brought the room into focus. As she held the cup to my lips, her arm was around me, holding me up. She was warm, caring, and smelled like wild ginger. The air smelled smoky, sweet, like the grasses used to start a fire.

"I'm very concerned ..." was about all I could sputter out.

"Yes, I understand. You were very cold, and you've been shivering, and I think you are dehydrated. Drink! You'll feel much better in a few minutes. I'll warm up a tamale for you to eat." I don't know why tears came to my eyes, but they did. Her kindness was so unexpected, and I needed *something* so badly. I sat wrapped in a blanket and sniffled.

"Do you remember why you came here?" she asked.

"Not really. I was cold."

"How long have I been telling you the stories?" she asked, giving me a penetrating look.

"Gramma Lamma, as long as I can remember, since I was a little girl," came out of my mouth. From where, I don't know, I swear.

"Drink your tea." And a couple of moments later, "Here is your tamale. Careful, it's hot! Now eat, and I will tell you the story of the three sisters."

Warm, cozy, safe. I curled up next to her, picked at the tamale, and said, "Yes, please tell me the story."

"I am the eldest of three sisters, born before time began, which makes me very, very old. My given name was Lamastu, but I have always been called Lamma. My children called me Mamma Lamma, which is a mouthful! And I like it when *you* call me Gramma Lamma, because *you* are the one I have chosen to inherit what I have left to give this world. After me came Lilith. She was beautiful and smart, and that was the problem. She was so smart that she was constantly in trouble. Lili questioned everything, would argue about *anything*, and was satisfied with nothing.

"My youngest sister, Lucy, was beautiful beyond belief. Where I was dark, Lucy was light. I had black hair, brown eyes, dark skin, like you, and Lucy was blue eyed and golden blond, with radiant golden skin — a true child of Heaven. And Lili? She had red hair, the color of trouble! Our mother had the most beautiful garden ever seen. That's where we grew up. Her garden was so blessed by good fortune that she was called the *Queen of Heaven.* I remember that she loved cats — small cats and big cats. She even told us that our father was a cat! But we also were told by the servants that our father was the ruler of the Sky, and that made *us* royalty.

"I remember my mother laughing. She was always so lighthearted and joyful, but there was something missing as we grew up. She petted us as if we were her cats, but we received more real mothering from the servants than we ever got from her. She was what you'd call a free spirit — and that didn't go over well with her brothers and uncles, or her father. They were all business, here to do a job, to mine the earth and to supervise everything. Lucy was like mother, in that she attracted the attention of all of the men. She was irresistible to them. They couldn't take their eyes off of her, and she loved the attention. But she incurred

137

the wrath of our mother, who would say 'Lamia, I command that you cover yourself when your uncles come to visit, and absolutely no flirting! I command it! Lucy! Do you hear me?'

"Lili and I understood the problem too well. Where were the boys for us to flirt with? It seemed so unfair that we were surrounded by boring older men, our uncles, and that the only other men around were the servants and those kept as pets.

"One day, when I was out gathering flowers, I noticed a wild-man at the edge of the garden, looking directly at me with insolent dark eyes. Instead of calling out for the guards, I took several deep breaths to calm myself, and looked *him* over. Oh, he was handsome! And strong. We touched.

"Child, you will learn this someday. I loved my mother and I loved my sisters, but I loved him more. Within weeks, I slipped away with him to live in the mountains far beyond the gardens.

"I spoke with Lili a great many years later. Shortly after I had left, our great uncle had spirited Lucy away to his home, and tried to make love with her. It was more like he *raped* her, Lili said. Lili and Lucy realized that neither of them could ever be safe again. At best they would end up being prize possessions with no life of their own.

"With Lili's help, and the help of one of the servants, Lucy simply disappeared. She traveled far and fast, wearing many disguises, and finally settled in a remote river wilderness halfway around the world, surrounded by a people who adored and protected her. We heard that she gave birth to many daughters, each as golden and remarkable as she was, but neither of us ever saw her again. And, at that same time, Lili went underground. She lived right under the noses of the royal families, but they could never find her, and they could never catch her. She did *what* she wanted, *when* she wanted, with *whomever* she wanted, *however* she wanted. She lived up to her name, *trouble*.

"None of us had any real idea of the upset we had caused by our decisions to leave the garden and find our own ways in the world. You would have thought that heaven had fallen to earth and that we were traitors who had sinned against the gods. Yes, they were angry, but maybe they would have gotten over it. After all, we were just girls, daughters of an unmarried woman. Instead, Lili made our already bad reputation worse. She was always meddling in their affairs — and for her, nothing was offlimits. She secretly told the servants that they had to grow their own food, that they had to avoid eating and drinking what was provided to them, because, she said, they were being kept compliant and docile with amnesia-inducing substances, along with birth control drugs and with potions that induced euphoria.

"Lili had seen one of the pets in the garden of one of our mother's brothers and had taken an instant liking to him. Which of course meant trouble. First, let me explain about the pets.

"It was rough going for the first crews and families sent to work on Earth. The conveniences that were taken for granted at home were nowhere to be found, and every little thing was so much more work and took much more time than anyone was used to. After much experimentation, *hybrids* were created to serve the royal families. They were blended to be three parts wild Earth people, and one part from the gods — just enough to make for willing and capable servants who could understand and follow orders.

"What was at first an experiment and a luxury enjoyed by a very few became a necessity; the harsh and dangerous work of mining, construction, and working the fields brought the sons of heaven to stop work in protest, in revolt against the conditions imposed on them. As a compromise between those Elohim on earth and those in high command in the Heavens, it was agreed that hybrids could be created in large numbers to do the hard dirty work, as long as they were conditioned, controlled and programmed to serve and obey. But occasionally, a hybrid would come along that was special — strong, beautiful, smart, funny, and full of personality — in short, irresistible. These special cases were taken in and kept as pets, and any offspring they accidentally generated were kept on, as well, and added to the servants and workers in the garden estates. The hybrids sometimes caused trouble, but they had such limited life spans that they never were trouble for long.

"Lili, on the other hand, was trouble forever! One year, she captured a pet that had caught her eye, Adam, and took him to her hidden caves, where she thoroughly and totally ravished him, for days on end. When she was done with him, this prize specimen was wrecked, dazed and confused. Adam's master was furious. Adam was the finest specimen that had ever been created, and it took months of medicating and reprogramming to restore him. It was decided that to keep Adam under closer supervision, he would be provided with a mate. They called this mate *Eve*, and gave her to Adam as a gift, programming her to stay close to him at all times.

139

"But instead of being compliant, and staying on task, Eve turned out to be an exceptionally bright and crafty young creature. She saw right away that the rules that had been ingrained into Adam, that he followed unthinkingly and unquestioningly, were simply made up for the convenience of the masters. And if the Elohim made up rules to suit themselves, maybe their proclamation that they were gods, to be feared and obeyed, was made up as well.

"Just to stay on the safe side, to these masters she kept an obedient, subservient, god-fearing front. She never answered their questions directly, even a question as simple as "Eve, how are you today?" Instead of answering, she would turn to Adam with a questioning look. This reassured the masters that all was well. But Eve had begun to question everything — where they could and couldn't go, what they could and couldn't eat, what beverages were off-limits, what fruit couldn't be touched because it was for the gods only. She had also discovered, and saw for herself, that those who caused trouble and violated the rules were sent off to the mines, never to be seen again. The masters were frightening.

"Lili had enjoyed her dalliance with Adam, and while considering causing *more* trouble with him, she took notice of this bright-eyed young girl. Lili began having conversations with Eve, secret conversations, early in the morning, or late at night, conducted in whispers at the edge of the garden. Lili could slip through the energized barrier fences that protected the garden from wild animals while keeping the many varieties of pets contained, and she reveled in the growing awareness of her student. Lili shared *many* things with Eve, but the single most powerful realization that Eve gathered from their conversations was the fact that what the gods were actually doing on earth was *exploitation.*

140

"Eve began carefully making sure that Adam ate only the food that she had harvested and prepared for them, without drawing any attention to her actions. Her hope was that she could gradually wake Adam up to the reality of what was really happening, and that together they could break free and share a life as free people, not as pets. She had asked Lili, the smartest person she knew, to speak with Adam, but he wouldn't listen to Lili for a minute. He would turn away from her, shuddering in revulsion, calling her a *snake* and a seducer.

"Lili and Eve came up with a plan. Lili would find a wise man of the wild people, and would ask him to speak with Adam man to man, as a brother. Mar-Sa, 'Son of the Sun' or 'Light Son' was his name, and when *he* spoke, Adam actually began to listen. Light Son told stories, wild stories of adventure, of other times and places. Adam listened because this was a man who spoke *with* him as an equal. He could *trust* him, and he felt good in his presence.

"The turning point for everything that has happened since those days occurred very early one morning, out in the fruit tree orchard. Mar-Sa appeared from the edge of the orchard as Adam and Eve were walking, and invited them to sit down and share some fruit with him. His invitation was so gracious, warm and friendly that they could not resist, and joined him under a tree.

"As they sat, Mar-Sa removed a small hand drum from his bag and asked Eve to keep a steady pulsing beat while he lit a small fire to ward off the chill of the morning air. He threw some sweet herbs into the small fire, and the smell of desert blossoms and open spaces filled the air. He asked Adam to reach up into the tree and to select a ripe fruit to accompany the figs and pears he had brought.

"Adam brought down a large pomegranate and handed it to Mar-Sa. 'Someday I'm going to have dreadlocks like yours!' Adam exclaimed.

"'Maybe sooner than you think.' Mar-Sa replied.

"Mar-Sa turned to Eve, and asked her to take the pomegranate. He took the drum, continuing the steady pulse. He stood, and turned to the east, to the rising sun, and said 'Adam, what would you say if this sunrise brought such bright light into our eyes that we could see the truth of ourselves, putting an end to our ignorance?'

"Turning to the south he asked 'Adam, can you be grateful to the masters for giving you *a life*, and also be grateful to your *ancestors*, who have given you the *gift of Life*?'

"Something stirred within Adam — the idea that he actually had a life because of ancestors had never occurred to him. 'Yes,' he said.

"Mar-Sa turned to the west and said, 'Adam, Eve, for *all of us*, becoming who we really *are* means letting go of what we are not. Are you ready to let your true self step forward?'

"And turning to the north, he concluded, 'Thank you! We don't know how this will turn out. But *Great Spirit*, we turn to *you* to guide us. *Kom.*' And with that, Mar-Sa sat down between Adam and Eve.

"Feeling unsettled, but impressed by Mar-Sa's simple, humble prayers, Adam said, 'You know, I'm not unhappy! The Master is kind to me. Look, he gave me Eve! Everything I could ever want is right here in this garden.'

141

"Mar-Sa nodded, and said, 'Eve, please peel open the pomegranate. Go ahead, break it open and hold it right here. Adam, let's look. What do you see?'

"'Many juicy red seeds.'

"'Are all of the seeds contained within the one fruit?'

"'Yes.'

"'Are some of the seeds *superior* to the other seeds?'

"'No.'

"'Eve, taste the seeds. How are they? Sweet?'

"'Yes . . .'

"'Here, Adam, taste.'

"And as Adam tasted the fruit of the tree of knowledge, he *woke up*. Adam saw clearly that he had been profoundly ignorant, that he had not seen what was blazingly obvious, that all of Creation's seeds were equally entitled to life, that the gods had used and abused the creatures of earth for their own benefit, and that their exploitation of life, along with the brutal suffering they caused, was *wrong*.

"By the time that Adam arrived back at the long table where the masters were gathered, taking their morning meal, his anger had transformed from a white hot flame to a calm and collected certainty. He knew what they had to do next. With Eve at his side, he strode up to the table where his master sat with the others and said in a loud voice to the collected gathering, 'May I have your attention?'

"Never before having been commanded by a pet, everyone continued to talk and eat, except for his master, who had a quizzical look on his face.

"'May I *have* your *attention?*' Adam asked again. Eve had walked to the far end of the great table. She took hold of the edge of the table, and with a nod to Adam, together they flipped it over on its side. Meat, fish, fruit, breads, glasses, cups, plates, silverware, flowers, napkins — all went skidding off onto the ground.

"'*You have corrupted this garden long enough, and I command that you leave!*'

"Sudden stunned, disbelieving silence fell upon those assembled. A single loud but distinctly feminine burst of laughter and delight rang out from behind a tall flowering hedge a stone's throw from the gathering of disheveled Elohim.

"Adam continued: '*You have behaved very badly! You call yourselves gods? You have caused great harm here, and you are no better than greedy thieves! Get out! Get out of our garden!'"*

"Gramma Lamma! What happened then?"

I knew what happened next. I remembered the story. But I wanted her to tell me instead that everything had come out for the best after all. I wanted to hear that Adam and Eve lived happily ever after.

"Oh, my child. What happened was that the masters tightened their grip. And they *twisted* the story. They made Lili and Lucy and me out to be monsters who ate people's babies. Lili especially. They lied. They declared that *God* had exiled *Adam* from the garden, because *Adam* had sinned. They forever slandered Eve, damning all women in her name. They lied. And everyone believed them.

"Yes, my child, they tightened their grip. For generations they systematically enforced their lies, and wherever they found even a *trace* of the truth, they destroyed it. They poisoned the world with war, with fear and hate, with division and separation. They set man against man, while *they* slipped into the shadows and erased the memory of their terrible deeds. The world is insane because of them. They are still the masters, and humans are still the slaves. Their total disregard for life on earth and their relentlessly greedy exploitation continue to rule the world.

"Until now. You see, they never found Lucy. Lili is still wild and free. And, they were not able to find *me*! My child, they couldn't stop me from giving *you* my story. And this time, I *know* that you will remember it.

"Now sleep. In the morning I'll walk you back to the Doorway."

Dreaming

Open wings reach for the sky
Wild winds are calling you to fly
With open eyes, it's so beautiful
Can you see it now? You're dreaming.
Angels say, "The time has come -
to let go, trust in love, trust in love."
So high above the whole world below you
Can you feel it now? It's freedom
With open arms we welcome you
Welcome you to heaven
Angels say the time has come
For you to be forgiven
Angels say, "The time has come
To let go, trust in love"
Trust in love.

"Row, row, row, your boat, gently down the stream, merrily, merrily, merrily, merrily, life is but a dream."

Yes, we're dreamers. Creation gave humans the gift of *dreaming,* and it's one of the best things about us.

Our dreams for the future are full of vibrant hope, our dreams for our children are a blessing on their lives, and our dreams for ourselves, for our lives, are in glorious radiantly brilliant color.

We touch the beauty of creation with our dreams of peace on earth. Our dreams of abundance for all, and our dreams of healing, wellness and wholeness for *everyone* show us to be capable of honoring the Sacred both in our hearts and our actions.

And yet, life is a struggle. And we struggle and struggle and struggle. And we're frightened; in fact, we're driven by fear. Under whatever daily charge of optimism we can muster is a sense of dread and the nagging conviction that something is terribly *wrong*.

What *is* it? What is it that keeps us in this state of struggle, instead of fulfilling our dreams? What blocks us from being the loving, life-enhancing dreamers that we really are?

Well, we all know the answer. It's death.

Death! Death is coming down the tracks. We see death in the future. It's an inevitable outcome. And death is coming down the train tracks towards *us.*

We're trying to dodge *this* way and *that* way, and we're *trying* to get out of the way. Every struggle becomes permeated with our struggle with death, because while we do everything we can to hold off the vision of death, death takes hold of our every move, inescapable, inevitable.

And when someone significant to us dies, it is a horrifying, horrible loss. It's unfair. It's unacceptable, and grief overcomes us. We become sad, depressed, wondering, "What does it all mean, and why go on living if death is there to take everything we love away from us, including our own lives?"

146

We'll do whatever it takes to fight death. Yet underneath this struggle for our lives, we know that death is coming for us, and that there is nothing we can do. Even so, we continue to struggle, we brace ourselves for the shock, and we try to hold it off.

The next step, a step *out* of this struggle and *into* creating the life of your dreams, is going to take a lot more than just reading or *thinking* about your relationship with *death*. A complex web of multiple strands of ignorance fuels our fear of death: we scare ourselves with our own thoughts, we frighten ourselves with our notion of *time* — dreading the inevitability of our coming encounter with death, and we can't help but feel that there is something terribly *wrong* at the very core of life.

Someone trapped in this web of overlapping strands would snort in disbelief at the suggestion that they are in a state of ignorant self-deception. So you can understand that the next step is so counter-intuitive as to be unbelievable. What is called for is an act of supreme surrender.

The next step calls for a complete reorientation, for an act of magic so *profound* that you are freed forever from the prison of three-dimensional reality, and you become the Dreamer, free to create, free to experience the joyful unconditional *YES!* of life, ecstatic, wild, free, and bold as love.

Let's prepare for this act of magic by unwinding the grip of these strands of ignorance.

Indigenous wisdom holds a completely different view of time. The old cultures didn't regard time at *all* like we do in this post-industrial age. Our mechanized deadline-driven Western culture is unlike anything seen on earth. Our notion of the end of time coming down the tracks towards us is a completely artificial construct. But we continue to believe it, taking our experience of the passing of time to be proof that the tracks aimed at us in our imagination are in fact *real*.

You're not going to believe how simple it is to completely derail this fantasy and realign yourself with time.

In the old cultures, the *past* is in *front* of us because what you see in front of you is the manifest world — the result of all the choices that have been made. You see the results of everything that has happened in the past and everything that has come into your life. And it's come into your life from *behind* you, from the future, which is behind you. The future flows through us into the past.

147

The absolute reality is that there is only this present moment. That is all we really have. We're always in the *present* moment, and the decisions and choices we make *now* flow into manifestation, before us, into the past. This is a different view of time, a view that offers us an opportunity to realign ourselves with death. Instead of struggling and fighting with death as an adversary, we now have an opportunity to change our relationship with death.

Let's take this in small steps: The past is in front of us. The future is unknown, behind us, flowing through us.

Yes, death will come for each of us, and yet, with our realignment of time, we have an opportunity to have death move into a different position: death is now just behind our left shoulder. The reality of death is unchanged, but Death now becomes an advisor.

Death looks over our shoulder and advises us:

This moment is *precious.* This moment is here, *now.*

This is life, to be celebrated! *Life is precious.*

This *moment* is a precious gift.

With Death as an advisor, things in the moment that previously caused us to feel irritated and annoyed, our feelings of anger, envy, jealousy, bitterness, frustration, impatience, or even worse — intolerance, hatred and abusiveness — become illuminated with the light of the *ultimate* big picture.

With Death as an advisor, what were *mountains* become *molehills,* and once again we see the magnificence of the gift of life. We see that we have a choice of ways to respond to any given circumstance.

The next small step is in fact a major act of *power:*

Allow your own death to advise you about the circumstances of your life — right here, right now — in *this* moment, the only time you really have.

Stand. Turn, and allow yourself to align *with* Death.

No more struggling with frightening illusions. Ask Death to advise you. Look. Listen. Can you see that every moment is too precious a gift to waste on petty reactions? Can you see that it has been your own *thoughts* that have frightened your body, and that you have needlessly been frightening yourself?

In this moment, you can see that *you* are not your thoughts.

You can see that your feelings are like the rain clouds of a passing weather system — *you* feel them, but they are not *you* — they pass through you.

And your body, the precious treasure that is the center of your experience of life . . . you see that even your body is a *gift* to you. *You* are an indefinable, indescribable celebration of life and love. You see that there is nothing wrong. Everything simply *is*.

The heart of *you* is the Dreamer. You have moved beyond fear, loving life, embracing life, embraced *by* life.

One and the same. Eternal, life everlasting.

Snakes

Exploring the shops along the back alleys of Cusco, capitol of the ancient Incan Empire in Peru, has always been great fun. There are shoe shops that make exotic looking tennis shoes while you wait, yarn shops, candle shops with candles four feet across — bead, button, and crystal shops — specialty shops of every kind imaginable.

Also in the plazas are shop after shop of vendors selling exactly the same things. It's kind of baffling — that vendors sitting side by side would offer exactly the same items for exactly the same prices. They count on odd patterns of tourist flow to ensure that everyone gets *some* sort of sales action — it's the least competitive environment you can imagine.

The food markets are also amazing and exotic. Take potatoes. In the United States, we see three or four varieties of potatoes — Russets, Red Potatoes, Yellow Finns, Yukon Golds, and what else? Anything you can think of?

In the markets of Cusco, *hundreds* of different varieties of potatoes are available — piles of potatoes in every color of the rainbow — plus, some potatoes that are specially cultivated to become the creamiest mashed potatoes ever, as if they were mixed with butter and cream, and some potatoes that are frying potatoes, becoming crisp and crunchy with the lowest heat.

Potatoes that are grown specially for stews, for soups, for baking, for home fries, for grating and making into patties — every possible application of potatoes imaginable can be found in the great *mercados*,

149

spread out on beautiful cloth mantas, in front of classically dressed Peruvian ladies, complete with little bowler hats.

Then, there are the chili peppers. Mountains of chilies. And beans, and vegetables — these markets make our "super-markets" look like sad monochromatic wastelands.

One of my favorite pastimes is to wander from street to street, from vendor stalls to *mercados,* to back alleys, exploring this ancient center of the universe — and it was up a side street off of the Plaza Armas that I discovered the shaman supply shop of Mauro Jesus Alvitos Mendosa.

I liked Mauro the minute I met him. He was small in stature, like most Peruvians, and had jet black hair, a big black moustache, expressive dark brown eyes, and a smile that included you in on the joke.

A small group of German tourists were trying to negotiate the price down on a striking large smoky crystal, and Mauro wasn't having it. The tourists were advising their companion, "you have to offer no more than half — otherwise you're being ripped off!"

This may be absolutely true everywhere else in Peru, but at the moment, it certainly wasn't true in Mauro's shop. The space was filled with crystals, strange little alabaster carvings, ceramic bowls and figurines, pipes, knives, carved wooden sticks, feathers, masks, piles of copal and palo santo, stacks of cloth mantas, glass display cases filled with shriveled dried lama fetuses, and all sorts of special incense and herbal preparations, including complete *dispacho* ceremony supply kits, with everything one could possible need for a ceremonial message to the Apus.

I was fascinated by the racks, cases and shelves *covered* with the coolest stuff I had ever seen in one place, and was simply observing the negotiations, while checking out the exotic spread of every tool of the trade a shaman could ever want, all gathered under one roof.

Mauro indicated a seat to me, and pointed, *please sit there.* He nodded to a dark beauty of a woman, who had been observing the negotiations as well, and she returned a moment later with a small cup of hot coca leaf tea. I sat and sipped the tea while the Germans made their point that the crystal was hardly worth buying at all, and that they were doing Mauro a favor to even consider such a poor specimen.

Mauro gestured to the group — his hand cut through the air — *finito.* No more talk — the crystal was not for sale for any price. He sat down on a small chair that faced my seat, and smiled a weary smile — these tourists were so clueless of the value of anything!

Then he gestured to me to set the tea down. He took my hand in his and closed his eyes. A moment later I closed my eyes as well and was standing with Mauro in a clearing at the edge of the rain forest obviously somewhere in the Amazon jungle basin, looking at a tree across the small clearing full of olive green parrots with bright red and yellow markings, squawking and carrying on like a group of rowdy German tourists.

An enormous snake slithered from the big banana leafy bushes on our right, entering the clearing and stopping suddenly, eyes glittering, tongue darting — tasting the air that we were exhaling. How could I not notice that it was absolutely beautiful? Its body coiled up behind it, as if its body had just noticed that its head had stopped and was motionless. The snake's head rose slightly as it turned towards us, its left eye focusing on two humans standing within a few feet of it.

Mauro was gesturing with his hands, making the motions as if he were taking off gloves and pushing them towards the snake.

"He is always hungry, and will taste us one way or the other — so we might as well let him taste our energy." Mauro spoke in Spanish, so no translation was necessary. I clearly understood every word.

I began to wipe my fingers towards the snake, as I stroked the fingers of my left hand I imagined that every note of every chord of every song I had ever played on the guitar was coming off like sausage links — an offering to this huge golden snake. What else could I do?

The snake closed its eyes as if savoring our energy, but its tongue continued to flicker in and out with a dry thrushing sound. A brilliant yellow and green snake, as big around as my arm, slid into the clearing, and undulated towards me. From under a small tree on our left, a trio of very small-headed black and white checked snakes crossed the clearing. A beautiful turquoise and gold snake was coming towards us from under the parrot tree.

We sat down, and continued to feed these snakes with the only thing we had, our energy. A red snake with yellow triangles on its face and back slid across Mauro's lap, coming from behind us. I felt sweat dripping down my arms, dripping off my elbows. The sheer number of snakes that were showing up was rapidly becoming more than I could track.

Mauro's eyes were closed. I was thinking yes, it's probably better that I don't see, when I noticed a small brightly colored snake directly in front of me. I immediately didn't like the looks of this snake. It had a black face with bright red eyes. Red, yellow, and black stripes circled

151

its body. It had an oily sheen that intensified the brilliance of its colors and a weird vibe, like the vibe you get from scorpions — a certain "don't even think of messing with me" vibe.

It was only about two feet long, and there were still at least 30 snakes around us, but it had my full attention as it was inching towards me, making small abrupt movements from side to side. I had been continuing to feed the snakes my energy, but now I sat absolutely still. I didn't want to make the slightest motion that could possibly provoke this snake.

Sweat was now pouring from my face, down my neck and back. I felt a salty sting in my eyes. I repeatedly blinked to clear the sweat from my vision. I noticed that Mauro had opened his eyes, and he was carefully observing the striped snake, with a look of real concern.

I cleared my throat — several times — and the snake stopped its advance.

Several large ants were making their way up my leg. Mauro had sat down cross-legged, and I had sat down with my legs to the side, and now it was hurting to stay upright, but if I were to swing my legs around to get more comfortable, I would be making myself a target for sure, and, then to top it off, more ants were starting to crawl on me.

"Oh, shit," I thought.

I had been completely taken by the vibrant colors and strange beauty of the gathering of snakes. I was also very aware that *this* was a rare moment of connection between humans and snakes, and that somehow I was participating in a look behind the curtain of our instinctive fear of snakes to something that we shared. Yet, even though I should have felt revulsion, I felt a certain strange *joy* at being a part of something so primal. All of *that* had stopped completely with the arrival of the red, yellow and black ring striped snake.

Then, suddenly, it was as if a crack opened into the infinite — and rushing into that moment like a gushing waterfall of bracing energy came the words, *"Face everything! Avoid nothing!"*

Beauty began again to pour into my awareness, with a flood of exquisite colors, a soft breeze of warm air, fat happy snakes, and jewel-like ants. What did I have to lose? Nothing. If life had brought me to this place to die, I would die singing!

I hummed to find a pitch, and softly began to sing:

> Oh what a beautiful stripe snake.
> Oh what a beautiful snake
> I've got a wonderful feeling
> Everything will be OK.
> There's a big golden snake in the meadow,
> There are black and white snakes in the grass
> These beautiful snakes are all telling me
> everything will be OK — yes,
> everything will be OK."

One of the small headed black and white checked snakes slowly slid between the striped snake and my legs, seemingly to get a better look at this crazy singing human — and its two fellow black and whites followed it — effectively placing a checkered flag of three snake bodies between the striped snake and me.

I had continued humming "Oh What a Beautiful Morning," and now I had no doubt. A rainbow snake the size of a freight train slid through the forest on the far side of the clearing, giving me a nod of it's huge head as it passed, as if it were tipping its hat. It took at least a minute to pass through the brush.

As soon as the rainbow had passed, I noticed that *all* of the snakes had slipped away into the jungle.

Mauro looked at me with very round eyes, and we both burst out laughing, tears and sweat in our eyes.

Mauro repeated *"Ay Dios Mio!"* over and over, and I exclaimed "Holy fucking cow!" We laughed so hard that I sat down again, and was immediately covered with ants. Mauro hooted and pointed. *"Si las serpientes no se obtiene, las hormigas!"*

"If the snakes don't get you, the ants will!"

We began walking, generally heading north, on trails that crossed the top of a number of small valleys. There was water, and we found some small fleshy fruit — nothing I had ever tasted before. We came to a small road, and a beat-up old truck, positively spewing black exhaust, slowed for us to hop on. We sat in the back with an oldtimer and a couple of kids, on top of wooden and chicken-wire boxes filled with hens clucking and complaining.

About two hours of bumpy truck jolting later, we got off in the market of a small village. We sat in a little park, and, within a short

153

time, a decrepit old bus lumbered into the small plaza, wheeling around one time to display the skill of the driver and coming to a stop. Mauro negotiated a deal with the driver. Neither of us had any money on us, and Mauro assured the driver that we would pay when we were dropped off.

We spent another several hours in the bus, stopping at every little village and junction. The driver had just turned his headlights on when Mauro stood up and indicated to him that we wanted to stop ahead. We got off, and I waited by the bus while Mauro went down a small hill to an adobe house, returning a moment later with a young man and woman excitedly hugging him, as well as cash and a small tip for the driver. *"Muchas gracias, muchas muchas gracias!"*

We were at Mauro's family home, a small group of adobe buildings, only the main house of which had electricity. A number of goats and chickens were wandering freely, and best of all, totally surprised and overcome with joy, Mauro's mother Francesca greeted him, and included me in her welcome.

Mauro's mother, probably in her mid-sixties, had the weathered, bronzed and timeless look of Peruvian women everywhere. She could have been 40. There's something about the beauty of these women. They hit a certain point, and then they hold there until their nineties, when they finally pick up a few wrinkles.

Mauro made a big deal about me being "Francis." Maybe she had given birth to me and not told anyone? Maybe I was part of the family? The young man and woman were Mauro's cousins, his mothers' sisters' childrens' children. Yes, I was confused too, but we enjoyed a meal of potato and quinoa sopa, and afterwards, I lay down and was sound asleep within moments.

We spent two days at Mauro's home. Mauro and his wife Mercedes lived and worked in Cusco and had a life there with their children, but *this* is where his heart was. He had studied and become a shaman here, a Maestro — an orchestrator of energy — energy which he described as colors of light.

He and I did a ceremony at the base of the countryside's Apus — a holy mountain, the living presence of the earth's divinity — calling violet light to illuminate us and to illuminate the land, the people, the animals and crops, and the world. He told me, "Hey Francis, you're looking pretty good in this violet light! It looks like you've lost a little weight!" We couldn't help it, we both laughed. In fact, laughter seemed to be the foundation for our friendship.

We caught the bus back to Cusco — teary goodbyes from his mother and all around. About 14 hours later, we got off at the big bus terminal — the TTC Terminal of Cusco — and caught a little cab back into the city to the central plaza, the Playa de Armas. We hugged and shook hands.

Mauro headed up his street, and I walked straight to my hotel, just off the square, to take a long hot shower, get something to eat, and sleep in a real bed. The next day I got it together by mid-morning to get out, head up to Mauro's shop and to thank him for such a great adventure. As I arrived at his shop, packed with everything under the sun a shaman could want, and more, I had to slip around a small group of German tourists who were argumentively gesturing to a large smoky crystal in a display case.

They insisted to Mauro that it was worth less than half of what he was asking. I had managed to get to the back of the shop, and was examining a group of alabaster carvings — carvings with mysterious, almost alien outer-space designs.

Mauro glanced at me, and pointed over to a chair, nodding his head slightly, silently saying, "Make yourself comfortable, I'll be right over," and his wife, Mercedes, went to the back of the shop to pour me a cup of coca tea.

I sat and sipped the tea while the Germans made the point that they were doing Mauro a favor to even consider purchasing such a poor specimen.

Mauro gestured to them — *that's it!* — his hand cut through the air — *finito.* No more talk — the crystal was not for sale for any price.

He came over and sat down facing me, smiling. "Hola amigo." I set my tea down, and we placed our hands together. He closed his eyes, and so did I.

After a long time in silence, with the noises of the street drifting in and no one but us in the shop, Mauro began to speak. He would speak a phrase, and I repeated what he said:

> I am alive.
> I am not afraid to live!
> I am not afraid to die.
> I face everything and avoid nothing.
> I see the beauty of this moment.

I love for no reason.
I am grateful for my life.
Thank you.

We opened our eyes, and both stretched slightly, no longer holding hands, but still holding this deep space.

"You know, my friend," Mauro said, "the Rainbow Snake, she knows you, and will come when you call!"

"Oh great," I said, "Just what I need, a really big snake!"

Laughter.

center

Deep Beauty

Your journey to Deep Beauty has brought you to this moment, to the beginning of a magical new world.

Here is a world very much like the one you have known, but existing in a different dimension, with different rules, and a language so ancient that it is the source of every language spoken today. Along the way to this moment you have become increasingly fluent. It hasn't been too difficult, because something about it has seemed so familiar.

You've heard it whispered in dreams, in moments of wonder.

You've heard it calling you to love wild and free, from the center of your beating heart.

And stepping to the center of the spiral, you stand at the heart of Creation, right here, right now.

Here, communication becomes *communion*.

Speaking becomes sacred poetry.

The Great Mystery, recognizing our sincerity, enjoying our celebration, and touched by our transcendence, drops her robes of material form, and reveals, from horizon to horizon, inconceivably vast realms of shimmering iridescent Light.

Language falls away, and we're speechless. Nothing can be said, and there is nothing to say.

Without effort, without trying, we notice beauty all around us. As we *see* the beauty, beauty speaks to us, and when we say, "Oh, this is so beautiful!" in grateful recognition of our communion, Creation *expands* her beauty. As we become increasingly delighted, Creation shines with increasingly beautiful Light. We are now speaking the original language, speaking with Creation, speaking the language of Deep Beauty.

We have arrived at the center of it all.

Beauty inspires us, beauty speaks to us, beauty nourishes us, and beauty encourages us.

Creation speaks heart to heart with us, loving us in return.

Speaking Deep Beauty

We had gotten up in the dark, around 4:00 AM. And, even if you *are* in a fine hotel in Aguas Caliente at the base of Machu Picchu, it's too early.

Our bleary-eyed crew began to gather in the hotel lobby. In a few minutes, our guide, Jorge, would be showing up, looking as fresh and happy as ever. We were up at this ungodly hour getting ready to take three specially chartered jitney buses up the mountain to Machu Picchu. Then, we would hike up to the Intihuatana, the Hitching Post of the Sun, for a special Sunrise Ceremony with don Miguel.

But *something* had gone wrong. Typical of modern Toltec communications gone awry, two thirds of our group thought that they had been told that we'd be *departing* for Machu Picchu at 6:30 AM — a case of wishful thinking — because the sun actually rises at 5:30 AM, if anyone cared enough to pay attention.

I knew what time the sun rose! Because the previous morning I had walked in the dark up to the hot springs at the top of Aguas Caliente and had been soaking at sunrise, having been advised by the locals that this was the best time to get clean water, before the herds of porters and trekkers arrived to rinse the Inca Trail off of their tired bodies. I'd made it back to the hotel for breakfast at 7:30 very relaxed and smelling only slightly of sulfur.

The confusion began when it came out at dinner the night before that the surrounding high mountains block the *direct* light of sunrise. The sun does not actually clear over the tall peaks surrounding Machu Picchu and shine on the Intihuatana stone until around 6:30.

And that was just the *beginning* of the misunderstanding. Because, as the sharper knives in our drawer pointed out to those protesting that they were *told* 6:30, to be at the Hitching Post by 6:30, you would still have to leave Aguas Caliente *before* 6:30, not just *be in the lobby* by 6:30.

This is the dark underbelly of spiritual power journeys.

And while people are just *people*, and sometimes inadvertently create these odd misunderstandings, the Toltecs seem to be significantly better at garbling information, due to the near total absence of anyone *not* in an altered state.

Rather than making us early risers wait, and we were already grumpy enough, Jorge decided to go ahead and send us up the mountain, and then take the rest of the group up whenever they were ready, still well ahead of Machu Picchu's normal opening time. We would no longer have a Sunrise Ceremony, it would now be a Good Morning ceremony.

The ride up the windy dirt road took almost no time. No one was on the road, and we whizzed up to the parking lot at the hotel. At that time, it was the real ruins at Machu Picchu.

There is a deep and quiet calm that sleeping people generate — no matter what their culture, no matter what era they live in, or what civilization, or even what dimension they might be in, *sleeping* is the same surrender to the night, to dreams. This is what the majority of our companions were still doing back at the hotel, and yet, all of our judgments and commentary began to evaporate as we went through the gates and onto the grounds of Machu Picchu.

It was magical beyond description, and to be with such a small group walking along the paths and climbing the stone steps of Machu Picchu with no one else around was primal. *We* were the ones called over and over again, across generations, to be present for the dawning of the light.

What had been a misunderstanding became a precious gift.

We hiked fast to get to the Intihuatana. It is perhaps the most sacred place in the entire Incan empire, the place where the Light of the Sun hitches into matter, where the divine presence enters into form, entering with love, with willingness to experience the darkness of existence, and then, to *illuminate* it.

A soft glow suffused the sky to the East. It was no longer black as night. We reached the Intihuatana, and people did their own things. Some meditated, some went from spot to spot, just gazing out at the beauty of Machu Picchu, and some of us gathered together along a short raised stone wall near the Inti stone, looking East towards the sunrise.

I counted — there were twelve of us. No guards. Jorge had ridden the bus up the mountain with us to make sure we had no problems getting in past the gate, but then had gone back down the mountain to gather the rest of the group, which included don Miguel and Gini. I was certain that there was a big *mitote* going on — a *mitote* being the chaos and noise of everyone shouting and arguing at once, kind of like what goes on in our minds all of the time.

(In fact, we heard later that people were running here and there, waking other people up, insisting that everyone get going, while others insisted that *no*, there was plenty of time, and there was no need to rush.)

Slowly, as the dawn broke over the far peaks of the holy Grandmother and Grandfather Apus, everything in my mind became quiet — hushed by the beauty of the early morning. A bank of fog had come in, below us, rising up from the river, so that we were floating in our own world, suspended between earth and sky.

It didn't matter what had happened this morning, or what was happening, or what would happen, or who would say what to whom. All of the drama of the morning became as ephemeral as the fog where the sunlight began illuminating it through the peaks of the ring of mountains surrounding us.

I had laid out a small mesa and put a special crystal in the center. The crystal had appeared on a shelf in a busy money changing shop in Cusco, just as I walked in, the previous week.

The shopkeeper didn't even know that she had it, and when I asked the price, she said, "Oh . . . 30 Soles" — around ten bucks! Vendors sold similar crystals on the street for several hundred dollars. There was something magical about this crystal, and there was absolutely no reason why it wouldn't have sold a hundred times at *that* price.

But the crystal had decided somehow that it would appear just when I walked through the door, and that it would go with me. It was in my bag in moments, the 30 Soles handed over in a flash.

One strikingly unique facet to this crystal was that it had a jagged lightning bolt fracture that spiraled down from inside the very top point, to deep within the crystal, and this morning, on the mesa, it glowed like a rainbow. A number of people commented, "Wow, *that's* pretty cool!"

I placed two small Peruvian cast bronze llama bells on the mesa, with three-leafed coca quintus at each of the directions.

Several conversations were going on. We were all very low key and relaxed, because it would be at least an hour before everyone else made it up.

Just for fun, I picked up the little bells and gently rang them. I had my back to the rising sun and was looking down into the valley where the Urubamba River runs around the base of Machu Picchu and turns west across the top slope of the Amazon watershed.

There was a distant rumble. Barely noticeable. I rang the bells again. This time there was an immediate rumble of thunder from across the valley, like a distant bowling ally strike.

I rang the bells towards the North, with the sound brightly splashing along the stone walls, and — ka-boom! A clap of thunder.

With this, most people had stopped talking, and were observing this bell and thunder conversation. One of the guys commented, "It certainly doesn't look like there is a rain cloud anywhere!"

It became a game. I'd ring the bells, very softly, and a rumble would emerge from a distant range in the direction I had rung the bell. Then I'd wait. No thunder. I'd ring the bells louder, to the East, and thunder would roll over us.

By now, everyone in our group was enjoying the conversation.

It was obvious that the thunderclaps had nothing to do with me personally. I was as surprised at the ongoing call and response as anyone. This conversation was happening between the sound of the little bells and the answer from the sacred mountains, the Apus, resonating through the mountain valleys and morning sunlight playing on the fog.

Several more times, for the joy of it, the little bells rang out, followed by claps of thunder. Then, the bells rang very softly, to a distant rumble.

I set the bells down, and the conversation was complete.

I felt deep gratitude. From my heart I spoke to the Apus, "Thank you for playing with me."

Other than that, silence. No one spoke. We turned and watched the sun's rays clear the far range and touch the very top of the Hitching Post of the Sun.

163

The light kissed the stone, and the universe would live another day.

This was my first lesson in *speaking* Deep Beauty, the language of Creation.

For the rest of that journey, it didn't matter to me what anyone was talking about. English was sheer babble and Spanish was just prettier sounding babble. I spent my time talking with rocks, plants, little spiders, flowers, hummingbirds. Everywhere *beauty* was speaking to me.

Hanging out with Quechua speakers later in the week, on the island of Taquile on Lake Titicaca, I began to feel more comfortable with the sounds that come out of human mouths. These people were textile artists, and welcomed visitors into their homes, to stay and experience life with their families. I felt right at home.

Like indigenous people everywhere, these people managed to get the maximum enjoyment out of the absolute minimum. At the same time, my host don Antolin informed me that the community was looking to create an online presence that would allow them to sell their textiles into the global marketplace of people interested in indigenous arts.

Maybe because I was *so* interested in the sounds of their language (one of 40 loosely related languages that is called "Quechua"), and, maybe because I had brought along my little baby Taylor travel guitar, and joined in playing music with don Antolin and his family, he decided that he would teach me to speak like a native.

It was fine with me that tripping over my own tongue was the source of such amusement for the family. I began to return phrases and comments — to much laughter.

"Allillanchu?" My emphasis was on the *chu!* This was like asking, "How are you" with a hearty sneeze.

Much of what I heard and understood reminded me of Tiwa, the "first" language, spoken by the Picuris people of Joseph Rael's heritage. Like Tiwa, many words in Quetchua are onomatopoetic — that is, words *sound* like the things they are describing. Also, like Tiwa, their language describes energies and vibrations *in motion*, and does not consider things *things*, but rather, processes in motion.

For example, in English, "I am thirsty" describes a state of being, it's static, and bereft of energy. "I am ker-plunk."

In Quetchua the expression is: *"Ch'akiwashanmi, yakunayawashanmi,"* which roughly translated is "water flowing over tongue is longing to flow down tongue river," expressing an *active* thirst, with water *alive*, water flowing over and beyond the tongue is desiring to flow down the tongue, just as much as the person's tongue desires it also.

Here, one's *thirst* speaks a revelation of the mutual interwoven love affair between water and human, between flowing river and the land that embraces its flow; in this case, the tongue.

The shape of *our* language has penetrated just as deeply into our psyche, and has shaped the gates of *our* perception.

An old callawaya, a healer from the highlands above Cusco pointed this out to me, in a combination of Quechua and sign language — *"movement, then, story"* — his dark rough old hand sweeping the air, *moving*, then suddenly *stopping*, palm out, and then pantomiming *"blah-blah-de-blah-blah."* He was teaching a foundational truth about energetic work, about the work of healing: *something happens. Energy moves*, and then, we *interpret* what we saw, we *explain* the movement that we perceived.

And our *interpretation* immediately becomes more real to us than whatever energy actually moved in the first place.

This old chakaruna said, "Move *into* the space between thoughts in order to clearly *see* what is going on with those who come to you for healing."

Spirit moves, and then we interpret the movement with a story, and then to us the story *is* the movement, and we expand on the story with additional related thoughts, information, and theories about the story.

This is, of course, why Hindu believers don't see Christ when Spirit moves, they see Krishna. Christians see Christ, Toltecs see Quetzalcoatl, and Incans see Tayta Inti.

The advantage that Tiwa, Quetchua, Amayra, Tungus and hundreds of other indigenous world languages have is that they describe the world as *vibration* — vibration that is the essence of what is being perceived — the essence of a flower blooming, or of a river flowing, or of the moon rising.

What I had discovered within myself at the Intihuatana, as the bells and thunder spoke with each other, is that *Creation herself* speaks a language of vibration — the very first language, the language of pure vibrating beauty, of the *deepest* beauty — of Deep Beauty.

Here's how a conversation goes in Deep Beauty: you are walking along a path, and weeds are growing out from around the tightly fitted path stones. You notice that some of the plants have little round yellow flowers and that they are more like little balls than flowers with petals. You stop, and lean down to look more closely. The little plants are shy, and look plain, weedy. Then, you get down on a knee, and say to the plants, "I love the way your flowers look like tiny suns. All of you together are looking like a galaxy of stars!"

The little flowers perk up, and *become* much more like a field of stars, growing in delicate spirals around the rocks, which have become infinite space.

"You are brave and beautiful little plants, and I *so* appreciate your courage in growing here on this path! I hope that some day you'll take over the whole path, and people will walk lightly on suns as they cross over you!"

The little plants sparkle, bursting with appreciation for being noticed, for being seen for the valiant effort they make to recover the path on behalf of Nature herself.

"Look, sweetheart," you say to your companion, "look at how really beautiful these little plants are . . . look at how stunning their flowers are. They're like little suns. Really, I've never seen anything so beautiful!"

And because beauty multiplies and begins to *sing* when it is shared, your sweetheart stops and notices too that these little plants with their tiny sun flowers are a *miracle* — and that she's never seen anything *so* beautiful in her life!

What has just happened? Do you remember the Toltec mythology that sees our language-based minds as a *parasite* that feeds on us? A parasite that continues its control over our lives and perceptions by convincing us that we *are* our minds? That *it* is us?

Well, the very last thing on our mind's mind is to stop and notice the beauty of Creation. "Yeah, yeah," it complains. "Lets get a move on here, or we'll be late!" And when the parasite is late, or becomes hungry, it uses fear to create drama and trauma, in order to feed off of the distressed energy. Eckhart Tolle calls this phenomenon the "emergence of the pain body."

Eckhart is speaking of the same thing that the Toltecs call the *parasite*. It's an entity, with an agenda of it's own to survive, and to continue its control of its host. Uh, and that would be *you*.

The Peruvian *chakaruna* who said, "First there is movement, and then we create a story to explain it," taught that *all* beings in Creation were part of the One being, and that I could *respect* parasites and entities as being sparks of life surviving in the ecology of the energetic world. He said, "Your life is a gift to you from Pachamama, from Creation herself. Now, what is *appropriate* is for life to flow through you, from your center, upwelling and pouring into manifestation as your body, your family, your friends, your work, your life.

"It simply is *not appropriate* for anyone or anything to take advantage of the flow of your life by *taking* your energy! And we simply remove these entities, and send them along to *their* source, back to their tribe. They were only lost and confused, and were just trying to survive."

Just like we have a *pain body* that emerges to satiate itself on

167

distress, we also have a *beauty body* that comes present and grows strong when we see beauty and appreciate it, moving towards beauty with love and enjoyment. The beauty body emerges from the center of the center within us. It emerges from the same Light that animates our DNA, from the vibration of life itself, which we can also call Love.

Sometimes when Creation speaks to us, we can only hear a subtle distant cry. It is Deep Beauty, longing to commune with us, longing to be seen, to be spoken with, longing to be shared, longing to be *cared* for. We hear this cry of love in our dreams, and in the myths of humankind that reveal our true natures to be as wild, beautiful and vibrant as Creation herself. We are, after all, her beautiful gift to ourselves.

As we become fluent in speaking Deep Beauty, and as we become saturated with beauty, it glows and radiates from us, and soon, the Deep Beauty of every moment is revealed.

Start by noticing the unexpected beauty of weeds growing from cracks in the sidewalk, and work your way up to conversations with the sun, the moon, and the stars. Speak with the beauty of seaweed washed up on the shore, and then speak with the ocean and the sky. The little hunting spider becomes your friend for life when you tell him that you appreciate the beauty of his dance, and *love* his little red back.

Soon, wasps become flying jewels, bees reveal themselves to be ambassadors of love, and the plants, trees, rocks, little mountain streams, mighty rivers, birds, animals, and humans *all* reveal the presence of the divine one.

And, it turns out that all are singing along with you in beauty.

You *know* this language.

It has always existed within your cells.

The love of Creation spoke the unique vibration of *you* into being, and Deep Beauty is your native tongue.

above

seeing

Seeing

WE DON'T USUALLY SEE THE BIG PICTURE, WHERE MAGICAL
opportunities are present and easily available to us, because we most
often look at reality through the narrow flashlight beam of our *attention*
instead of seeing from horizon to horizon in the bright sunlight of
awareness.

Your journey through the spiral has brought you to the center of
this awareness — where beauty permeates you, beauty radiates from
you, and the Deep Beauty of every moment is revealed. This is the
homeland of shamans and seers, of visionaries and mystics. Here, in
these fields of light, are the resources so desperately needed on planet
earth, brilliant flashes of illumination, lightning bolts of inspiration,
visions of the Divine entering the affairs of mankind.

Here in the big picture, magic is not the exception, it is the rule,
and in this time of transition, at the beginning of a new world age, what
were once tightly closed gates of perception have swung wide open.
Around us we can clearly see the "kingdom of heaven" that surrounds
us. As a species, we're at a new evolutionary moment. We are entering

into the time of the *flowering* of humanity. The ancient promises made deep in our hearts — of life caring for life and of sharing the gift of life as a single family — are coming true.

It used to be that shamans, seers and visionaries would bring messages from *this* place back to what was called "normal" reality. Translating these visions of deep beauty and encouragement into something that frightened people living in a world of scarcity and limitation could understand was a daunting task.

Now, we're in transition, between an age of ignorance and an age of enlightenment. At this moment, these worlds are overlapping. Love is overtaking fear, peace on earth is *here* as each of us turns to embrace peace within ourselves, compassionate loving kindness is upwelling everywhere, especially within our children.

Now, the challenge is not how to communicate the messages from another realm of being, but how to *navigate* through the changing landscapes of one world falling apart as a new world emerges.

While there are no *maps* to chart a course, there *are* guides — like this one, *A Shaman's Guide to Deep Beauty.* And while old-style guidebooks told you *where* to look, in this time of global transition you will need to know *how* to look.

We each have this little flashlight beam — it is our ability to pay attention. This function of our mind's eye — the ability to focus, concentrate and direct our attention — helps us eliminate vast amounts of extraneous and unnecessary information that would only clutter our perception of what we think is important.

That's a kind way of saying it: the reality is that instead of attention focusing and showing us what is actually *present*, it operates in service to its master, the mind, and *only* shows us what we *believe* we're going to see.

And what it shows us is *proof* that we're *right*. Our attention blots out anything that would make us *wrong*. After all, our view of the world, based on everything we've learned and everything we know to be true, has *got* to be right, because that's the way we're certain it is. Even though it's just the tiniest of flashlight beams that we're seeing the world through, we trust it completely. We trust it because it is *our* perception.

And what do you think this flashlight beam of attention constantly finds? It finds *evidence* that we're right! It finds solid, reliable, undisputable evidence that we're right. This is not a whimsical fantasy generating function of the mind, it's hard core, tactile and tangible.

Everything it focuses on proves that "I'm right." If it passes across evidence that indicates, "I might not be right," or "I'm definitely *not* right," or even "I *might* be wrong," it quickly scans away and lands on the reassuring evidence that proves that while there might have been some erroneous information, it turns out that "I'm right" after all!

As long as our focus is on evidence that proves that "I'm right," we are *incapable* of seeing another point of view. The evidence that we're not right can be overwhelming, but we will find the tiniest fragment of evidence that supports our view, and we will continue to see only what we believe we're going to see.

Shamanic wisdom has a phrase for this phenomenon: "our attention follows our beliefs."

What we've been calling our "attention" is referred to by shamans as our "first attention," because it is the *first* way in which we have learned to use this tool of the mind's eye. You can witness the *attention training program* in action by watching parents and families repeatedly capturing an infant's attention. This *is* the tool used to domesticate a child into the belief system of the family and culture.

By themselves, just in terms of how they function, tools are neither good nor bad, and there *are* increasingly useful ways in which the tool of attention can be used. More on that in a moment.

173

First, though: can you see that in the rising light of the blazing sun of awareness, tracking everything you experience and perceive with the tiny little flashlight beam of attention is no longer useful?

As we have been talking here, in the relative safety of this book, your mind has naturally and easily switched from attention to awareness.

We all know, and can agree, that for the most part, our views are self-serving and designed to protect what we believe to be true. So, the information that our view of reality could be so tightly limited and controlled comes as no shock.

But how do we re-learn how to use our attention, in a way that includes reality, rather than excluding what we don't believe?

Well, a traditional path to an expanded worldview is to start with entertaining small paradoxes and from there to progressively expand our capacity to contain alternative and even opposing points of view.

My mother, Marita, greatly expanded her worldview in her final months by allowing the uncertainty of paradoxes to exist in what had been a highly organized and disciplined mind.

Marita was a brilliant psychoanalyst and critical thinker. She and I had long discussed psychology, attachment theory, brain development, child development, and the foundational premises behind various psychoanalytic theories. She would defend and explain the position of modern science, and I would counter with ancient shamanic views. And of course we continued these arguments — I mean discussions — when she became ill. In fact we spent *more* time together, because as her eldest son, I was responsible for much of her caretaking, along with my cousin Christina and one of my brothers, James.

I had the night shift, which gave us plenty of time to talk. During one discussion about self-imposed limitations, self-defeating behavior and our tightly held identities, I told her, "You know Marita, you are not your mind!"

"If I'm not my mind, then who am I?" she exclaimed, as if it were obvious that *not* being her mind meant that she would not have an identity, and the proof that she *was* her mind, and *exactly* who she thought she was, was the obvious evidence that she *was* herself!

As she came to the end of her life, she broke free of the constraints of limiting self-imposed identities. In fact, she broke free of time and space and left this life unfrightened, in awareness, in a blaze of illumination. But, she began on this path to ultimate liberation from the tyranny of her mind with small steps, by first proclaiming, "You really do have to absolutely STOP and smell the roses!" And in the very next sentence, she'd add, "But you've got to get going, and act quick, because there is not a second to waste!"

From there she grew to be able to contain the truly unsettling paradoxes of human existence. Why do we *fall* in love? And then, why do we hurt the ones we love? And because she was a thinker, how could one be subjective and objective at the same time if one could be neither without opposing the other?

Finally, she advanced to what might be the greatest of paradoxes, that this world is *perfect* just as it is, in *this* moment, and yet, within us we find an irrepressible drive to advance, grow, learn and evolve — an inborn drive to make the world a better place and to care for all those who have been broken, injured and damaged along the way.

Along her way, Marita saw that instead of attention following belief, the *first attention*, she could direct her attention to follow her growing awareness that she was not her mind, not her emotions, and not even her body — that the essence of her self was mysterious, and much deeper, broader, and greatly expanded than she had ever imagined.

As a testament to her beauty, courage and unflinching intent to know the truth, her final act was to embrace the Great Mystery.

"Attention follows awareness," So, this is the *second attention*, where our capacity to pay attention allows us to focus within the field of awareness, instead of being exclusively focused within the field of our *beliefs*. In the second attention, we are able to see what *is*, revealed in the light of awareness.

It would seem that the leap from the first to the second attention is over a chasm so deep and treacherous that few have the courage to jump. From the desperate insecurity of the first attention, it seems that only being forced by ultimate circumstances, like the certainty of immediate death, could compel one to make this leap.

And yet, as dramatic a shift in perspective as it is, the second

175

attention is simply another stepping stone on the way to an even deeper experience — the penetrating perception experienced by a Seer — a shaman who *sees* in the "dark."

In fact, the word "shaman" is a Siberian word for "one who sees in the dark." It was adopted as a general label for any and all indigenous "medicine people." Also, remember that the actual Siberian word for shaman is not a noun, like Doctor, or Lawyer, but rather it is a verb. It describes an action being taken, the act of seeing.

So, a *shaman* is a *seeing*, a saturation of awareness that floods through us. We see in the dark, we see in the light. There's no difference.

However, this *seeing* in the *third attention* is more than just a shift in perspective. This is the realm of the *visionary*, the one whom Creation is able to look *through* into creation.

In the common parlance of our Western world, a *visionary* is one who sees into the future. But the true Visionary, that we speak of here, is *Creation* seeing with keen awareness into the many dimensions of being, to the place where a radically compelling alternative view is offered as an expansion of awareness. Here in the third attention, *attention serves awareness*.

For the visionary, this experience was always reported as being otherworldly, dream-like, and the result of a state of greatly expanded awareness. But this *is* the realm of the shaman, the place where the shaman has gone searching for solutions to whatever situation that calls for care, healing and movement.

The *vision* of the visionary, the seer, and the shaman is a natural evolution of our human potential — to be free to roam infinite numinous awareness untamed and unobscured. This is the essential wild beauty that the shaman has long been in service to.

And, *this* is the world that is now overlapping us here at the beginning of a new age. Creation, *life* itself, is looking *through us* into life here on planet earth, and we are seeing the gift of this evolutionary opportunity being offered to us now.

As we turn to cooperation and collaboration with Creation, we find a renewed willingness to *change* the ways we do things — the ways we produce energy and food, the ways we care for natural resources, like the water in our ground, lakes, rivers, and oceans. We are entering a time of miracles. The time has come for us to globally revision and reinvent everything, from healthcare, education, and the economic system, to the environmental impact we make on the world we share with all living things.

The gift being offered to us is not just that we can *survive* the changes that are upon us, but that we can *thrive*, cherishing and celebrating life, having heard the message that the world is not ending, and having seen the light, that it is always beginning.

Coming deep from the heart of Creation is a call for us to *wake up*, to *grow up*, and to *take care* of life on earth. And *this* is what you have been preparing for, to taste this water of life and to *see* for yourself. You speak Deep Beauty like a native. And the ceremonial work you have done in this guide will help you to effortlessly shift your focus to this realm, to the third attention, where *you* are of service to Creation.

A simple ceremony can change how you *see* forever:

Walk out into an open field just before dawn. Have a flashlight, and use it to watch where you step.

As the sun comes up, continue to point the flashlight around.

Experiment with clenching the flashlight tightly in your hand and then totally loosening your grip. Does a tight or loose grip change what you see?

Set the flashlight on the ground — it's a useful tool, and there is no point in throwing it into the creek! You can retrieve it later.

Now, face into the rising sun.

With closed eyes, notice the rising light of awareness *within* you. You begin to see everything clearly, as it is. You have been seeking the Light, and here, now, you have found it. The rising sun is within you as it rises into the morning sky.

Turn around.

The search is over. Open your eyes and let the Light stream through you into all of creation.

Seeing Double

The symbol of the double-headed serpent that is used to represent the energetic process at Teotihuacan is far more ancient than it's use by the Aztec religion. For them it represented the presence of royalty. The Aztecs associated serpents with many gods — Quetzacuatl, the Feathered Serpent being just one example.

For the ancestors of the Nahuatl people, the double-headed serpent was a metaphor for the profound effect that *black light* — the energy fields that were marked by the temples, plazas and pyramids built at Teotihuacan — had on the human energy system.

That effect, which continues to be active and can be experienced today, can be most likened to *digestion*. The process that occurs at Teo is one of being *digested* by an enormous snake.

At its simplest level, this ceremonial process, recovered and shared with us by don Miguel Ruiz, involves entering the body of the snake through one mouth, having all beliefs, inauthenticities and artificialities digested away, and finally leaving the body of the snake through the second mouth — with everything stripped away but the essence of divinity.

The second mouth was seen as *speaking* the essence of one's divinity back into the world, as Light. A new universe was born, and — just like in the Bible, "In the beginning was the *word*" — the vibration of Creation reborn.

Arriving at Teo, the first step before entering the mouth of the snake involves seeing our *attachments* and gathering small rocks as symbols of the people, places, things, relationships that we are, for better or worse, attached to.

The next step is seeing that we each have created an island of safety, where we clutch our attachments, in the great sea of hell that surrounds us. In other words, we can see that our personalities are constructed to protect us from the infinite sea of frightening possibilities, and our attachments are our safety net.

We see that we must *leave* the island of safety in order to discover the truth about ourselves. At the great Temple of Quetzalcoatl, we enter the mouth of the serpent and are no longer in the world we have constructed over our lifetime. By releasing our attachments, we are accepted by the great serpent, and taken in. If we continue to cling to our attachments, we are not appetizing, and we are spit back out until we are willing to surrender ourselves.

In the first plaza, of *earth*, we conduct our own funeral and burial, saying goodbye to our bodies and to the life we knew.

Progressive stages of digestion involve next washing away emotional responses with *water* — with a baptism into spirit — in a plaza where we are washed clean of emotional reactions.

Then, in the plaza of *air*, black light radiating from a small pyramid at the center of the plaza works through the tangles of our beliefs, and vaporizes the artificial constructs of language and judgment that are like a parasite feeding on our own life energy. Dispensing with the tyranny of the rational mind allows our natural intelligence to heal.

We will become the creative artists of our own lives, creating poetry, art, and music. Our lives will be based on a foundation of *love*, rather than living with the ever present *fear* that is the foundation of the rational thinking mind.

In the final plaza of transformation, *fire* burns away our identities as human males or females, burning away everything that is not the absolute essence of our being. Here we experience the revelation that we are all one being, one life. In a small temple that is an opening into heaven, the *Palace of the Butterflies*, this all embracing love can be experienced.

And at this point, all that is *left* is love. And yet, one final stage awaits us — to be *spoken* by the serpent back into the world.

179

During my first journey to Teotihuacan, I experienced this process, and saw and felt the possibility of gaining personal freedom, along with freedom from fear. But like a tough nut, I passed through the body of the serpent relatively undigested.

I knew that this was a process unlike that offered by any psychological or transformational system, and I wanted it to work. The problem was that I continued to attempt to steer the course of transformation as if I already knew what would happen every step of the way. I can describe this now as the arrogance of the *mind* co-opting everyone and everything for its own self-aggrandizement and protection.

On my second journey to Teo, I was ready.

Don Miguel told us, "If I can do it, *you* can do it!"

Over a period of days the eighty or so people on this journey experienced the process at Teo, split into small groups of around twelve people, each group with a teacher guide under the supervision of don Miguel and La Dona, Gini Gentry, who would also conduct morning and evening teaching sessions.

Besides don Miguel's confidence, I had the good fortune of having a very experienced and gifted teacher, don Allan Hardman, along with his wife at that time, Randi, guiding the small group that I was in.

With eighty or so people going through deep personal processes, the slightest incident could hang the whole group's journey up for hours. But it was easy to be patient — the plazas and temples were exquisitely beautiful, and going slow benefited everyone.

Just by luck, after the plaza of fire, our group was held up by a group stalled out at the next stop, the mouth of the serpent at the plaza of the Pyramid of the Moon.

We stretched out in the warm sun in a small temple complex next to the plaza of fire, and I fell asleep and dreamed the dream of Teotihuacan. From that dream state, I was awakened, and we began walking down a long open avenue, towards the Pyramid of the Moon where we would hold a ceremony celebrating our passage through the snake.

Don Allen whispered to me as we walked, "Create a *double of yourself* — an exact replica of *you*, only larger — and with every step, give it your personality and energy."

This double would be offered to Creation in gratitude during the ceremony — a sacrifice of what we had been, made in gratitude for what we found ourselves to actually be.

Don Allan continued his whispered suggestions a moment later, "And if you should happen to see an *opening*, be sure to go for it!"

I was in an altered state, still dreaming from the short nap, and I had no idea of how offering a double of myself made any sense in the scheme of things, or what he could possible have meant by seeing an opening and taking it. I didn't ask for an explanation, I just walked along, creating my double as he had suggested.

We got to the platform and sat together in a tight circle. Don Allan had placed two couples in the center, back to back, with our group tightly gathered around them.

We began a soft humming *om* chat together. Within moments, a loud roar filled my ears, as if a large motorcycle gang had pulled up surrounding our little group, and were revving their engines.

My eyes were closed. The ground was vibrating and shaking under me. Behind me I could *feel* a funnel cloud of energy opening between me and the Pyramid of the Moon. I remembered that don Allen had mentioned that if an opening were to appear, I was to go to it. I didn't need to be told to go to the opening, it was calling to me, it was irresistible. I turned and quickly headed for the opening in the whirling energy. As I turned towards it, I noticed that my body was still sitting with the other people. Whatever!

I was *almost* at the opening when I heard a scream coming down from out of the sky and glanced up just in time to see an *enormous* red eagle with claws extended, dropping from the sky. *I was about to be caught*. I spun, trying to elude it's grasp, when the eagle attacked and grasped my double in its claws.

181

My double was 10 times larger than me, and the eagle snatched it up like it was a field mouse. I dove towards the opening, hanging in the air, everything now in slow motion.

There, beside the portal, which was beginning to tighten up and close just as I began to touch into it, was a striking creature — a woman? With black hair, black eyes, golden skin, topless, with a skirt of writhing snakes, she grabbed my left arm at my elbow and propelled me into the opening, and just as I slid through, behind me the portal snapped shut.

I was gliding up through the Earth's atmosphere, the Earth becoming smaller and smaller below. I was heading towards the sun, now moving at tremendous speed, and it got hotter and hotter. I couldn't bear the heat. I looked at my outstretched arms and hands in front of me as the flesh burned off, and my bones blackened and then vaporized — directly into the center of the sun — silence — no longer hot.

Far away, the sounds of waves crashing a spray of stars, like delicate rainbow foam laced against the black velvet of infinite space, still moving, moving towards the *black sun,* at the spinning center of creation.

My heart beating — the beating heart of all of life. Endless close touch, of myself everywhere, all at once, my beating heart. My eyes open, and every eye opens — I see from every open I simultaneously.

Perfect peace. Love. And such affection for all — an iridescent torrent of being — a rainbow waterfall of *yes* — life gushing, flowing out in every dimension. I remembered that I once had a single form, and now it was unnecessary.

Why return? Why depart from bliss when all of life is bliss? Go back to the limitation of a point of view?

I was being called back by Randi; she was holding my body, cradling me, rocking me, whispering "come back, come back, come back."

Wasn't it just as beautiful and amazing as anything else to be in a body? Why not? For love? To love?

I came back into this body, only partially fitting — with the majority of myself including everyone that was climbing to the top of the Pyramids of the Moon, of the Sun, everyone in the plazas and courtyards of Teotihuacan. I had come back to the body of the snake.

The group climbed from the Moon plaza to the top of pyramid; I floated to the top, effortlessly. Someone commented, "I wonder if the tourists that are coming up here have any idea of what this place really is."

I looked at my hands and arms, curious. I had just seen them burnt to a crisp and vaporized, and now I was seeing *through* them, through to the rocks of the Pyramid of the Moon where I sat looking out at the whole body of Teo.

I looked around. The tourists who had no idea of what this place was were illuminated from within. They were so beautiful that my eyes welled up with tears. The soccer clubs that brought their young teams to run and explore Teo were now making their way to the top of the pyramid to join us, a positive swarm of children, and the *children* — precious jewels, flowering, sweet gifts of life celebrating life.

Why on earth would they need to know anything?

For all of us, there is a time for seeking, for seeking the light, and turning *to* the light.

And then, for each of us, there comes the moment when the search is over, when the light is all there is, when all of Creation is illuminated.

It is here, and it has been here all along. If you *look* with eyes of love you will see light flooding out from within you, from within the radiance of the Presence of love.

cosmic center

nothing

Being

Ultimately, awareness permeates Creation.

All sides, all beings are seen at once. The dreamer is awake.

The great mysterious presence of Creation's love permeates and surrounds everything and everyone. This awareness, this love, is your gift.

At the center of it all, Being.

Peace.

Blessings.

Coming Home

The old Nepalese shaman held out a small oval grey rock. He was no longer looking at me; he was looking through me, and he was muttering a guttural sing-song incantation that included little squeaks and whistles accompanied by *tablas* and a splashing mountain stream. I've heard Tuva throat-singers singing harmonies with themselves, but this old shaman had other realms harmonizing with him.

I had asked Surendra to take me to visit a "holy one" for a blessing for my return trip to the United States. After two months in northern India and Nepal I was ready to go home.

Yes, the ancient mountains ringing the hills and tea fields of Darjeeling had been exquisite, and visiting the great bodhi tree where the Buddha had become enlightened had been a totally disorienting collision of crisp hyper-reality and an intensely vivid dream state; it was the living history of spirit mixed with my own burning desire to find the "answer," all overlain by the omnipresent deep droning chanting that sounded like I had entered a huge hive of large orange bees on another planet in another dimension.

I was ready to return to my dimension. But two things were absolutely true:

One, this had been a great journey; I had visited temples and holy sites, had made a lot of friends and had played a lot of music; and two, Indian antibiotics had not even touched the dysentery that had been my nagging, egg-shell-walking companion for the past couple of weeks. I was ready to go home.

Surendra was whispering, "He says the full moon, the full moon!"

"The full moon? The full moon what?"

"The full moon gate will open in two weeks' time. And he, I mean you..." the shaman was pointing the small rock at me, and I noticed that it was now as black and shiny as his eyes. Surendra continued, "He says 'you have come for this moon, and the moon is coming for you.'"

I shuddered, like a jolt of voltage had just hit me, and immediately my mind protested that the moon was sure to shine just as bright back in the States.

The shaman held the rock above his head, holding it with two fingers. He brought it to eye level and investigated it, turning it as if he had never seen anything like it. Then, holding it high again between us, he balanced it on one short, thick, callused finger and closed his eyes, still as a statue.

I swear, he didn't move — not even an eyelash. The rock fell, and without thinking, I reached forward and caught it.

In addition to being a very competent guitar player, Surendra has the best connections — within hours he had arranged for me to hitch a ride from Katmandu up into the highlands of the Anapurna Range on a big, smoking, old Russian helicopter chartered by an English rock star and his son who were on a tour of Nepal's mystical places. They were planning to visit a monastery high in the Anapurnas where they would stay for three days. It was arranged for me to meet up at the monestary with Surendra's bass player's uncle, Tjeno, a trekker guide, who would supply the tents, stove, potable water and other supplies we'd need for a ten or eleven-day trek to a valley even higher in the Himalayan-Tibetan range.

The Nepalese people are the sweetest, most gentle, good-natured, good-humored and considerate people I have met anywhere, but this took the cake. Tjeno had arranged for two young nephews, Billy-one and Tju, to porter our gear.

Of course we became great friends. I taught the boys chords on my traveling guitar, a "Baby Taylor," and together we created a lot of laughter, silliness and fun.

Late every afternoon, at our cooking time, Tjeno would ask me to bring out the stone. He would mark in the dirt the tiny image scratched into one side of the stone: three tiny lines, like Roman numeral III, with a small dot centered above:

.

III

He would talk and talk, in an elegant flowery Nepalese dialect I had never heard before, Billy-one and Tju nodding, listening intently. He would include me in the dialogue, and I would nod and say "yes." I would set out the Peruvian "mesa" (altar cloth) I carry, with its electrically bright colors — hot reds, shocking pinks, bright greens, earthy brown blacks, sky blue. It looked exactly like highland Nepalese or Tibetan woven fabric.

(What is it about these thin-air people that, worlds apart, they create the same insanely brilliant fabrics and love the same scratchy, clanky, wailing music?)

187

On the altar I would set my favorite Peruvian healing crystal, a small brilliantly-patterned little bag containing a small rock from the four-leaf clover cave at the center of the great pyramid at Teotihuacan in Mexico, a small medicine bag I carry, fresh leaves and grasses gathered on the day's trek, and finally, the rock.

Tjeno would pick it up reverently and hold it high; then he would pass it around, each of us holding it, eyes closed, then opening our eyes, holding the stone up to the setting sun, the evening star, and to the growing moon.

Tjeno explained that the stone was our passport, our ticket, and it was the justification for our presence on the trail that was increasingly populated. There were groups of robed monks with shaved heads, small groups of oddly-clothed, shiny-eyed travelers, a group of Mongolians, a group of Sikhs, groups attending to an old one, carrying him on a stretcher-type affair, covered with blankets. There was a group of 20 nuns all in rust-red robes, with cloths covering their heads — they were very serious, very focused on the next step — there was no distracting them or catching their eye. The trail had people ahead of us and behind us.

Each day our trek would stop in the mid afternoon when we would come to a small, rocky, flat area on the trail that would hold two-dozen tents and five or six cooking fires. Those encamped nearby would be curious, but very polite. Had they seen a Peruvian mesa before? And the rock, instead of being inspected, passed around and admired and talked about, would simply be acknowledged. The monks and travelers would just nod their heads, a distinct "Yes, I see," gesture that made me feel included. I was wearing Western clothing (as were my three Nepalese companions) and hiking boots instead of sandals, but with my Peruvian bag, mesa and the stone, I blended right in with the growing flow of brightly colored travelers.

I had been keeping a journal, which was lost (along with my sleeping bag and a wool knit hat my mother, Marita, had made) in a river crossing. Snow was melting, as spring had arrived, and passes and gorges were running with fresh ice cold water, which I happily drank. I had my jacket, a blanket, my Peruvian shaman bag with mesa, crystals and the stone of destiny.

My hair was long, curly, tangled and as wild as that of the wild-men from the Ganges Delta. My skin had turned from my normal brown tan color to a very dark brown. I caught a glimpse of my face in a stream pool, and my Spanish-brown eyes looked back at me, intoxicated, no longer "me" but one on the path, the high trail to the Wesak.

"The Wesak," Surenda had informed me, "is a *big* festival, held in a high mountain valley. All of the world's holy people are there, and all of the lamas and the top disciples of the different schools. There's even a special section reserved for those elsewhere who dream that they are there!"

"Great! In that case, I'm heading back home, and I'll dream that I'm there. *Ouch!*"

I had put the rock in my pants pocket as we left the old shaman's compound, and it was now burning a hole in the pocket. I pulled it out; it was definitely really warm to hold. I handed it to Surendra: "Check this out!"

"Listen, Suren, I would like to know more about this, you know. . . . What am I getting into here? Do you have anything written about this? Have *you* ever gone to it? Who could I talk to who has?"

There's a certain "sinking stomach" feeling of inevitability that you get, when the only way out is through, where you just have to jump. I was fighting it. I told myself, "I'm tired. I'm not physically well. It's been a great trip, a really great adventure, and I've met enough shamans, saints and holy people to last a lifetime, but now, it's really time to go home."

"Well," Suren offered, "I heard that Dekendra is back from the south — I think he got back last night, I talked with his son."

Dekendra was the old shaman-healer I had gone to Nepal to see in the first place. Meeting him, hanging out, doing ceremony, doing whatever I could with him was a key part of my plan, my mission being to visit and learn from the indigenous healers and shamans of the world before they were gone.

189

"And I was going to surprise you! We are invited to lunch with Dekendra and his family, *this* afternoon!"

That's the way things happen in Nepal; a non-stop, rolling train wreck of synchronicities, higher consciousness and power outages.

Dekendra, now in his late eighties, spent his winters in southern India and his summers in a small village that was a two-hour, winding, cliff-hugging bus ride north from Katmandu.

I had understood that he would be returning by early April and had planned my trip around that. Now, at almost mid-May, I had sadly written off meeting him. Just like the old Toltecs, Dekendra used smoke and mirrors to cleanse energy and to call in healing energies. Smoke served as the temporary body of beings of Light, and mirrors were used as portals to see into alternate dimensions where gifts of wisdom, opportunity and practical resources were offered for use in this reality.

To find this ancient Toltec practice alive and well and being used by shamans in Nepal was evidence to me of an ancient wisdom still alive on our planet. I could hear don Julio's voice: "First, see how it is done, then do it, then, show others how."

Now — finally, suddenly — I was going to meet Dekendra, maybe extend my stay a week or two if it was possible to spend time with him, to observe, to learn. I was thrilled! The bus ride was a white-knuckle affair; finally, I surrendered. If I was going to die, so be it.

Dekendra's house was musty and water-damaged from the past winter's snow, so a long table was set outside in the courtyard. Women were cooking for us in a small shed-like structure next to the building, a shed dug down into the earth, and full of smoke (no mirrors) as the cooking fire had just been lit. Dekendra and a son had gone out for his "constitutional" and would be back soon.

I took the opportunity to peek inside the house; maybe I'd see a shrine or altar, maybe some shaman's tools, crystals, a skull, whatever. I was curious.

What I saw was a shock.

On the wall of the main living room was a large framed portrait of Elvis Presley on black velvet. Elvis was outfitted in his most gaudy Las Vegas style, big collar with a gold cross flashing on his exposed chest. This was pure, 100% country hick schmaltz, although Elvis's half-raised lip sneer/smile was absolutely perfect, as inscrutable as the Mona Lisa's.

Elvis, as it turned out, was Dekendra's hero. In fact, Dekendra had a full head of silver hair that he combed in a pompadour just like Elvis's. When he returned from his walk, I was formally introduced by Suren, and we sat together in the courtyard. Hot tea was brought, and I got out my guitar. I played "Jailhouse Rock" first, followed by "Hound Dog," "Love Me Tender" and "Fools Rush In."

Dekendra demanded a repeat performance of "Jailhouse Rock" — and we were friends for life.

After dinner, a fire was lit in the courtyard. We gathered around it, and Dekendra said, "So. What is the situation?" I handed him the rock.

He holds it in the palm of his hand and says, "Yes, the Buddha *will* be there."

I've studied many shamanic and indigenous traditions, and I'm comfortable with things being true and untrue at the same time. It's true that all we have is *this* moment. And in *this* moment I was planning to return home, but hoping to stay for two weeks more to work with Dekendra, if he would let me. And now I was being compelled to consider trekking to a mysterious festival called "Wesak."

"It's like a Bob Dylan concert," Suren translated (Dekendra had clearly said "Boo Deelan"). "Every year for eleven years the Boo Deelan concert plays his music, everyone sings. Then, on the twelfth year, Boo Deelan comes in person — same songs, same music.

"*This* is the twelfth year. It is a very established and very old festival — very organized, too. There are special places for the different groups. It is a great honor to be there with the masters, the lamas and seers and their disciples, the yogis and yoginis, row after row of holy people arranged in concentric circles around the giant altar where the Three Great Lords stand."

I was oddly touched that Dekendra had made it a Bob Dylan concert in his explanation — here was the Elvis generation reaching out to the 'youngsters.'

He scooped coals from the fire into a small copper pan, and placed several chunks of something tarry on the coals. He gently fanned the pan with his open hand, humming, eyes closed to slits.

"You did not come here for smoke and mirrors."

The smoke was billowing, and I moved slightly to avoid the aromatic clouds. If I moved one way the smoke would follow me, if I moved another, that's where the smoke would go. Ah . . . for some fresh air.

Dekendra looked directly at me and spoke in clear English: "If you leave, life will go on. But, you came a long way — you came for this.

191

Take the rock! The full moon is coming and so is the Buddha."

⟳

Trails from two other directions converged at the entrance to the valley.

With Dekendra's blessing in mind, I thought that somehow there would be a special place for me at the Wesak, someplace up front, near the altar, because my long journey "meant" something, because of the rock, because there was a higher purpose, a higher plan.

I was wrong.

There was something else that these people all knew that I didn't, because they all looked freshly washed and scrubbed, with crisp, clean, ironed robes. Had they teleported here? Hadn't they been on the same dirty rugged trails? I looked like a dusty vagabond, wild eyed, wild haired, rough around the edges, unshaven and still a little damp from my stream-crossing mishap.

The valley is shaped like a beer bottle, with the entrance to the valley through the neck — at the base of the neck, in the center, stood an enormous stone mesa. That was where the ceremony took place, on the grand altar.

There were thousands of lamas, yogis and monks, robed and turbaned people sitting in curved rows close to the altar, and stretching back in tightly organized groups of orange, rust, white, and brown — very formal and serious. How many people came to this thing? It looked like a major concert at a football stadium. The entire field was covered with people.

Everywhere I walked I got stern looks — "No, no — not here, go back, back" — hands waved — "This is *our* space. Move on!" Finally, way, way back, Tjeno spotted some Nepalese monks he knew, and we moved to sit with them in the worst seats in the place, at the very back.

I felt uncomfortable and restless. This sucked. It was just so tight, and so uptight. What was the chance of anything good happening here? It was mid-afternoon, sunset and moonrise were at least five or six hours away, and I didn't fit in anywhere. Even Tjeno's friends were giving me disapproving looks.

I decided to explore the little valley. All I could see coming in was that it was filling up with people, and that it was so highly organized that I wondered, "Where the heck is the space for the dreamers coming from other dimensions?"

Now, I noticed that the valley was very dry, with sparse brown grasses, and no trees or bushes. As I turned and looked around I saw that the valley was ringed by the high mountains of the Himalayan Range. Suddenly, I was home, I was in Peru, these were the Royal Andes. I could see, and name, the Apus, the holy ones, Apu Ausangate, Apu Salcantay, Apu Wakac Wilka, Apu Pachatusan. Wow, I was feeling better.

I sat down in a little raised area, on the hard rocky dirt, at the base of the west-facing slope of the valley, close enough to see and hear the now-chanting gathering, but out of the way. I just relaxed and began to enjoy the warm late afternoon sun. I opened my coat and shirt, letting the sun warm and dry me. "This is their culture, this is their religion. They've been doing this for hundreds, maybe thousands of years. As kids, growing up, they heard about the Wesak, they dreamed about it, and listened to the stories of those who went, and imagined that one day they would come here. Now, they *are* here. And they worked to get here too, they studied, they were tested."

As I was thinking, a group of four people were making their way past the back rows of the assembly. Maybe they noticed me, because they headed right toward me. Was it the funny, protected and comfortable spot I was sitting in that attracted them? Or did I have an energetic sign above my head that said, "Misfits Here"?

They certainly didn't look like the assembled crowd — a middle-aged Moroccan-looking black man wearing what once had been a white dashiki, his neck wrapped in a half-dozen folded scarves of different lengths who was helping an elderly oriental gentleman walk, holding his arm for balance, sometimes with his arm around him when walking over the rocks. Two short, barrel-chested sherpas followed, carrying a camp stove, pots, stool, bed rolls, maybe a tent — the typical baggage of those who walk the trail. My first thought was to search for the reassuring sight of Tjeno and the boys. I had left all of my gear and my guitar with them, my sleeping blankets and my pack with toothpaste and toothbrush, plus spare T.P. and baby wipes in case my intestines acted up again — not that I had eaten enough in the past few days to cause that, but my drinking water was also in the pack. I spotted them, far across the valley floor. They were with the group that had welcomed them, perfectly at home with their crew. At least I had my most valuable possessions with me, and

193

I relaxed again. I knew that they would find me.

But how this frail, old oriental gentleman made it to this spot, in this valley, was incomprehensible. I've seen it before in Mexico, in Peru and in Bolivia — ancient, decrepit old-timers, who would have been in nursing homes in the States, could be found carrying wood, baskets of vegetables, or jugs of water along steep trails in remote places. And they would always respond with huge, gummy smiles when you greeted them, as if here, on this trail, you, their beloved grandchild, had finally appeared to help with the chores.

This old gentleman smiled as they approached — ah, he has teeth! He wore a threadbare blue wool Mao suit and a white shirt with a ragged collar buttoned to the top.

"Please, make yourself at home — you are welcome, yes, right here is fine!" I still felt just a little stung by the chilly reception I had endured, so I made damn sure that this motley bunch felt welcome to my little patch of dirt and rocks. "Please, set up your tents right here, yes, set your stuff down here."

As the old gent came creaking into this little clearing, smiling, I spread out my spare blanket and indicated, "Please, let him sit here," and helped the African gentleman ease him to the ground.

"There, there," the African said — he wasn't speaking English, but the "cluck-cluck" sound was unmistakable. "Make yourself comfortable, we'll have hot tea in a moment."

The African turned to me and smiled. He had been 100% focused on the logistics, and I think he was surprised to find that a blanket had appeared to cushion the spot where he set the old guy down.

194

"Jesus! You have incredible eyes!" I couldn't help exclaiming, because almost blinding in the bright, shining light of his absolutely radiant smile was the surprise of ultra-blue eyes flecked with turquoise and gold. His smile, impossibly, widened further.

"Uugh," said the old gent, tilting precariously to one side, almost going over.

"Uuugh." We had inadvertently set him down on a sharp rock I hadn't seen when throwing down the blanket. The African dove to catch the old timer, and I pulled back the blanket and removed the offending stone — folding the blanket over a couple of times to make a softer landing surface. The porters were slapping their thighs with laughter — now *this* was *funny*! We got the old gent tilted back up and comfy on the blanket. He was happy, with a hand on his lap and a hand in the dirt; he closed his eyes and seemed to immediately drop off into a nap. Now, *that's* old.

Within a few minutes water was boiling for tea, and a tent had gone up directly behind the old gent, so that it looked like we had set him down on his own front porch. The sun was still shining, the kind of warm that happens at high elevations, where individual rays of sunlight prickle your skin.

The African and the sherpas were gathered on the far side of the tent, just out of my sight, but I could hear them talking in low tones. They all had a lot to say. I sat in silence with the old gent, facing into the late afternoon sun, with a fine view of the still-gathering assembly — row after row of robed pilgrims facing the giant stone mesa that was the altar.

Finally, tea-time; the African and sherpas had finished their conversation. One of the sherpas, who turned out to be a short, powerfully built woman with very clear all-black eyes and hair almost as tangled as mine, handed me two small cups, nodding toward the old gent, whose eyes were still closed. I took a sip — ah, excellent! Strong black tea, no salt, no fat, no stinky fermented anything in it — just hot, black tea.

The old gent moved just a little; his eyes opened to "where-the-heck-am-I" slits. I held one of the cups toward him, saying, "Sir, sir — this tea is for you." He stretched his fingers, took the offered cup, and to my absolute and utter surprise said, "Don't 'Sir' me."

"What? I'm sorry! You speak English?"

"When you get as old as I am, you pick up many things, many languages, a little here and a little there." He smiled.

The shock was wearing off. His voice was light, delicate, but crisp — nothing sloppy, pidgin or old-fogie here. He looked at me — polite — but obviously sizing me up. He was not reluctant to look directly into my eyes. He took a couple of sips of tea and let out a long, slow, "Ahhhh."

"He's not your father, you know."

"What? Who's not my father?"

"Him," he pointed at the African, who had just sat down with us, along with the sherpas. "Right there, the one you called 'Jesus' — he's not your father." The porters and the African all nodded their agreement.

"What? You all speak English?" No one responded; they all sat quietly, sipping their tea. "Hey, I know he's not my father!"

"Do you?"

I've had many strange conversations in my travels, apprenticeships, and work with shamans and mystics, and I was wondering how this old oriental man got to this . . . this something about my father. And what was that about Jesus? What? Strange. And then it got stranger.

"And, I am not your grandfather."

The ground began shaking, rocks were moving on the surface of the hard-packed dirt, and dust was rising in odd spirals. Strange, the sherpas continued sitting quietly as though nothing was happening. The African smiled in my direction, a sun-like burst of light. The old gent sat calmly on the front porch of his tent. The ground was now shaking violently, accompanied by a horrific, shrieking, wrenching sound of mountains tearing apart.

I've been through several major earthquakes in the Bay Area. Now, we were out in the open, so there were no buildings falling, but instinctively I jumped to my feet, and then down into a low crouch, ready for anything. I'd also experienced a serious earthquake in the highlands of Peru, and I knew that these high places were geologically unstable. Still, how could they just sit there as if nothing was happening? A grinding vibration tore at my stomach. I sat back down.

The old gent's gaze was so compassionate, so understanding, as if he was saying, "I'm so sorry it ends like this." A deep, booming explosive crash sounded just over the rise of the valley, and crash after crash, like depth charges, came closer, closer, closer. The old man reached down with his hand, touching the earth, and everything disappeared.

◎

Silence. The grinding stopped. Crying, someone crying. Peeling an onion. Crying. Each layer of the onion peeled, bringing more tears, more tears. Why? Why am I doing this? What am I doing? Why am I this way? Why am I hurting? Layers peeled away. Crying. Wanting. "I want Mama." Crying, "Papa!" No answer. Peeling, peeling — there! The center. Nothing. No hope, no choice, no light. Nothing.

Marita was a frightened teenage girl, pregnant, abandoned, desperate and alone. Her parents, Juana and Pedro, matriarch and patriarch, in a post-WWII world that made no sense, being abandoned by their own children, took their youngest child in. After all, how could a child raise a child? Suddenly, the world made sense again. Family.

Suddenly, and what a relief, Marita was a teenager again. And Juana had a job. Taking care of the baby. Pedro's place once again was at the head of the table. "Are you my little man?" Bouncing his little treasure on his knee. "Marita — he has the ears of an alien! Are you certain his father was human?"

And what a delight to be a treasure. With Mama, Papa, Mommy. Children thrive on love and attention, and I was thriving. But the treasure was put away when after four years of living with her parents, Marita left home, to make a life with her strong, handsome, American military hero husband. From a home where lentils cooked in a big pot on the stove, and only Spanish was spoken, Marita and her hero went to live in a crisp Lysoled and waxed military housing unit, where anything foreign, like Spanish, was forbidden.

I moved, too, from the exuberant, curly-headed, curious, goofy, singing, dancing, hopping, laughing, jumping center of attention to *"children are to be seen and not heard"* with a military style buzz cut. Kept out of the way of his Lord and Master. I was four years old and suddenly I was in the Army.

Marita was just doing what she had to do to keep in the good graces of her hero. Jerry Hayhurst was the man of her dreams, her answered prayers, her security, her rescue from life as a second class citizen. She could not risk his displeasure. It was her duty to serve and obey him, to keep the child out from under his feet.

"Mama Juana, Papa," I cried, sucking my thumb, consoling myself, too anxious and distressed to sleep each night.

197

Of course, I rebelled. First it was escape into the world of music on my grandfather's guitar. Later, it was *to hell with the military!* To hell with the church! Fuck the war in Vietnam, and fuck the United States of America! And to Marita's horror, the greatest sacrilege of all: fuck the flag — the flag that for Marita represented salvation and rescue from the Los Banos prison camp in the Phillipines where she and her sisters had been interred by the Japanese. The flag represented everything good. It represented her true identity, and it represented her husband. It was holy.

If being an alcoholic, womanizing, abusive, self-serving, self-aggrandizing, over-bearing, dogmatic, mindlessly patriotic and obedient military asshole like Jerry Hayhurst was what it was to be a *man*, well, fuck that!

I became a rock 'n roll musician, and played electric guitar for peace.

I was bright and curious. I read widely. I was always able to get excellent grades with no effort. However, there was no man or woman, no teacher or adult that I could see who deserved a single iota of respect. Adults were stupid, compromised, sell-outs. The world was changing fast and *they* were obsolete, their great accomplishment was that they had screwed the world up royally, and what could be done about that?

Where was the wisdom? Where were the answers? I read the Upanishads, the Tibetan Book of the Dead, the I Ching, the Koran, the Bible, the complete works of the Sufi masters, the ancient poets, and went from Zen meditation to Maharishi's meditation, always searching, certain that somewhere there was a sane, healthy, helpful way of life, with wise mentors to guide and help one on the path, the path to happiness, to wellbeing, to the sacred.

Anything organized was out. Because I played in front of groups of people as a musician, I was not eager to join in anything that involved groups of people. I was a performer, not one of the herd. As early as eight years old I had rebelled against the Catholic Church — and had memorized the names of the Popes and their heinous deeds —

198

information which I used to torture the poor nuns who were entrusted with my spiritual education in catechism.

Then, in my mid-thirties, I was introduced to shamanism by way of don Miguel Ruiz. Here was a completely disorganized religion. Maybe I'd finally find some real answers. And don Miguel — here was a man who was a medical doctor who set his profession aside in order to teach the Toltec Path to awakening, and he shone with the brilliant light of unconditional love.

From the pyramids at Teotihuacan in Mexico to the highlands of Peru, to Machu Picchu and places of great mystery and beauty, first with don Miguel, and then on my own for many years, I searched out and worked with the old shamans and mystics of the world. These old ones were people I felt respect and admiration for. They felt it, and saw it in my eyes, in the obvious love I expressed for them, and in return they opened doors of perception for me.

I was so obviously happy to be in their presence that they gladly gave me the keys to their strange kingdoms. I became free of the constraints imposed by time and space, and walked away from the world of civilization and structure into a world of wild beauty, finding a new home in the Great Mystery. I became a shaman, healer and seer myself in the process.

And the whole time, I was just trying to get back home, to be with my Mama Juana, with my Papa.

A chill. A shudder. The sun was setting; it had gotten cold. The old gent was getting up, shaking hands and hugging the African and the sherpas. I got up, confused, stiff and cold. "Are you leaving?" I asked.

"They must go, to prepare the ceremony, the Wesak. Time to get to work!"

What? The sherpas weren't a porter and a cook? They were conducting the ceremony! I pulled the rock from my pocket and held it out.

"Yes," the old gent said. "There are three and one. The Christ in the center, the Lord of Humanity and the Lady of Creation on either side. And Above, the Buddha."

"What?" I dropped the rock — surprised again. It immediately blended in with the other rocks, happy to be home again, looking no different than its brothers and sisters, just another rock, its mission complete.

"Yes, they must prepare. They must go now. But you," he pointed to me, "you will stay and keep an old man company?"

It was a question, but it was also a command. The African and I helped lower him back to his seat — a quick, radiant smile, a hug, and hugs for the sherpas, to the Lord of Humanity and the Lady of Creation — then, they were gone.

"Christ," the old gent slowly shook his head, "*there* is a new wrinkle for humanity! What a smile, what a gift."

"The other two," he gestured to the empty ground, the place where the sherpas had stood a moment before, "They were ancient before I was born." Looking directly at me, he smiled again. "I *was* born, you know, just like you. The difference is, I never wanted for anything as a child." He continued:

> I had my own zoo, you know, with creatures from all over the world — I had elephants, giraffes, tigers, monkeys, birds — all well cared-for and healthy — our grounds were magnificent! My father was a king. His kingdom was very large, and very wealthy. It stretched from the foothills of these very mountains down into the richest farmlands the world has ever seen — beautiful valleys and vineyards. There was plenty of good water — three rivers flowing from the snowmelt and the rains that came up from the jungles.
>
> You'd think that life was perfect — and I thought so, but my father was always worried, as if something was not right. You know, he and my mother, the Queen, had four daughters, my sisters, before me. He wanted "me," he wanted me so badly — he wanted an heir to his throne, his kingdom. Any one of my sisters could have done a fine job running things, but no, that's not how he wanted it. Tradition, you know, his pride, his manhood — he wanted a son.
>
> Can you imagine? My father, the King! My mother, the Queen! Four sisters who cared for me and played with me — I was their Precious. I had the best of the best of everything. When I had a little sniffle, doctors were called in from all over the land. I had the best teachers — in fact, the wisest men of the country had been assembled at our palace before I was born!

My father had been so worried. "Is it a male child?" he
would demand of them. "If it is another female child there will
be hell to pay around here!" "It will be a male, Your Majesty,
for a great white bull announces his coming. He will be a noble
being, we are certain, and we all agree. The ancient scriptures
have foretold his coming, Your Majesty, and the stars agree that
you are the caretaker of destiny."

Great white bull, indeed! If it was another female he would
have taken them all out to the river and had them drowned!
"Caretaker of destiny" — now, *that* worried him.

My father was so concerned for my well being that he
became unhinged — obsessive, beyond protective, a fanatic. He
expanded the palace to include a small lake and some woods,
along with many fantastic and beautiful buildings. Around
the grounds he built an enormous high wall, with a special
set of three gates. Only young and middle-aged people were
allowed within the grounds of the palace; old people had to
leave. Anyone with an illness or disease was banished to the
outside; death itself was forbidden. His subjects still loved and
revered him — it was a peaceful and prosperous time — but
they couldn't help but notice and speculate about his extreme
concern for bathing; if you were not freshly bathed, you could
not enter the palace grounds.

Of course, I knew nothing of this. I loved my papa, my
mama, my sisters Ninjie, Shajie, Alreci, Ciari. I loved them and
they loved me. I loved my animals. I loved my toys. I didn't love
my teachers — they were stiff and difficult — but I did love
arguing with them. I especially loved studying the stars at night.
I absorbed knowledge like a thirsty sponge. I wanted to know
everything about everything.

I discovered my penis! It worked perfectly! Such pleasure! I
began 'experimenting' with our serving girls, and they told my
sisters, who told my mother, who told my father. In very short
order, I was married! On my sixteenth birthday, at my grand
party, with dancers, singers, jugglers, magicians and musicians,
my father and mother gave me a very large present, a most
beautiful jeweled box, and inside was the most exquisitely
beautiful girl-child I had ever seen.

I was astonished. "For me?" "Yes, this is your wife." "My
wife?" She was exquisite — her eyes were downcast, her
delicate lashes trembled. "What is your name?" I asked. "What

would you call me, Your Majesty?" she softly replied. "Hey!" I exclaimed, taking her hand in mine and gently raising her face with my other hand under her chin.

"Hay? Your Majesty, hay is for horses!"

This beautiful girl child became my best friend — she was athletic, smart, and fast, my equal in every way. My sisters loved her. Soon she was pregnant, and on her sixteenth birthday gave birth to a beautiful baby boy, my son! My father was in heaven. His son had produced a son! His lineage was secure! And perhaps he was destiny's caretaker.

A year later, she was pregnant again. One afternoon I came into our chambers and saw that she was crying, crying while changing little Baji's diaper. "Maya, what is it that distresses you? Whatever could be wrong?"

"My mother is gone."

"Where did she go?"

"She's gone! Gone for good. She died this morning."

"What? I don't understand."

"Here — help me pin this diaper."

Maya had said, "Govi, I know so little, and yet I see that you, my dear husband, know nothing."

She was wrong! She was crying and beside herself with this "my mother is gone" business; it had made her say crazy things. "Govi, you do not know what is beyond the wall. You don't know."

To be honest, I had never considered that there even was a wall — I knew it was there, but it was a fact of life, like the roof. I gave it no thought.

Then, driven by Maya's sad statements, stung, curious, I demanded to be let through the three gates, and at each gate the keepers and guards bowed and, with lowered heads, saying, "Yes, Your Majesty," they let me pass.

I wandered through streets that often reeked like Baji's soiled diaper. I met a beggar and a dying man. I saw a man beating a poor creature loaded with heavy bags, stumbling to a stop only to be beaten until its poor body bled. I demanded that he stop immediately and unburden the poor animal, and he told me to go to hell, and to "beat it or I'll beat you!"

I saw horrible things — a woman dying in childbirth, a child with no legs, a body crawling with maggots.

"When were you planning on teaching me about this?" I was

angry and frustrated at the stupid obstinacy of these supposed 'wise men.' I taunted them. "I know everything you know and I know nothing! Your maps are a joke. They do not show reality. They are entirely made up — everything you've taught me is a fabrication."

I was becoming really angry, and I was just warming up. "Do you know what I did today? Do you know where I went?" Ashen faces, serious looks among them. I went on. "Today I saw a man, or what had been a man, twisted and broken, with an empty cup next to him. He was moaning, 'Help me, help me,' and when I went to him — and he smelled rotten by the way — when I asked him what I could do, he begged me for money for a bottle of forgetfulness to escape his misery.

"*Misery!* I slammed my fist on the table. "And then, I saw a man, pale and thin as a reed, all bones and scabs, crying bitter tears. 'I have wasted away to nothing because I cannot afford medicine,' he sobbed when I asked why he was in this condition. "For want of *money*! In our rich land? How is this possible?"

"Maya," I whispered that night, "you were right. I know nothing. Forgive me, my darling, for I love you beyond words, but I must go into the world and see it for myself."

The following morning I left and went in search of answers. Why do we suffer? What purpose does death have, other than making life meaningless in its presence? Who are we? And who am I? Why are men capable of such brutality and cruelty? Is there a Divine Presence? What does Divinity think about this troubled world?

I traveled to many schools where wise men claimed to teach the answers. I was always asked to leave when I would ask, "If you have the answers, why aren't *you* happy?" Or, "Why are you so fat?" "Why are you always drunk?" "Why do you abuse your position, hitting on the young students?"

I visited many monasteries and ashrams where I was told that only by serving the master for many, many years would I begin to understand. I spent a season chanting, singing and praising Her, the goddess who birthed this creation. My questions were offered to the fire of my devotion, until the morning I awoke to chant, and as I sang my praises, I felt myself become more and more comfortably numb. I jumped up and ran out the door!

Years had gone by, and as far as I could find, no one knew the answers, no one told the ultimate truth. Every system of knowledge claimed the truth but came up empty-handed when it got right down to it.

I spent my days and nights alone. Solitude felt better than the company of humanity — corrupt, self-congratulatory, self-serving, lying, cheating, stealing humanity. Months became years, foraging alone, living in a dream state in caves, in the forest, oblivious to cold or hot, day or night, oblivious to hunger, to wild creatures and finally, after many years, surprised that a community of sunburned ascetics had joined me in denial of the flesh, in fierce refusal of pleasure in any form, a community of tormented skin and bones who had gathered, waiting for *me* to speak!

"Am I boring you?" he asked with eyes still closed. Still naked in the hot desert.

Startled, I protested, "No, no, this is fascinating, but to be honest, my attention did shift. The assembly is moving together, it's like a weird dance, a synchronized dance making symmetric figures. I can't make out the chant. What is that? 'Amma, amma, dough-gi, dough-gi, amma, amma, dough-gi go!'"

"They are calling me. They are calling me their mother and father, which I am not! But they are my people and I can't help but love them, although I must admit that they cry out for a sign of Divine Presence, a sign I told them could only be found within. Well, they are so insistent, that they see my hand whether I'm here or not — which, true enough, I am and am not."

I could make out three figures on the great altar, standing at the center of the big stone tabletop. The last rays of the setting sun cast three immense long shadows — either that, or they had grown ten feet each, because they looked hugely larger than life — and they had changed clothes, because now they were wearing sparkling iridescent shimmering robes, impossibly beautiful to see, even from this distance. They were very slowly moving from one tai-chi-looking posture to another; here must be the origin of showbiz, because Christ, in the center, repeatedly gestured up, while the Master and Lady gestured simultaneously out to either side, or in toward him.

"Do you see how they demonstrate that the work of creation in the service of all beings is love, unconditional love?" And the old man continued his story:

> So many years of dedication to escaping the big wheel of birth and death, finally coming to the centermost point, the end of karma, the end of all cycles, the Nothing and All-things created.
>
> A dozen starved, naked, beaten men sat around me, waiting for me to speak. In the distance I heard the tinkling of bells, perhaps a traveler on the road at the edge of this wilderness. I had nothing to say to these men. My solitude was ended. When I moved to get away from their eyes, their questioning postures, they followed. When I stopped, they stopped. Where I sat, they sat.
>
> On impulse, finally done with this desert, I got up and strode toward the distant road, cutting through the scrub and rocky wasteland, diagonally, on a path to intercept the far-off tinkling bells. The bells stopped at dark, and I stopped too. Twelve skinny ascetics stopped as well, waiting, twelve pairs of wary eyes on this unexplainable but seemingly purposeful new direction I was taking them in.
>
> What could I tell them? The sum total and truth of my years of monasteries and ashrams, of gurus, guides, mentors, teachers, yogis, lamas and wise men could be expressed in two simple words: 'Not this.'
>
> Not this, not this, not this, not that! What kind of a talk was that?
>
> The following day, just before sunset, I cut through a sunny ravine intercepting the source of the tinkling bells, a caravan of beer carts, seven bull-drawn carts carrying three enormous barrels of beer, on the road from Dikacarta to Balitma, from the wheat beer-brewing capital of the land to an apparently very thirsty sister city. The drivers were jolly, heavy, happy blokes, in stark contrast to the skinny, burned, crazy-eyed wild men that appeared like ghosts out of the desert.
>
> "We might as well park right here for the night, easy, boys! Round out the wagons! Bulls to the middle, boys! Fire right here!"
>
> "Gentlemen," the road boss surveyed the skeletons before him, "would you join us for dinner?"
>
> "Such disgust and spitting on the ground from the twelve! As if he had asked if they would join him in hell."
>
> "You! You lead this sad-looking crew? Would you like a beer?"

"Yes, thank you!"

The beer was delicious, a delicate golden ale with bubbles that took the top of my head off. "It's *good!*" I exclaimed. The road crew laughed and laughed, delighted at this confirmation of what they knew to be true — this was damn fine beer!

The light of the moon was beginning to glow in the sky behind the altar — a lone star appeared — an omen of things to come. The assembly was again seated. Before them on the altar stood a huge crystal bowl, faceted and shimmering like an enormous diamond. A last ray of sun sparking red, an amber inland sea. A gentle continuous "Om" sounded, with the slightest rise and fall, a soft sea of sound. Behind the bowl, facing the rising moon, the three stood stock still, like ciphers, a symbol of patient waiting.

Disgust! Years of patient waiting down the drain. Instead of revealing all, the supposed 'Holy Man' had gotten drunk with a bunch of fat beer merchants. Years wasted on this fraud!

Years wasted, indeed. Now, burning like the sun, my single desire, my single intent, my single focus and most compelling and absolute commitment was to liberation — liberation from illusion, liberation from ignorance, liberation from all constraints, however constructed, that kept me in darkness, that kept me from knowing the blazing Light of Truth.

I got off the wagon, leaving the beer merchants, I was near a small grove of ancient trees, miles from nowhere. I resolved to sit with my back resting against a great beauty of a tree, and not to move from this place until the Light of Liberation shone in my heart.

This was it. I sat, telling the tree, "Thank you, old beauty, for being here, and it is here that I surrender. Whether I live or die, here in your shade, I will know the Truth."

Days, nights, months, years, I do not know. The stars spun in the sky — seasons came and went — my resolve remained — unshaken. Liberation! Men wearing the orange robes of monastery monks approached. "This is no place for you, old holy one! We have a tent, with a hot meal and a warm bed, prepared just for you. Come with us — allow yourself this comfort, surely you deserve that."

Unmoved, unshaken. The wood nymphs danced and cavorted, nude, shimmering young bodies, graceful, splendid in their sensual flowering of life, juicy and sweet. Deer, usually docile, gentle, bucked their heads, snorting and chasing the girls down into a remote meadow.

A messenger appeared, accompanied by the Palace Guard, resplendent in purple and gold shimmering uniforms. They stood to attention, saluting. A proclamation from the High Council: "Your Majesty! The Queen, your wife, has passed from this world, leaving the reins of government hanging, unguided. Surely this great nation will perish and its nearly infinite riches will be plundered without the wisdom you have gathered these many years. We ask for your guidance and leadership. Please, we beg you, Your Majesty, you must come at once!"

Looking up, I saw a tiny speck vibrating the top surface of the moon, the huge mango moon rising directly behind the altar, throwing rays of orange light into the eyes of the enraptured assembly, now standing, heads and arms raised, diving into this light.

"Observe!" the old gent quietly commanded. He gently moved a finger, horizontally, back and forth. The moon speck glided back and forth across the edge of the moon in response.

The assembly gasped — an explosive "Aaaaahhh!" that reverberated in the valley. This *was* it! The Buddha was coming! Every story told was true!

"Get up, you poor ragged skin-and-bone excuse for a man!" an angry voice commanded. Standing at the edge of the clearing, a tall burly woodsman stood, dark, scowling, with a sharp double-bladed axe held threateningly. "Get up and get out! This is not your forest! These are not your trees! GO NOW!" The grinding menace in his voice shook leaves from the trees, cutting into their bark, the hot sap fear of being brought to the ground.

Unshaken.

Black clouds gathered, a thunderclap, lightning strikes illuminating the fierce black-robed figure pointing a sharp finger at the seated man. "I command you, ants of fire, wasps of pain, snakes of wrath, go! Attack him! Bite! Sting! Move this foul demon from our midst!"

The ants marched, pincers held high, snapping like bloody shears; the wasps swarmed, furious at this still presence stuck like a stick deep into their hive; snakes writhed hissing and striking, and swarmed in a poisonous wave moving close to the

207

seated one — then, something strange occurred.

The ants, recognizing the sweet smell of the Queen of All Queens took up protective positions, antennae touching with tender regard for their very own mother; the wasps landed gently, forming ornamental patterns, living jewelry on the body of their Beloved. The snakes encircled the tree and the seated one, protective, alert but relaxed and calm: there is no threat here, only us.

"Now I'm angry!" roared the Lord of Illusion, dark clouds of foul smoke trailing from his black robes. "Attack!" He commanded vast legions of warriors armed with sharp swords, and long pikes with flashing metal points, and many thousands with long bows, battle arrows set, quivers full — this snarling spewing mad dog of an army, the largest ever assembled, gathered like monster storm clouds intent upon their enemy, one ragged little man, serene, quiet, sitting cross-legged with his back against a tree.

"Shoot, shoot, shoot!" Black Robe screamed, enraged, frustrated, impatient, commanding this vast army to commit carnage on this one still figure.

Flights of arrows sang out, a deadly humming whine filling the air with hundreds, then thousands of arrows darkening the sky, a storm of Death arriving now at their target.

Flowers.

Hundreds of bouquets of flowers of every description, every scent filling the air with the sweet smell of heaven on earth. Flowers radiating out in every direction like Spring, then filling the hands and quivers of the archers, bouquets held by swordsmen looking suddenly like bridesmaids at a very posh military wedding.

"Damn! The Lord of Illusion exclaimed. "Damn! I've never seen anything like this." With a wave of his hand the multitude of baffled warrior bridesmaids disappeared.

"Well, you're not human, that's for sure." The Lord of Illusion, erasing spiraling paisley formations of guard ants with a gesture, sat. "And you're not superhuman, or Elohim. No being from any planet could have withstood that."

"Hmmm," he mused, "there's only one explanation: you are one of us!" A smile, a bemused shrug of the shoulders, a sigh.

"Well, congratulations, dear brother. I don't know how you got here, but here you are, one of us, a Master of time and space, a Lord of Lords, a Creator of the fabric of Being. Look, my dear brother," a soft smile, a wink, a tilt of the head, "we're getting together this evening — a banquet, in fact, now in *your* honor, and I will most happily introduce you, our lost brother, to the Gods of Creation, to your family — for you have shown me that you are one of us!"

Soft stirring, a gentle smile overtaking the face of the seated Buddha, clear eyes, engaging directly the eyes of the Lord of Illusion. The Buddha slowly lifted a hand from his lap, displaying an open palm — a simple gesture indicating "I see," then slowly he allowed his hand to drop into the earth, fingers reaching into the dirt, coming to rest deeply connected within the soil at his side, his smile radiant with compassion for the Black Robed one, now positively twitching in front of him.

"My place is here," the Buddha spoke. "My time is *now*," and with the light of many suns shining from his eyes, with stars and moons of infinite times and places suddenly radiant, transparent and present, he said, "and *this* is my family."

The assembly gasped, many fell to the ground, many with tears streaming down their faces. "My sweet Lord, my sweet Lord, my sweet Lord," they chanted.

There, emanating like an iridescent splash of bubbling foam from the heart of Creation, from the overflowing full moon, came a bejeweled throne, glittering impossibly.

Seated cross-legged on the throne, in a robe of the deepest saffron ever seen, was the unmistakable presence of the Holy One, the Lord Buddha. A quarter the size of the moon, the throne was rapidly growing, coming closer, closer, not a dream — real. Dizzying, impossible, unbelievable, *real*!

"Good. Now, put it in your shoe!"

What? Startled, I clenched my fist, surprised to find that I was holding a sharp little stone.

"In your shoe. Good. Now walk. Right here," he pointed to the little clearing, making a little clockwise circle with his finger. A huge gasp went up from the assembly behind me. A quick thought flashed through my mind: "He could be a little more careful with that finger!"

"Here, now!" Spoken softly but unmistakably, a command, "Walk!"

Ouch, ouch, ouch! That really hurt — walking normally was out of the question. A number of times around the circle and I managed to work the rock toward the arch of my foot, still painful, but from a hopping hobble I was able to limp around — uncomfortable but managing.

"That's right — keep going," he instructed. "The journey of a thousand miles, every step full of pain — you look around, yes? You see everyone and everything suffering. Some, like you in this moment, manage to work the stone to a less painful spot. You manage. But others are not so fortunate. They look and see others so much better off, and they ask, 'Why me? Why am I so unfortunate? What did I do to deserve this?'

Walking in a circle, encouraged by the old gent who continued to gesture, walk, walk — the discomfort would almost disappear as the otherworldly scene came into view of the huge assembly of chanting, praying, dancing, yoga posturing monks, lamas and holy people under the now lemon-yellow light of the still-rising full moon. Then as I turned back toward the tent and the seated old gent — sharp, hot bursts of pain would shoot up my leg. "That's it; I'm stopping this right now," I thought to myself, but there was the old gent gesturing, yes, yes — walk, walk.

"This is the pain of existence that you are feeling. It is the price you pay for having a body. We are born with pain, we live with pain, and we die with pain."

His face, now fully lit by the yellow light of the moon, was changing, shifting — what? A young wide-eyed girl, an aboriginal with three white lines across his forehead, a young Chinese boy, a dark-eyed Spaniard, a round-faced grandmother, a grey-bearded blue-eyed Merlin, the old gent, a slow smile, a twinkle appearing in his eyes. "Pain," he spoke very slowly, "is a given. But suffering, suffering is optional!"

Surprised, I sat, kerplunk, happy to be off my feet. "I thought suffering was the 'given,' the condition of mankind. Isn't that why we have compassion?"

"Misunderstanding," he replied. "I said 'pain' is an inescapable condition of all humankind, but 'suffering' is optional. Do you see how simple this is? You can be in pain but choose not to suffer! Suffering is the story we tell ourselves and others about the pain. We are not 'conscious' when the two are blended and indistinguishable.

"*Ah*" he said, looking up toward the moon, the throne of the Lord Buddha sparkling like a jeweled broach, now over half the size of the moon, rapidly coming closer, from the moon to the valley, the altar, the awestruck assembly.

"Ah — it is almost time."

"Yes, take the rock from your shoe," he spoke, as I already had my shoe unlaced and was pulling it off. "Take the rock and hold it in your hand. Good. Now, with that hand, please pour us a little more tea."

It was awkward, but doable — the kettle was still hot, over half full, and the metal handle pinched and hurt my thumb as I poured.

"Now, with the same hand — use this hand only — open your pack and retrieve your neck scarf."

The teakettle had been merely awkward. This was the "awkward Olympics." I gripped the rock in my palm with my third and fourth fingers while using the thumb and fingers one and two to push and tug at the straps and buckles, working at tight straps while not bearing down hard, which squeezed the sharp pointy little rock painfully into my palm. "Ouch!"

"Come on!" he said, "We don't have all night!"

"Hey, it's harder than it looks, and it hurts too." Reaching into the pack and tugging at the inner Velcro pocket — "How am I supposed to get this apart with one hand? And this stupid rock . . ." Jeeze. Then, pulling out the scarf, "There! I did it. Here it is."

"Drop it back in." He spoke, more gently, without a trace of impatience. "Yes, put it back. Now, open your hand and look at the rock."

I opened my hand, noticing both the rock and the white bloodless skin indentations it had made in my palm. I had been clenching my hand tighter than I thought.

"You are conscious of the rock, yes? Less pain than in the shoe, true? But even more story!"

He was right — I had complained almost the entire time I was undoing the pack, and was still complaining as I held the rock in my open palm.

"This rock is the unavoidable pain of existence that you were given — the price of admission into embodiment — and every incarnated being has a rock, and they all are in pain, the pain of birth,

211

the pain of life, the pain of death. And pain is pain — there is no lesser pain, no greater pain."

"What do you mean? Everyone is in pain? Even you?"

"Yes." He gently nodded.

A deep stillness surrounded us. His eyes, black pools, glistening, suddenly far, far away. Welling up, with what? With tears? Down the valley, the assembly was in full roar, a deep resonant organ chord of "om" ringing off the canyon walls, and impossibly, there above the altar like a big helicopter coming in for a landing, was the dazzling jeweled throne of the Lord Buddha, glorious, amazing, the Buddha radiant, sparking white light in a corona, like the sun, his features serene, his eyes dark slits, all knowing, all seeing, his left hand open, palm up, thumb and forefinger touching, his right hand reaching down toward the altar.

"Yes. Pain is a condition of existence, but suffering," he paused, "suffering is optional."

A huge dizzying swell of sound washed over us, like a wide-open Hammond B-3 organ kicked into fast vibrato overdrive.

"The journey of life is full of suffering when the rock is in your shoe. Every step hurts. That's all you know. You are conscious of nothing else. Then, a ray of light, a small awakening, a longing, yearning, searching for something. What? A way out, a way in, a way to the truth."

As he spoke, an iridescent rainbow wheel, spinning slowly, appeared behind the throne, with Lord Buddha at the center, the nub, and spokes of every color radiating out, astonishing, beyond beautiful. I felt my body jerk and shake, as if caught in the sharp teeth of a huge predator, a Tyrannosaurus Rex, the bottom was falling out, like the death rattle of a 747 going down hard, losing altitude fast.

"The wheel of creation, birth, life, death, over and over, many times, until you look where? To the center. You look, for the first time, at the rock, now in your hand, and you see that you have a choice.

"If you throw it, it returns like a great bird to its nest, back to your shoe, back to the outer rim of the wheel, back to endless suffering. When you hold it, you become more conscious of it, but you have also fully entered the realm of illusion, of perversity and confusion, of power and corruption, of wealth and poverty, of sex and separation, the realm of duality."

I agreed, nodding my head, a seasick sailor who felt fortunate to not be vomiting over the side of the boat for at least this moment. I had, I recalled, felt hard-done-by, the victim of "the boss" telling me what to do and how to do it, just moments before when I had retrieved the scarf from my pack with one hand holding the rock.

"Well, I certainly felt like the victim of circumstance, and I caught myself complaining like crazy," I confessed.

"Yes — imagine being proud! Imagine displaying your rock to others: 'See, see! I am the victim of childhood abuse, and one *never ever* recovers from *that!* See! My father was an angry, frightened man — and what he did to me *cannot* be undone! You must make allowances for me. I was raped and one never is the same, one can never again be open and vulnerable!' You see?" The old man was quite a master of illusion himself, bringing each complaining and justifying victim to life before my eyes.

"And it is just as bad to claim certainty as to the Truth and the Way that one is to manage the rock in the hand. Everything that arises from this compromise is compromised. Do you see it?

There was such urgency in his voice; he was leaning forward, asking, almost begging me, "Do you see?" His eyes glistened, brimming. Was it a tear that ran down his cheek? Hard to tell with the stars now spinning in the sky, the great wheel of life rotating behind the throne, now a mere 100 yards above the altar, thrumming the earth, whisking the moon, throwing flashing rays of color every which way.

The assembly undulated as if underwater, swimming, darting, congregating like huge schools of orange fish at the coral reef head of the altar. The ground shook; I was trying to gain my balance, my perspective in this wheels-within-spinning-wheels, crazy, undulating acid-flashback, many-ring-circus gone tilt, thinking, "Get a grip, get a grip," when an alternative came swimming into view. I could let go, surrender, and simply be.

If this was "it," then this was it. Absolutely nothing was under my control anyway, and it was all deeply beautiful in an extreme, 'that's it for this lifetime' otherworldly way.

"You're crying!" I suddenly noticed that this radiant Buddha, Lord of the Universe, was a frail, elderly man, tears streaming down his face,

213

sobbing, trembling. I reached out to touch his shoulder, to somehow console him. How bony and fragile he felt, now thin and worn his coat.

My hand felt warm, very warm. I imagined vitality, life energy, flowing to him. Why hadn't I noticed that he was this distressed? And *wow!* I was still holding the small rock, third and fourth fingers pressing it into my palm; it was red-hot, stuck to my skin like a burning ember. I couldn't shake it off. Ouch, ouch, ouch!

"Yes," he spoke so softly.

Completely forgetting the red-hot ember that I couldn't shake loose, I leaned forward very close in order to hear what he was saying, "Yes, this is my offering. You understand? My mother was not my mother. I have seen her in dreams, I remember her smell. She lived less than a week from the time of my birth. She cried and cried, and made her sister promise to raise me as her own, to take my father as her husband, to become the Queen, to assume her life. I was never to know. She made her promise! And all of my life, I searched for the Truth, I searched for Her, just as you searched the world for your grandfather." Tears streamed down his face.

Unsuccessfully trying to choke back my own tears, I was touched that he had remembered my story, and at the same moment I felt poked in the center of an extremely tender and bruised, not-yet-healed wound.

"Offer it to Creation, to the Divine One, as I am doing." He pointed to my hand, to the rock. I opened my hand completely, looking at him, looking at my open hand, looking down into the valley, to the altar, to the strobing, spinning wheel of light, to the glittering throne, to the no-longer-serene Buddha, tears streaming down his face, falling like rain into the huge crystal bowl, everyone, everyone with arms raised, hands outstretched to receive the blessing of these tears cried in such longing and grief.

The little cooking fire, almost out, flared as an ember sparked into flame. Without thinking, I pushed the remnants of a small branch into the flame, and as it ignited I recalled every fire I had ever been warmed by — cooking fires, bonfires, beach fires, fires in every fireplace of every home, the fires that were central to every ceremony, used by every shaman of every tradition in every country I had ever been in.

I felt my love for the sun, that great burning fire that I once leaped through, being burned to a crisp on my way to the greatest fire of all at the heart of Creation. Yes, this was the place to offer up the pain of my existence, "this fire is my sacred place," and ever so gently, I set my rock down.

A wild celebration was going on in the valley. Hundreds of thimble-sized glasses were being filled at the big crystal bowl, passed out to cheering, howling, chanting, dancing, stomping monks, nuns, yogis, holy people, sherpas, pilgrims and fellow travelers, all delirious with joy.

Overhead, the throne of the Lord Buddha, now a bright spot of gold at the center of a huge mandala of light within light, crazy glittering beyond-psychedelic, with diamond sharp crisp light at the center, becoming softer and softer, then sweet and diffuse, a shallow tropical sea of light at the outer edge of the rotating spokes of the wheel, then with a swirl like water down the drain, gone.

Silence.

Overhead a chill, cold white light, the moon, full and crisply defined. The assembled crowd, who a moment before had danced with joyful abandon, stood with faces uplifted, hardly breathing, quiet and still in the pale light with the dust of the dance settling back to the ground.

Silence.

Peace.

Blessings.

Welcome home.

How to use this book

Experiences of real magic, along with increased wellbeing and happiness, will come your way if you are willing to experiment and work with the practices and processes offered in this guidebook.

Start at the Beginning: There are as many paths to the center of the heart of Creation as there are individuals — however, this guide offers the benefit of time-tested shamanic wisdom and traditions, a definite advantage if you are willing to do the suggested work. Practices are designed to create new neurological pathways, allowing for new responses to the challenges and opportunities of your life. Generally, practices take 5 or 10 minutes, and are adopted for 30 or so days. They are to be used until they become unnecessary because they have become internalized and automatic.

Processes are acts of intention. Once you have completed a process, you're done, and you move on. You'll need to create a special time and place in order to enact and complete a process.

Take the Next Step: Each step is designed to open the doors of perception to the next step. It helps to have community support, and working with a group can provide companionship as well as accountability. Ultimately, however, Spirit is calling you to take action — to take the next step — whether or not you have a teacher or community. Life itself is your community, and these steps lead to increased communication, communion, cooperation and collaboration with the divine Presence. You can do it!

1. Enlightenment Is Easy.

The clenched fist / open hand practice (page 14) is designed to wake us up from unconsciousness. It seems counterintuitive that paying attention to our distress is the path to awakening, but it is our distress that drives us into habitual patterns of unconsciousness. Enlightenment is easy because it's our nature — we're designed to open. Also, enlightenment is not the goal of our work, but merely the first step! This practice takes 30 days to re-wire your responses to stress from avoidance and withdrawal to acceptance and openhanded engagement.

2. Forgiveness Is the Key.

With open hands, eyes and hearts, the first thing we see is that our energy is bound up and obstructed in protecting ourselves from past injury and abuse. Forgiveness is a process of returning toxic energy belonging to others back to those who injured us. This process (page 40) releases us from the perpetual effort involved in protecting ourselves and recovers that energy, returning it to flow freely within our energy system, increasing our vitality and capacity in life. Starting with central life figures, our mothers, fathers, brothers, sisters and family, we methodically work through those who have impacted our lives, offering forgiveness, asking for forgiveness from others, and forgiving ourselves.

3. Suffering Is Optional.

The suggestion that we can choose not to suffer seems to be impossible, until we consider and come to accept that we are responsible for every aspect of our experience. The practice (page 57) involves representing the pain in our lives with a small rock and then choosing how we handle it: Do we walk on it, unconscious that we have a choice? Do we hold it in our hands — in consciousness — and define our lives by it? Or, do we offer it to divine Presence, in awareness? This ancient practice takes a full 30 days to assimilate.

4. Wellness Flows Like Water.

Wellness flows through us, and it is this flowing life energy that is the fabled fountain of youth. The process of discovery of the obstructions and kinks in our energy system involves locating an old garden hose and playing with unkinking and recoiling it (page 76). The practice of flow will be a lifelong one, involving your choice of full body exercise combining flexibility and strength with awareness. Choices include yoga, tai chi, chi gong, many martial arts, and, of course, surfing.

5. The Great Mystery Is that You Are It! This

seemingly impossible truth is revealed in the process of making a Mobius strip (page 96). This physical model is tangible proof that there is no "inside" and "outside" — there is only one side — you! Your practice is to acquire a drum, and begin playing it, for fun, with yourself, and with others. You will find that drumming does not put us into a trance, but rather, it lifts us out of the cultural trance that has overtaken us, along with the habitual patterns we allow to govern our life experience. Drumming takes us off of "autopilot" and into the living experience of the same living presence within and around us.

6. Alignment with Creation. This is the foundation of all

ceremony, and your alignment practice (page 114) will help open the doors of perception for yourself and others, bringing you a lifetime of resources and access to vast fields of awareness and energy.

7. Freedom. Our focus on freedom from lack, from hunger, and

from oppression, prevents us from seeing that freedom is to be found in movement, especially in the movement of a special but mysterious and little-known aspect of ourselves. The practice involves acquiring a small bell and using it in a special way (page 124). This practice brings new meaning to the phrase "let freedom ring."

8. Dreaming. Your dreams for your life, the dream of heaven on

earth, can come true because we are dreamers. What prevents us from realizing our dreams? Fear. And the biggest fear is the fear of death. This practice (page 147) helps us realign our lives, flowing with the seasons of our lives and completely shifting our relationship with death. Surrender and acceptance at this level is very advanced work, and all of the earlier steps are a necessary for the taking of this step.

9. Deep Beauty. In the beginning was the word, and the word was YES! — spoken into manifestation in the language of Creation, Deep Beauty. As you practice and become fluent in this original language (page 165), beauty permeates you, radiates from you, and the deep beauty of every moment is revealed.

10. Seeing. We continue "seeing" what we expect to see, because out attention is directed by our beliefs. In other words, what we see proves that we are right in our beliefs. Here we practice seeing what is (page 177) without the limiting filter of our beliefs and discover the illumination of radiant Presence within everything we see, including our selves. This is a lifelong practice — a way of being — but you will notice a greatly enhanced perspective within days, if you've done the work and the energy of the spiral flows through you.

11. Being. Moving from constant busy "doing" to the ease of simply "being" is the key to the power within all spiritual practices. The practice of "being," oftentimes called meditation, takes us below the surface ripples of our lives, into the depths where we are refreshed and reinvigorated. Shamanic practice brings this potential into every moment of our waking and sleeping lives — the depths, the surface ripples, and the cosmic environment we find ourselves in are all included in one experience of being (page 185). We are rain — the liquid Light coming from the thunder and lightening storm clouds of the Great Mystery, nourishing the Earth and filling the streams and rivers, the lakes and oceans of being with the flow of Life itself. We are the Earth, we're the sun, the stars, the galaxies and the infinite cosmos, and the practice is to simply be.

Acknowledgments

My life is blessed with love — Dodi O'Neill inspires me with her artistry, her honesty, and her beautiful open heart. She just now said, "Don't forget to thank Maria and Angel," our feline companions, whose opinion is that they co-wrote this book.

I'm eternally grateful for the love and wisdom of my mother Marita, Dodi's mother Betty, Grandma O'Neill, Mama Juana Puerto, and my grandfather Pedro "Papa" Fernandez Ormaechea.

I deeply appreciate the friendships that have graced my life, giving me both the support and the reality checks necessary to speak about deep beauty. My musical partner Richard Hughes has been rock solid, as have Blair Hardman, Jim Corbett, Don Connolly, Rogelio Herrera, Captain Mike Hiebert, Antonia Greene, and my cousin/sister Christine Oss LaBang.

It takes a village to produce a book — and I'm grateful to Paulette Millichap and Sally Dennison of Council Oak Books and the Tri S Foundation for including me in their vision of creating beautiful books. I'm grateful to my muse, Terrie "Tink" Cowgill, and to videographer Jessica Varga, who helped shape *A Shaman's Guide to Deep Beauty*. Extra thanks go to Ted and Peggy Raess, of Raess Design, who created the mojo graphics that make this book magical. Thanks also to Carl Brune for a beautiful book design.

I'm thankful to those who have inspired and informed my work — Joseph Rael, don Miguel Ruiz, Gini Gentry, Jorge Delgado, Mauro Alvitos, Onye Onyemaechi, Eugene Albright, Frank Fools Crow, Martin Prechtel, Eckhart Tolle, Allan Hardman, Heather Ash, Raven Smith, Lee McCormick, and Larry Andrews.

Angels have helped me every step of the way, and I'm grateful to Gail and Hal Forman, Surendra Rai and Ellen Zalman-Rai of Clone Digital Print, Marcia Gabriel, Gary Doty, Dexter Leland, John Heidi, Bill Prange, John Reidy and Sabina Domenici, David McNair, Carla Hess, Gretchen Lawlor, Brooke Kaye, Lisa Dintiman, Michael Bates, Preston Bailey, and the angel who called me back, Randi Hardman.

Finally, my eternal thanks to the elders who continued our traditions through the ages and left their gifts to be shared in this time of need. Extra thanks to those who told me, "Now, *you* are an elder. Get to work!"

About Francis Rico

Francis Rico combines ancient and modern shamanic wisdom with a gift of sight to assist his students, clients, and fellow adventurers in awakening to the truth of their magnificence, and to the gift of their lives.

He has studied with indigenous elders in the American Southwest and throughout South America, and has led shamanic journeys to Teotihuicán and Peru for the past two decades, working with Miguel Ruiz *(Beyond Fear)*, Gini Gentry *(Dreaming Down Heaven)*, and Jorge Delgado *(Andean Awakening)*.

Francis Rico, under the name Frank Hayhurst, is also a musician and recording artist — who earned a Grammy for his work creating Musicians Helping Musicians, a musician health/crisis response organization. He is also a radio personality, whose weekly program "Face the Music" is popular in the Bay Area. For over thirty years Frank owned Zone Music, a popular destination for both musicians and music lovers who enjoyed the frequent events held on the courtyard stage. Twenty five bands and over one thousand grateful friends gathered to celebrate "Zone" when it closed last year.

Francis lives in Northern California, where he shares the beauty of the wild coastal mesas, cliffs, and ocean in support of his counseling and healing practices. He conducts community-based Peace Ceremonies, Solstice and Equinox observations, visions quests, and home and business clearings and blessings — along with classes, workshops and private sessions.

Francis Rico can be contacted at: francis@shamanzone.com